Interpreting: An Introduction
Revised Edition, 1990

Nancy Frishberg

Illustrations Designed by Marian Eaton

RID Publications
Registry of Interpreters for the Deaf, Inc.
8719 Colesville Road, Suite 310
Silver Spring, Maryland 20910-3919

Copyright © 1990 RID Publications
All rights reserved
Printed in the United States of America

Library of Congress Cataloging in Publication Data

Frishberg, Nancy
        Interpreting: An Introduction

        1st Edition 1986
        2nd Printing 1987
        Revised Edition 1990

    Bibliography: p. 227
    1. Interpreting I. Title
Library of Congress Catalog Card No. 90-62400
ISBN 0-916883-07-08

General Editors: Members of the 1983-1985 Publications Committee
                Marina McIntire, Chair, CSC-CA
                Richard Hagen, CSC-CA
                Margaret James, CSC-WI
                Andrew Keith, CSC-NH
                Robin J. Titterington, RSC-GA
                Janice Hawkins, Board Liaison, CSC-IA

Revised Edition Contributors:
                Marty Barnum, CSC-MN
                Gail Bedessem, CSC-IL
                Gay Belliveau, CSC, Prov: SC:L-NJ
                Charleen Brewer, CSC-NM
                Jan Kanda, President, RID, CSC-CA
                Kellie L. Mills, CSC, Prov: SC:L-MA
                Donna Reiter Brandwein, Chair, CSC-IL

Contents

Table of Figures

Key to Diagrams

Deaf Interpreter		Hearing Interpreter	
Deaf Participant/ Client		Hearing Participant/ Client	
Deaf Audience		Hearing Audience	

Acknowledgments

The preparation of this book was made possible with the encouragement and assistance of many people. W. Fred Roy, former Executive Director of RID, was a constant source of positive energy and solid ideas. I relied on his vision of this project at times when my own failed me. I appreciate the support also of the RID Boards of Directors (1982-83) and (1983-85).

Anna Shalhoub was an excellent research assistant, hunting down bibliographic sources, with some assistance from the NYU Bobst Library staff who performed their normal miracles. The NYU Linguistics Department housed the growing stacks of notebooks, files and diskettes, permitting me access at all the weird and wonderful hours when I like to write.

Thanks also to Marshalee and Robert Douty for their assistance in providing equipment and facilities necessary for the preparation of artwork, to Marian Eaton for the design of the artwork and graphics, and to Telecommunications for the Deaf, Inc. for the sharing of their Macintosh computer for the final graphics.

The many interpreters who shared their comments on communication challenges, ethics, settings, and the business of interpreting deserve acknowledgment as well. Of special importance in this regard are the members of the U.F.G. ("Unidentified Flying Group"), a totally *ad hoc* cohort of freelancers in New York City who met for about a year to bat around ideas and share work-in-progress intended for performance. I have gone back to those discussions in my head and my notes often. These interpreters, as well as many others who have been part of conventions, workshops, and teams that I have participated in, motivated this work.

Robbin Battison and Christina Edenas opened their home to me at a particularly difficult juncture, and took good care of a struggling author in the dark of winter. Mark Seiden provided much appreciated editorial and technical assistance, and lots of TLC.

RID Publications wishes to thank the members of the 1983-85 Publications Committee for all their editorial work on this text. In addition, we'd like to thank Nancy Creighton for her copy editing and production work on the final draft of this book.

All photographs are by Pentafore Photo Group, except Figures 9-7 and 9-8, by Nancy Frishberg.

Preface

The 1990 revised edition has expanded the sections on educational, legal and medical interpreting, and has brought the text up-to-date on the RID evaluation process. RID Publications wishes to thank Nancy Frishberg and the members of the Revision Committee: Marty Barnum, CSC-MN; Gail Bedessem, CSC-IL; Gay Belliveau, CSC, Prov: SC:L-NJ; Charleen Brewer, CSC-NM; Jan Kanda, President, RID, CSC-CA; Kellie L. Mills, CSC, Prov: SC:L-MA; and Donna Reiter Brandwein, Chair, CSC-IL. Although working under impossibly tight deadlines, they were able to produce work of high quality using their expertise and experience so that all who read this book will benefit. The RID home office staff, especially Debbie Prevost, NTS coordinator, and Sylvia Straub, executive director, has been indispensible.

Introduction

This book is about interpreting between people who do not share the same language. The two primary audiences are expected to be students of interpreting, and working interpreters, both novice and experienced. The book is not designed in the way that one might expect an introductory textbook to be designed. An introductory textbook generally includes study questions or suggested assignments at the end of each chapter. Perhaps it will be better to consider this book as a reference manual. While reading this book—or any other single book for that matter—will not turn an interested and hardworking student into an interpreter, it can offer a framework for understanding the field of interpreting. Interpreting requires both a base of knowledge and a body of experience. This book is designed to begin to provide that base of knowledge. Instructors in interpreter education programs will find it necessary to supplement the reading here: observations of working interpreters, practical exercises to simulate the complex array of tasks an interpreter takes on, additional reading, and discussions of accepted practice in the locale where the interpreters will be working. Nor does this book pretend to have all of the answers to the working interpreter's questions; it can only attempt to put those questions in perspective. Working interpreters will benefit from discussing questions raised in this book with colleagues and co-workers inside interpreting and in related fields. And, while we have not said it yet, we anticipate the largest audience to be interpreters who translate between hearing and deaf people, sign language interpreters.

This volume's goals are more modest than other publications for sign language interpreters, in that it focuses specifically on interpreters or those studying to become interpreters. The relationships with clients (both deaf and hearing) of interpretation services will be dealt with in several sections, but from the perspective of the interpreter. Insofar as interpreters are the ones who educate the public about interpreting, much of the material will be relevant to tasks beyond the immediate work situation, including client relations, working conditions, logistics, and advocacy for interpreting. Only the final chapter on "Practical Considerations" is written toward the audience of non-interpreters, those hiring or preparing to accommodate interpreters and mixed groups of hearing and hearing-impaired people.

At the same time, this volume is more ambitious than previous ones, since it makes general statements about interpreters and interpretation wherever possible. Sign language interpreters are becoming more aware of similarities between themselves and spoken language interpreters. While twenty years ago the goals of interpreting with deaf people related to certain circumscribed spheres of action, such as rehabilitation, medical and legal emergencies, and the occasional phone call, nowadays changes in public laws and public attitudes have increased the integration of deaf citizens into the worlds of business and professional life, recreation and arts, education and all aspects of social service. The increased opportunities for deaf people have expanded the dimensions of the interpreter's work as well. This book, then, attempts to identify the parallels between spoken language interpretation and interpretation with deaf people (whether presented in signed or other visual forms). We will be reminded of differences which cannot be ignored, as well.

International conference interpreting is the most well-studied, highest status and most strictly codified subfield within spoken language interpreting. Therefore, international conference interpreting is one model we can refer to frequently. At the same time, we recognize that conference interpreters function within constraints that community interpreters cannot assume. Conference interpreters can expect to prepare for an assignment by reading the specific documents which will be discussed at the treaty negotiation, technical meeting, or policy briefing. International conferences generally are conducted within formal procedures of etiquette and diplomacy among people of similar educational and social backgrounds. Spoken language interpreters are just now beginning to be educated for work in medical settings, the courts, union negotiations, and a variety of other mundane settings that interpreters with deaf people know intimately. The inability to anticipate the content of a particular assignment implies the difficulty of knowing how or what to prepare. For interpreters in the community, spontaneity is often the hallmark of each assignment, and expecting the unexpected the inter-preter's motto. Therefore, taking a new look at sign language interpret-ing will give breadth to the field of interpretation.

Interpreting involves competence in at least two languages, an un-derstanding of the dynamics of human interaction in two quite different modalities (for the signing interpreter), an appreciation of social and cultural differences, the ability to concentrate and maintain one's atten-tion, a good deal of tact, judgment, stamina, and above all a sense of humor.

Interpreting between deaf and hearing people can be thought of as a process or as an event. The process of interpreting involves several steps which we can separate out for the purpose of analyzing the task. In actual performance, these steps are accomplished nearly instantaneously, often with no discernible break from one part of the process to another. The interpreter must perceive and understand a message in one language, extract the meaning of the message from the words, intonational fea-tures, gestural behavior, pausing, and any other cuing mechanisms, and reformulate that meaning into the language of the listener. The inter-preter must also monitor his or her own output to check that all the intended information comes out in the intelligible form as intended. So, for example, the grammar of the original message is in most cases of no interest to the person receiving the interpreted message; it may be of use for the interpreter later in the exchange and therefore such details are probably saved in memory for at least a few minutes. The process sketched above is primarily of interest to the interpreter (and perhaps to the cognitive scientists who study human language processing), but of less importance to the sender and receiver of the message. The par-ticipants can only evaluate the interpreted events according to whether their purposes in communicating were accomplished.

Eleven chapters follow this introduction. The first outlines the his-tory of both spoken language interpreting and sign language interpret-ing. Special attention is given here to formal recognition of interpreting as a profession through legislation, certification or professional organiza-tions. The next chapter is devoted to defining terms. As with any area of specialization, interpreting uses its own terminology to talk about the practices, the people and the problems. Sign language interpreters will find the special vocabulary used among spoken language specialists suffi-ciently general for our purposes as well. The terms introduced here are language-neutral wherever possible.

What skills and competencies do we expect interpreters to have? Are our expectations realistic? The chapter on skills and competencies gives some overview of the attributes of accomplished interpreters. These skills are not limited to language manipulation, but include the application of knowledge of interpersonal relations, small or large group behavior and cross-cultural communication. The description of research about inter-preting and translation will elucidate what is known about interpreting both from the laboratory and from field observations. The research re-viewed here includes work in experimental and survey methods, as well as proposals for future investigations of interpretation and interpreters.

It has been said that half of the job of the interpreter is translation; the rest is logistics: finding the assignment, getting to the right place, arranging the participants for everyone's maximum benefit, getting paid for one's work. Of central importance here are the issues relating to ethical practice and appropriate etiquette on the personal level. At the community level are concerns about the marketplace and the expected or required working conditions. The interpreter's inclusion indicates a willingness on the part of the people involved to admit their lack of communication or language skills, and their openness to trusting a third person to fill that lack. Interpreters, especially community interpreters, often come to the profession with admirable attitudes about performing a needed social service. Realistic understanding about some of the dynamics that shape local markets, and about how to conduct oneself as a business person can lead to positive work experiences in interpreting. A single chapter gives some perspectives on education and evaluation. These topics are addressed from the point of view of sign language interpreters in particular, with little or no emphasis on spoken language practitioners.

One long chapter orients the reader to some of the more frequent or visible interpreting assignments. The choice of which settings to focus on depended on a combination of factors. The author's own experience as a working interpreter and thus familiarity with these settings naturally shaped part of the decision. The availability of additional written resources on the settings was also an important element in the selection of the eight focused settings. The current legal requirements spelling out the rights of disabled people to access in employment, education, health care, government and legal institutions motivated the choices as well.

The chapter on special communication techniques lumps together several additional aspects of the interpreter's skills. Interpreters may find clients with communication needs unlike those described previously. To mention just one example, deaf people with serious visual difficulties may require different communication techniques. Alternatively, the circumstances of the work situation may require additional skills. For example, where the communication takes place over the telephone rather than face-to-face, the interpreter will need additional preparation. The final chapter, as mentioned above, gathers together the practical issues relating both to logistics and to language. In this section we prepare for diverse conditions in the optimal manner.

Interspersed within the text are anecdotal reports from the author and other working interpreters which are intended to be instructive, as well as entertaining. Instructors can easily supplement these anecdotes from their own experience. The bibliography includes many familiar items for those who have been involved in the field of sign language interpreting. However, readers will also find a number of less familiar sources from beyond the immediate realm of sign language and deafness. Students and working interpreters are invited to browse this bibliography for additional references to those cited directly in the text.

As we said above, books alone cannot teach the skills and sensibilities of professional interpreting. Formal classes with instructors guiding the curriculum and the activities can supplement books. Supervised internships also contribute to an interpreter's development. In addition, let us include the peer support and sharing of professional concerns that can come from joining professional associations of interpreters.

Local organizations provide the most immediate source of support for individuals, and offer an active setting for testing ideas, working through difficulties and in general sharing professional issues. Because interpreters often work alone, they may lack a sense of what is usual and customary treatment on the job, and what is an unusual experience. Discussions in local forums can give some perspective. Local organizations also can support continuing professional education.

State associations are crucial in providing leadership in setting policies and laws affecting interpreters and therefore in the development of the interpreting job market. State-level decisions might include the determination of Department of Social Service statewide fees, legislative measures dictating how and when interpreters will be employed in legal and administrative settings, and whether to license interpreters. Interpreters who have banded together and who can present a unified, organized proposal will be taken seriously by state government agencies and elected officials. This implies that interpreters need to be talking to each other to come to resolution on each issue as it comes before the government personnel.

At the national level, interpreters have much to do in creating the kind of responsive professional organizations we want. Nationally standardized evaluation of interpreters has been and will continue to be a high priority. Communication among the various state and local organizations is a must. A national organization can be active in promoting public awareness of and reliance on professional interpreters. These few specifics only touch the surface of the benefits we can gain from supporting our professional associations.

1 History of Interpreting

It is interesting to contrast the growth of the field of spoken language interpreting with that of sign language interpreting. The former truly became a profession because of pressures among representatives of nations. The latter is emerging as a profession primarily out of the needs of private individuals. The contrast between the two arenas is instructive.

History of the field of spoken language interpreting

Sign language interpreters and others involved with deaf people will be interested to learn that interpretation for spoken languages underwent tremendous growth and recognition as a profession only after World War I. Of course, before that time, interpretation existed, but the demand for work of uniform high quality and for relatively large numbers of conference interpreters did not exist.

On any occasion when people meet who do not all speak the same language, they will solve the problem of how to communicate in one of several ways. They may attempt to speak one another's languages and do so imperfectly. This process is known to linguists as the creation of a pidgin language, and it happens all over the world where languages come in contact. Another alternative is available if one person in the group knows both languages; that person may be designated the interpreter. The degree of expertise in both languages and the practice at the task of instantly rendering messages from one language into the other can vary over a wide range of proficiencies. The interpreter may improvise, barely being understood, or may present a fluent and idiomatic message, full of local expressions, while at the same time remaining true to the original sense.

Under the usual conditions, the interpreter who appropriately fulfills the requirements of the role will not be noticed, appreciated or applauded. Longley, in her brief work on conference interpreting, reminds us of the Turkish sultan who built a mosque in Istanbul to his interpreter (1968:2). This acknowledgement of the contribution of the interpreter is definitely noteworthy, because it is so exceptional. Ordinarily, the interpreter will do the job and remain unnoticed. Bowen of Georgetown University's Division of Translation and Interpretation reminds us, "Only when interpreters make errors, or are otherwise inept, are they noticed. If they are very good in their profession, they achieve an absolute anonymity, they do not exist" (New Yorker, 1984). The title for a recent article on sign language interpreting reflects the same sentiment: "Being Ignored Can Be Bliss" (Fink, 1982).

It was during the Paris Peace Conference in 1919 that the field of conference interpreting got its start. The first practitioners were experienced civil servants, journalists, or diplomats with fluency in four or more languages, and passive understanding of probably several more. The job that these interpreters did was consecutive (not simultaneous) interpreting.

A consecutive interpreter initially would intersperse a few sentences of, say, French, after the speaker delivered the opening paragraph in English. The advantage of alternating between speaker and interpreter throughout the address was that a whole segment of the audience was not sitting idle and uncomprehending through the length of the whole speech (or its interpretation). The choppy technique was rapidly replaced in favor of a system whereby the whole address was delivered by the original speaker, followed by the interpreter who worked from a set of notes. The individualized notetaking systems of consecutive interpreters are discussed in depth by Keiser (1978), Lambert (1984), Kanda (1984), and Mikkelson (1983).

Interpretation of whole speeches in a fluent and continuous manner gave a certain pace to the proceedings. The delegates became accustomed to using the time while the languages other than their own were presented; they carried on deliberations within the delegation, negotiated privately, drafted proposals, and so forth.

Mehta (1971), writing about an exceptional interpreter and the process of interpretation, reports that it was largely due to the presence of

Edward Filene of Boston (who knew little French) that the present system of simultaneous interpretation developed. Filene, according to Mehta, was active in the work for peace carried on by the League of Nations' International Labor Organization. In smaller meetings where everyone except him could speak and understand French, a friend would whisper in English to him. It was merely the mechanization of the whispering technique that became simultaneous translation via microphone and headset that is familiar to us today.

Filene financed the production of a headphone system permitting six languages to be translated simultaneously and sent to different users. It was first used in 1931 at the League of Nations Assembly, improved and reliably introduced as a regular part of the Nuremberg trials following World War II. With simultaneous interpretation, the amount of time allowed in the program specifically for interpreting into the various necessary languages diminished to a few inconsequential seconds. The expense of the equipment was immediately offset by the savings in meeting time, personnel, and so forth. Of course, the quality of interpretation had to be superior for the simultaneous system to be acceptable. With respect to the Nuremberg trials specifically, the standards of accuracy and faithfulness were under more careful scrutiny than ever, because the immediate outcome would be decisions about the lives of accused war criminals.

Some people continue to argue that consecutive interpretation is more accurate or more faithful, that the time for reflection that comes with it is a positively valued attribute. The potential gain in accuracy and time for reflection is weighed against the savings of time and the more natural interchange of ideas possible with simultaneous interpretation. The United Nations has adopted simultaneous interpretation as the usual method, although consecutive is provided on request in the Security Council, where time for deliberation is often crucial. Consecutive interpreting might also occur where the meeting room is not outfitted with necessary equipment for simultaneous.

Court certification

In the United States, Public Law 95-539 (The Court Interpreters Act of 1978) requires that interpreters be certified by the U.S. courts in order to serve in bilingual proceedings. As of this writing, Spanish-English is the only language pair which is being federally certified. Of 1,334 candidates who took the written examination (testing language competence) in the first year (1979), 412 (or about one-third) passed and were eligible for the oral examination (based on functional aspects of court interpretation) (ATA Chronicle, 1980:4/5:15). Anticipated in the near future are similarly rigorous examinations in other languages.

Education

In recent years, professional spoken language interpreters have been called upon in settings where previously they were unknown. Sometimes this occurs because the multilingual aspects of the setting are now being acknowledged, as in the involvement of interpreters with farm laborers, unions, and management. Increased contact between previously isolated language groups and the majority language is another area of growth for interpreting, as in the projects to increase literacy and educational opportunities for speakers of Native American languages.

For these and other reasons, interpretation and translation (which often are taught in the same program) are being offered by a number of colleges and universities, such as Georgetown University and the Monterey (CA) Institute for International Studies, where the expectation originally was to instruct people for diplomatic service and conference interpreting. Other institutions are accepting students whose bilingual fluency is not natively acquired and whose goals may initially be more modest than the highly demanding field of conference interpreting.

History of the field of sign language interpreting

Sign language interpreting did not grow out of the needs of diplomats and nations. Rather it developed from the increasing acknowledgement that deaf people, like others with disabilities, were prevented from achieving their full potential as citizens (Bruck, 1978). Among the key elements in making sure that such potential is not blocked is the removal of communication barriers facing deaf people.

Interpretation for deaf people had, of course, always been taking place in the doctor's office, in church, and in other settings, in a haphazard and *ad hoc* manner. Few of the "interpreters" were compensated for their time and work; fewer of them had been educated in any formal way for the role they fulfilled. Often the interpreters were family members, neighbors, or friends who obliged a deaf relative or friend by "pitching in" during a difficult personal communication situation.

Since the people doing the interpreting were not professionally educated nor compensated, they rarely considered their own obligation to maintain attitudes of confidentiality, impartiality, or the right of the deaf person to know and understand the full proceedings. To compare these signers with the situation of spoken language conference interpreters is silly. A better comparison would be with the bilingual individual pressed into service for a neighbor or family member.

Amateur or professional

In the United States, the story of interpreting begins with the introduction of the language of signs to the public education system with the founding of the American Asylum for the Deaf (now the American School for the Deaf) in Hartford, Connecticut, in 1815. We know from recent work by Lane (1984), and also from research by Eastman for his as-yet unpublished play of Clerc's life, that Thomas Gallaudet interpreted for Laurent Clerc, the French deaf man brought to America to help found schools for deaf people. We assume that during the nineteenth century and the first half of this century, interpreting happened because hearing signers were available from schools for deaf people, from among deaf people's family members, and from churches which integrated deaf members through the use of signing. Alexander Graham Bell, among the staunchest advocates of oral education for deaf children, did nonetheless know how to sign and fingerspell. According to his biographer, Bruce, Bell would interpret on public occasions for adult deaf friends (1973:383).

The historical record does not focus on interpreters, but merely alludes to them by noting that various deaf leaders participated in administrative or policy-making positions in mixed hearing and deaf groups. Lane (1984) lays out in great detail the changes in attitudes towards sign language from its introduction as an educational tool through the nineteenth century.

There was no distinction, however, in the decades before the 1960's between a "helper" (any hearing signer who might help out) and an interpreter. A neighbor who might be relied on for assistance with the telephone could also be called upon to go along to the physician if necessary. The minister or his wife who signed Sunday services might intercede on behalf of a deaf congregant with the insurance agent. These hearing people might offer advice, translate messages from a deaf person to a hearing person and a hearing person to a deaf person, or even make decisions for the deaf person. We now understand that "helping out" in this way may reflect attitudes that deaf individuals are not able to take care of their own business, social and personal affairs without the intervention of a hearing person. Of course, not all hearing people who took on the role of interpreter would act in this paternalistic manner.

Grosjean discusses children of deaf parents in the context of bilingual children in general, and how they become responsible for translation at a young age (1982:199-201). Lauritsen (1973) and Royster (1981) give two firsthand accounts of their experiences as hearing children of deaf parents. Greenberg's (1970) story includes a fictionalized version of a hearing child of deaf parents. Walker (in press) reveals her own feelings as a young interpreter within the family and in the larger community.

Federal legislation involving interpreters

In the 1950's and early 1960's more hearing-impaired and deaf individuals requested the services of an interpreter in conjunction with their work or civic involvement. The Vocational Rehabilitation Act Amendments of 1965 (Public Law 89-333) authorized hiring interpreters as part of the vocational rehabilitation expenses when a hearing-impaired client was involved. If the federal government was willing to hire or pay for interpreter services, then it needed to know if the requisite professionals would be available in the work force. So we see that, as the communication issues touched on employment and training opportunities, the role of interpreters began to expand and become formalized.

Indeed, further legislation through the 1970's has only led to more awareness that support services are crucial to ensure disabled individuals' full participation in society. For example, Public Law 94-142 (Education for All Handicapped Children Act, 1975) mandates that children shall be educated "in the least restrictive environment." What this means differs for each disability group and to some extent for each individual; many school districts, however, have chosen to permit hearing-impaired youngsters to be mainstreamed in public schools with support services, such as tutoring, speech training, and interpreting services in the classroom. (For further discussion of educational issues and mainstreaming, see Greenberg and Doolittle (1977), Neisser (1983) and Moores (1982)). The Rehabilitation Act of 1973 prohibits discrimination against disabled people, and requires accessibility in employment, education, and in other health, welfare, or social service programs. The 1978 amendments to the 1973 Act clarify what accessibility means for each disability group: for blind and mobility-impaired people, accessibility generally means removal of architectural barriers to participation; for deaf and hearing-impaired people, accessibility means removing communication barriers. One means of accomplishing this is by bringing in an interpreter to bridge the communication gap. The staff of the National Center for Law and the Deaf have put together a clear handbook that describes *Legal Rights of Hearing-Impaired People* (DuBow *et al.*: 1982).

Individual states have, in the past ten years, become more active in protecting the rights of disabled citizens. By establishing commissions for deaf people (as in Connecticut, Texas and Michigan), state level agencies for employment and service provision (as in New Jersey), or in working with state associations of hearing-impaired and deaf citizens (as in South Carolina), the states are expanding on and clarifying government's responsibilities to deaf and hearing-impaired citizens. In this way, interpreters have been recognized at the state and local levels, through the legal system, mental health and medical care delivery systems, and in education.

Founding of the Registry of Interpreters for the Deaf

A historic workshop for rehabilitation personnel, educators, and interpreters held at Ball State Teachers' College in Muncie, Indiana, June 14-17, 1964, led to acknowledgement that professional interpreting would have an increasingly important role in the lives of hearing-impaired people. Mary E. Switzer, Commissioner of the Rehabilitation Services Administration at the time, is credited with promoting this new view of interpreting.

At this first workshop, Edgar Lowell and Ralph Hoag, two prominent educators of deaf people, proposed a national organization of interpreters. The group supported this proposal, and founded the National Registry of Professional Interpreters and Translators for the Deaf for the purposes of recruiting and educating more interpreters, and maintaining a list of qualified persons. They agreed to develop and present a code of ethics for interpreters.

A second workshop, held in Washington, D.C., on January 28-29, 1965, was devoted to drawing up and approving a constitution for the new organization, now called the Registry of Interpreters for the Deaf (RID). With the support of a Rehabilitation Services Administration grant for seven years, administered through the National Association of the Deaf, the RID began to organize nationally by setting up an office in Washington, D.C., publishing a registry of interpreters, investigating evaluation and certification systems, and informing the public about interpreting services. Incorporated in 1972, the RID redefined the purposes of the organization: maintenance and distribution of a registry of accredited interpreters, establishment of certification standards for qualified interpreters, recruitment of qualified interpreters, advancement and education of qualified interpreters, and preparation of literature relating to the methodology and problems of interpreting. A third workshop, sponsored by the Vocational Rehabilitation Administration, was held at the Governor Baxter State School for the Deaf on July 7-17, 1965. The result of this workshop was the first manual for interpreters in this field, Interpreting for Deaf People (Quigley and Youngs, 1965).

Since the early years, RID has become an independent national association. As a national association, it now has over 3,000 members from the U.S. (with members also in Canada and several other countries). RID administers a national evaluation and certification system, maintains state and national registries of certified interpreters, and advocates on behalf of interpreters and interpreting.

Evaluation system

In order to develop the evaluation and certification system, RID asked the Southern California chapter of RID to modify and expand the local evaluation system originally implemented by the Texas Society of Interpreters for the Deaf (TSID). Following a two-year pilot project, a committee of hearing-impaired individuals, interpreters, professionals from related fields and representatives of the Vocational Rehabilitation Administration reviewed the evaluation system for use nationally. From October 21 through October 23, 1972, representatives from forty-three affiliated local chapters came to Memphis, Tennessee, to take the certification evaluation, and be trained as evaluators. These individuals each became the chairpersons of their respective local evaluation teams.

Since then, evaluation materials have been revised several times. Special certificates have been offered in the areas of legal interpreting and performing arts interpreting. Also, procedures were developed for recertifying those whose initial certifications expired. More than 6,000 evaluations have been conducted, with over 2,500 individuals having received interpreter certification under RID's evaluation system. Most recently, uniform standards of evaluator training have been instituted. Some state agencies or organizations of interpreters continue to perform their own screening or evaluation in addition to offering national certificates through the local evaluation teams. (Evaluation is covered in more detail in Chapter Eight.)

Interpreter education

Federal support has also been instrumental in instituting interpreter education. Early in the 1970's, support from the Rehabilitation Services Administration (RSA) funded the National Interpreter Training Consortium (NITC), which included six institutions: California State University, Northridge; Gallaudet College; New York University; St. Paul (MN) Technical Vocational Institute; Seattle (WA) Central Community College; and

13

the University of Tennessee, Knoxville. The five-year grant was renewed for a second five-year period, and each of the institutions was responsible not only for offering basic interpreter education to individuals in their geographic area, but also for being a resource and educational center for the surrounding area. In the most recent period, federally-supported interpreter education programs include ten institutions, while more than thirty other colleges, universities and agencies offer interpreter education.

In 1979, the Conference of Interpreter Trainers (CIT) was founded as an organization to provide professional development opportunities for educators and instructors of interpreters for deaf people, and to develop liaisons within the field of interpreter education and among related disciplines and organizations. Educational programs may offer certificates of completion, college level degrees or no formal credit and vary widely in their entrance requirements and length of programs offered. The chapter on education and evaluation gives more information about the components of interpreter education.

The comparison of professionalization of spoken language and sign language interpreting highlights some differences between the contexts in which different language specialists work. Conference interpreting, the most prestigious and perhaps most difficult of interpreting specializations, came from the needs of diplomats. Filling the positions initially were people from similar spheres of operation, e.g., other diplomats, journalists, and the like. These people were already multilingual from circumstances of birth, education, or previous employment.

Similarly, sign language interpreters were originally drawn from among those who had deaf parents and siblings, whose language skills were natively acquired. While there is still a large proportion of interpreters with deafness in their backgrounds, many others come to the field from quite diverse motivations. For example, some interpreters come from total immersion experiences at schools for deaf people, while some teachers at these schools practice interpreting part-time (some teachers move into interpreting as a career option, and vice versa). Some interpreters come from social service backgrounds, and return to college for a degree in interpreting. And finally, some interpreters are recruited from disciplines such as intercultural communications, psychology, sociology, linguistics, anthropology, and communication theory.

2 Terminology about Interpreting

The terms "interpret," "interpreter," and "interpretation" have several senses in English. We speak of an actor's interpretation of a role, and mean the actor's choices about how to portray the character. We interpret the speaker's remarks, by which we mean we make our own understanding, we construe the speaker's meaning in a particular way. The interpreters hired by the National Park Service and other organizations offer explanations of the site; they act as guides, elucidating the meaning of the place we visit. However, none of these senses involves the use of two languages or codes of communication. This book is about interpreting between people who do not share the same language or mode of communication.

In order to talk about interpretation without being restricted to considering only particular language pairs, interpreters for spoken languages have developed terminology which is language-neutral. The terms involved describe the language skills of the interpreter, and the techniques of interpretation or translation involved. Since this volume focuses heavily on interpreters working with hearing-impaired and deaf people, we can also introduce terminology related to sign language at this time.

Language skills

The language from which one interprets is the *source* language (sometimes simply SL), while the language into which the interpretation is made is called the *target* language (also TL). Interpreters refer to one another's language skills as "A," "B," or "C" depending on one's ability to interpret or translate into that language. The "A" language is the interpreter's first language, or mother tongue, in which the interpreter continues to have fluency. Any other active language which the interpreter commands—i.e., can interpret into accurately—is called a "B" language. An interpreter may have one or more passive languages, which can be understood well enough to interpret from them, but not used fluently enough to interpret into them: these are "C" languages. Thus, the interpreter can have A, B, or C languages as source languages, but only A or B languages as target languages. The usual, and generally preferred, practice among interpreters of spoken languages is to interpret into one's first (or A) language. Keiser (1978) discusses some of the issues in the selection of interpreters and opportunities for employment based on language combinations.

Among sign language interpreters, only those with deaf signing parents can be said to possess American Sign Language (ASL) as an A language. They can be called native signers. Among that group, not all have English as an A language. For some, English may have been learned well, but as a second language, in the context of school, neighborhood, or with more distant relatives. As the field of sign language interpreting grows, the proportion of people entering the profession who have deaf parents decreases as interpreters with ASL as a B language increases. Thus, the practice among sign language interpreters is to interpret into one's B language from one's A language as often as the opposite. Sign language interpreters who can communicate using foreign sign languages or idiosyncratic gestures have these forms as B or C languages. Some situations require the use of one interpreter's A and B languages (i.e., English and ASL) and a second interpreter's A and C languages (i.e., ASL and a foreign sign language). (See the section on teams in "Special Communication Techniques".)

Sign language varieties

American Sign Language, French Sign Language, Swedish Sign Language, and Chinese Sign Language are names of a few sign languages used by deaf people within specific national regions. ASL extends to some parts of Canada and Mexico, and has been exported to several other areas. Puerto Rican deaf people, for example, use a variety of signing which has diverged from ASL for only the past seventy to seventy-five years, and continue to have contact with ASL signers. Each of these sign languages has its own lexicon (signs), repertoire of non-manual behaviors (facial expressions, body movements and the like), and conventions of grammar. (For more about the grammar of deaf sign languages, see Klima and Bellugi (1979), Deuchar (1983), Baker and Battison (1980), Moody (1983), and several of the articles in Siple (1978). The proceedings of several international research conferences also give more details of particular signing traditions, as well as comparative and universal features of deaf signing.)

While the several sign languages mentioned above represent at least three separate historical traditions, there are some characteristics which have been found to be present in all true sign languages that have been investigated. Such grammatical elements as classifiers, the use of spatial locations and directional movements for showing grammatical relationships, and the general size and shape of the signing space appear to be constant features of the category of deaf sign languages.

When one of the languages involved in interpretation is a sign language, the interpreter must know which variety of sign language is required. The diglossic relationship between the spoken language and signed language of a community has been described in detail by Baker and Cokely (1980), among others. One can produce signs—that is, the lexicon—of any particular sign language using the grammatical principles of natural sign languages of deaf people.

Alternatively, one can represent the spoken language through coding into manual-visual symbols. The system of coding involved might be any one of several approximations of English (or another spoken language) rendered visually and gesturally. Fingerspelling is one familiar form of coding spoken language gesturally. Some countries use a "hand-mouth" system instead to represent the sounds (rather than the spelling) of the spoken-written majority language. Morpheme-by-morpheme re-coding and the use of invented forms to correspond to English grammatical forms lacking in the sign language may also be employed to represent English. Most of the systems of coding the spoken language follow its word order, including mouth movements of words along with signs. Most commonly, one uses the lexical repertoire of the sign language, in the word order of the spoken language, omitting modulations and non-manual signals. (No attempt is made to represent all the grammatical features of the sign language in such coded forms.)

Thus, in the U.S., English can be interpreted into a distinct language, American Sign Language (ASL), or into any of several forms of Manually Coded English (MCE), including a pidgin (or relatively stable contact language) called Pidgin Sign English. Great Britain uses British Sign Language, Sign-Supported English, and Signed English. Italy has spoken-written Italian, Italian Sign Language (LIS), and Signed Italian. Similar distinctions can be drawn for most of the communities in which education for deaf people has incorporated modifications of the deaf community's sign language.

In communities where formal education has not been adopted, or where the deaf person involved has not had contact with the insti-

17

tutionalized educational system, these distinctions may be less sharp. Deaf and hearing people tend in these situations to give less importance to the specific form of the communication and concentrate more on the transmission of the message through whatever codes or channels they can mutually use. The section on Minimal Language Skills in Chapter Ten of this volume expands on a portion of these complex issues.

Translation and interpretation

In ordinary language, the terms "translation" and "interpretation" might be considered synonyms for one another. Among the people working in these fields they refer to quite different processes.

Interpretation refers to the process of changing messages produced in one language immediately into another language. The languages in question may be spoken or signed, but the defining characteristic is the live and immediate transmission.

Translation may be a more general term referring to changing messages from one language into another. Brislin (1976) allows that the form of the languages might be written, oral, or signed; the languages might have standard orthographies—written forms—or not. In a more narrow or technical usage, it refers to the process of changing a written message from one language to another.

When interpretation for deaf people began to be regularized and talked about nationally and internationally, the term "interpretation" was used to refer to rendering between two languages and "translation" to renderings between codings of one language. Since then, in order to avoid confusion with its usage in reference to written-to-written work, the term "translation" has been replaced by the term "transliteration". Still, some imprecision and possibly confusion remains in the choice of terminology.

Transliteration is a term that has one meaning for spoken and written language manipulation, and a related but separate meaning for signed language interpretation. In the first instance, transliteration refers to the transcription of a written text from a non-Roman print or script form to Roman letters. Thus, a Sanskrit utterance, as in Figure 2-1, which originally was printed in the Devanagari orthography might equally well be transliterated into Roman letters, enabling an English speaker to pronounce the message. The message would still have to be translated in order to be understood by a person who does not read Sanskrit. In the figure, the first and third lines are given in Devanagari, while the second and fourth lines are transliterated. The *gloss* of the first line might read "Here-beginneth Nala-episode." That is, a gloss gives a literal rendering of each element from the source language in order into the target language. The gloss of the next line might read "great-horse called." The translation would be given in more appropriate English, as "And now the story of Nala, called Great-Horse." Transliteration permits the reader of Roman print to pronounce but not necessarily understand the source language message.

18

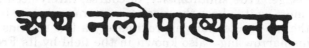

atha nalopākhyānam.

बृहदश्व उवाच

bṛhadaçva uvāca.

Figure 2-1
Devanagari script

Sign language interpreters have used the term "transliteration" to refer to the process of changing an English text into Manually Coded English (or vice versa). An interpreter who transliterates, also called a "transliterator," gives the viewer English in a visually accessible form. For the audience who knows English well, this may be the preferred form of translation. Interpreters who work with deaf people are schooled and tested on both sorts of renderings: the rendition of American Sign Language (for example) into spoken English (or the reverse of this process), and the rendition of Manually Coded English into spoken English (or the reverse of this process). Therefore, terms are needed to distinguish the two types of interpretation.

Interpretation is the generic term for the process which results in one language being transformed live—in "real time" to borrow from computer terminology—into another form, and will be used to include both "interpreting" and "transliterating" as used by sign language interpreters. Translation is the most general term for rendering of one language by another, and we will use "translate" to mean written, spoken or signed transformation of one language to another.

Simultaneous and consecutive

Simultaneous interpretation (also confusingly called simultaneous translation by the general public) describes the most familiar case in which the interpretation is delivered nearly instantaneously after the original message. True simultaneity, of course, rarely occurs, since the interpreter must wait to hear the speaker's utterance before interpreting. Typically, the interpreter lags approximately a few seconds behind the speaker. This narrow lag—also known in the field by its French name, *décalage*—is minimal enough though to call the process simultaneous, particularly when contrasted with the consecutive method. Simultaneous interpretations are expected to be integral; that is, each thought will be represented in full form as given by the original source.

For spoken language interpretation, there are at least three simultaneous methods which are used: whispering, use of booth and microphone, and sight translation.

1) *Whispered* interpretation, also known by its French equivalent term, *chuchotage,* occurs when one or a small number of people speak one language, which is not the language the group is using. An interpreter will whisper the translation for the benefit of this individual or small group. Before the development of appropriate technology for simultaneous spoken language interpretation, an interpreter seated near enough to the rostrum to hear the delegates' speeches would whisper the translation into a microphone which would be attached to earphones at the delegates' seats. This *hushaphone* device was an accepted form of simultaneous interpretation before the availability of technical facilities as employed in the next example.

2) Interpretation using a *dumb booth* or sound-proof booth is now fairly common for international scientific, diplomatic, or government related meetings. Spoken language interpreters occupy specially equipped booths from which they speak into microphones attached to a system of headphones attached to each seat or some sections of seats. The booths may be semi-portable, being set up for the purpose of the specific meeting and later removed from the meeting room, or may be built into the meeting room. Generally, the booths are raised above the height of the meeting room floor, affording the interpreters a good view of any visual aids (slides, overhead projections and the like) and of the interpersonal interaction. This makes it possible for a speaker from one language group to address a community of listeners from another language group on a topic of mutual interest. The listeners need not wait to have the speech repeated in their language, but with the assistance of technology can hear the interpretation simultaneously.

3) *Sight translation* is a special case of ordinary interpretation in which a written text rather than a spoken text is the source for the interpreter, who reads it off in the language of the meeting or audience. For example, a report from a German scientist might be read to an English-speaking conference by the interpreter who sees German on the page and speaks the equivalent message in English for the attending group. Sight translation has comparable usefulness for sign language interpreters. For example, a deaf signer who does not read English, or read English well, might request an interpreter to read the questions on the driver's license examination. The interpreter then reads the English and produces the equivalent expressions in the appropriate signing variety.

Consecutive interpretation involves the interpreter's ability to repeat the message in the target language following the original speaker's presentation. The interpretation may interrupt the proceedings at intervals of a phrase, a few sentences or a whole speech. In the U.S. Courts, currently, this method is used with spoken languages where a non-English speaking witness is giving testimony. The question is asked and then translated, following which the answer is given and then translated. Traditionally, this was the method of interpretation used by spoken language interpreters in diplomatic circles, before the use of technological aids, such as headsets and microphones. The interpretation may either be full or abbreviated in time; that is, a half-hour speech may be consecutively interpreted in a half-hour's time or in somewhat less time. Accomplished consecutive interpreters place high value on the individual interpreter's ability to adjust the length of interpretation on demand, while maintaining faithfulness to the meaning and intention of the original text. Indeed, among professional spoken language interpreters, for many years this form of interpretation has been considered higher in quality than simultaneous.

Consecutive interpretation may take place either from the rostrum or from the floor of the meeting. Another type of consecutive interpretation, which Herbert reminds us is "wrongly termed 'semi-simultaneous'" (1968:7), involves the quality of translation associated traditionally with consecutive interpretation, but the assistance of technology associated with simultaneous. Following the original speaker, one interpreter will deliver his or her consecutive interpretation in front of the assembly, either from the floor of the meeting or from the rostrum. At the same time, from the audio booths, the remaining several interpreters each relying on their own notes will deliver their respective interpretations. Each interpreter is making a consecutive interpretation independently, but all of these interpretations are happening at the same time.

The interpreter usually will be aided by notes prepared while listening to the original speaker. The system of note-taking used by consecutive interpreters deserves a more careful look (Mikkelson, 1983; Lambert, 1984). In the notes, abbreviations, symbols borrowed from other alphabets or scientific notations, and single letters serve to represent words, grammatical tense, relationships between ideas and complex numbers. Although consecutive interpreters' notes are said to be highly individual, so that one interpreter could not reproduce a speech from another interpreter's notes, many consistent principles and even shared symbols are used by all who have learned the method.

Sign language interpreters have begun to recognize the relationship of good note-taking (in the ordinary language sense) to interpretation. Consecutive interpretation requires the development of a personal note-taking system as a conjunct to the process of interpreting. Note-taking may aid the memory by being an external storage device or by contributing to efficient encoding and at the same time keeping the listener-interpreter attentive. Note-taking, such as practiced by spoken language interpreters, however, has not been used where sign language is one of

21

the languages in the situation. The neglect of this technique stems from some practical difficulties and also from prejudice left from the early years of professional interpreting with deaf people.

The interpreter translating from a sign language realistically cannot look at the note paper and watch the signer at the same time. Instances of consecutive interpretation into sign language are most often marked by exchanges that are so brief that they do not make note-taking worthwhile. Because consecutive interpretation into signing has been the usual method for the young child (interpreting with deaf parents) or the bare-bones beginner, professional interpreters have avoided this technique to distinguish themselves.

With a re-examination of the value of professional interpreters' notetaking techniques, we may begin to see the incorporation of this specialized method in educational programs or even in use in conferences and meetings.

Liaison interpreting may be contrasted with *conference* interpreting, in that the former defines situations in which the interpreter may have little or no special preparation and accompanies an individual or group in one or more meetings, tours, and activities. The State Department of the U.S. maintains lists of individuals who are qualified to interpret for groups of business, civic or cultural leaders in their official visits to the U.S. Individual interpreters may make themselves available to business people to aid in negotiations, sales meetings, trade agreements and the like. Liaison interpreters, also known as *ad hoc* or *escort* interpreters, usually work without taking notes and interpret one or a few sentences at a time. Conference interpreters are likely to be qualified to interpret at larger meetings and conferences, where not one but a team of several interpreters will be hired to provide continuous high quality interpretation. Conference interpreters may be expected to perform either simultaneously or consecutively. The same individual may perform liaison interpreting and conference interpreting on different occasions.

Relay interpretation occurs when one interpreter must rely on another interpreter's output to serve as input for his or her interpretation. For example, if a presenter is speaking Russian, and Russian is not among the languages known by the interpreter responsible for making Spanish interpretations, that interpreter may wait for the Russian-to-English interpreter's version, and interpret into Spanish from the English. In a similar way, a deaf interpreter may make a tactile interpretation for a deaf-blind audience member using the (hearing) signing interpreter's version as the source for the tactile translation. The term relay interpretation works equally well for this second example.

Audience

The audience for interpreting can be referred to in several ways. We will talk about an audience member, a participant in a conference or meeting, a student or a member of a particular profession, where the example under discussion can be labeled explicitly. When we are making general statements that are true of many contexts of interpreting, two terms have been used frequently: clients and consumers.

Like social service professionals, interpreters refer to the people listening and viewing the interpretation as clients. This term makes no particular claim about the audience's role *vis-à-vis* the interpreter. In some cases, the client may have been the hiring party. A hospital, for example, employs an interpreter for specific hours in the out-patient clinic each week: the hospital or its personnel can be considered the client of the interpreting service. In other cases, the client may be seeking assistance from an organization which provides interpreters as part of its usual business. A deaf out-patient, to continue the example, is also the interpreter's client at the hospital's clinic hours.

Interpreters sometimes adopt the usage of other businesses that sell a product. In this usage, the audience is referred to as the consumer. Consumers of interpreting services have no implied relationship to the hiring procedure, but are simply on the receiving end of the interpretation. Under this terminology, consumer education is the process of orienting deaf and hearing people to the practices, role and functions of interpreters. Unfortunately, both deaf and hearing people who are unfamiliar with this usage—that is, the largest bulk of potential consumers—are often confused by this term. They think of a consumer as someone who can walk away with a tangible product, rather than someone who has received a service.

In this book we have usually referred to the audience as the clients of the interpreter, in order to avoid the misunderstandings sometimes engendered with the term consumer. Readers who prefer the alternate term consumer can use that in their discussions of the topic of interpreting service.

Summary

We have introduced a series of terms which can be used to describe the language skills, interpretation and translation techniques and sign language varieties currently in use among interpreters. Terms which are common in use among spoken language interpreters can often be adopted directly by sign language interpreters. To reiterate, the term "translate" will be used in this book in its most general sense, except when specifically noted as a technical term referring to the transfer from one written language to another written language. The audience for interpretation will most frequently be called the clients of the interpreter in this book.

3 Interpreters' Skills and Competencies

What are the communication skills that are required of interpreters who interpret between signed and spoken languages? We can look at several broad categories of skills: language skills, interpersonal skills, public speaking, cross-cultural communication, and advocacy.

Language competencies

1) spoken language

Hearing interpreters need exemplary spoken and written English, with ready access to a wide range of specialized vocabulary items, and an ability to understand many regional and foreign accents. Their spoken language must not show too marked an accent, and spoken delivery must avoid a monotone, or dull quality.

2) signed language

They must also have excellent sign language skills, including a range of variation from American Sign Language through a multitude of ways of incorporating English into a visual-gestural code. They must be able to recognize diverse regional terms, recent coinages, borrowings and non-standard usage. They must be flexible in their own usage in order to accommodate clients from differing age groups, ethnic origins, social and educational backgrounds.

In both language modes (spoken and signed), the interpreter needs to be able to match any speaker encountered for register (intimate to formal varieties). The interpreter must adapt to circumstances, as Herbert (1968) puts it, attending to subtle nuances in government or diplomatic conferences, technical accuracy in academic circles, elegance and aesthetic qualities in literary or dramatic settings, matching forcefulness, reservation, humor, and poignancy as each arises in the interaction.

3) spoken-to-signed interpretation

Beyond fluency in each language, the interpreter is expected to be able to interpret from spoken language into the appropriate signed form, according to the preference or requirements of the consumer.

4) signed-to-spoken interpretation

The ability to interpret from these same sign language varieties into the appropriate register of spoken language is equally required. In fact, until recently, these two last categories of skill have been the only ones tested under the certification program of Registry of Interpreters for the Deaf.

5) simultaneous communication in sign and speech (Sim-Com)

As soon as one begins to take on interpreting assignments, it becomes clear that the ability to talk and sign simultaneously is a valuable asset. At times, one must explain one's role as interpreter to both deaf and hearing individuals. By signing and speaking simultaneously, one can avoid putting either party off, giving both the information and attention. Sim-Com is not formally taught in most interpreter education programs, and it has not been consistently tested. There is some evidence that Sim-Com abilities vary quite widely, and that in the hands of unskilled users it does not communicate much (see, for example, Baker, 1980; Marmor and Petitto, 1979).

6) sign-to-voice interpreting with Sim-Com

The sixth language skill is really a combination of several of the above, and yet requires astounding facility. It occurs in the situation where a group includes several deaf people who cannot see one another. Interpreters are expected to be able to watch a signed message and simultaneously interpret into spoken language while signing the same message. The folklore of interpreting instructs us to shadow the signing while voicing, but observation and experience say that what we actually do is watch and understand the signing, then interpret into Sim-Com. That is, the signs which the interpreter produces are generally the signs which re-translate or re-match the voiced output.

This last task is so demanding that many cannot do it. When one of the deaf members of the audience makes a comment without using voice, the interpreter is obliged to provide voice translation for the benefit of non-signing hearing people, while at the same time repeating the signed message for deaf people who cannot see. The size and shape of the physical space would lead to this situation: a lecture hall, a crowded classroom, a narrow hallway all might cause such an interpretation mode.

If two or more interpreters are working as a team, then one can take on the voicing interpretation while the other handles the repetition of the signing. In this way, neither interpreter is overtaxed, and the team approach can be truly effective.

Interpersonal skills

The interpreter needs to quickly survey a new situation to understand who is in charge, how the participants will interact, and then make sure that each participant is acquainted with how the interpreter functions.

At times the interpreter takes on the role of "communication cop." This term refers to the traffic regulator part of the interpreter's role. Hearing people, even those who do not share the same spoken language, share many of the same conversational regulators and turn-taking behaviors. I can recognize question intonation in another language after some brief exposure to the language. I will begin to anticipate when the speaker is coming to the end of his or her remarks. In contrast, the (hearing) speaker and (deaf) signer are probably not attuned to the same set of cues for who speaks when, how to interrupt, how to know when someone is simply pausing or is finished speaking, and so on. Baker (1976, 1977) has described some of the sign language turn-taking devices and conversational regulators that occur in ASL. As interpreters, we must have competency in using both sorts of regulators (those for spoken language and those for sign language).

What is the responsibility of the interpreter? Shall we wait for deaf persons, for example, to interrupt for themselves? But how will they know when an appropriate opportunity comes up? One interpreter comments on past practice in the profession and offers an alternative (this long passage is taken from a taped conversation with an interpreter who is also an instructor):

... I think that our profession has said that deaf people need to interject on their own and that we [interpreters] shouldn't interject for them; I disagree. I think we should take the intent of the deaf person to interrupt and use the proper turn-taking device and do it.

For example, in a classroom, a big problem that deaf people often complain about is that they feel that the interpreter interrupts at the wrong time or they don't interrupt at all, in which case the interpreter tells the deaf person that it's really their responsibility and they raised their hand at the wrong time, and their timing is all off, and deaf people get very embarrassed and the interpreters get embarrassed and subsequently the deaf person stops asking questions.

So, I think that there needs to be more communication between the consumer and the interpreter about when that question wants to be asked and just the fact that it wants to be asked. ...

And the interpreter needs to take that on as part of their role, as "communication cop," because they're the bilingual person in the situation, and they're going to know the timing and the rhythm and the pause sequencing and the languages and know when is an appropriate time.

So I think it's very foolish to pretend that . . . well, I've heard a lot of interpreters won't do it, or being very strict they won't.

Let's say you're in a college classroom and the deaf person says they want to ask a question. The teacher's going on, and you've picked up that it's not the right time to ask a question just by the tone of voice. The deaf person doesn't get that information, can't hear that. If they say, "I want to ask a question," some interpreters will interpret that, no matter what. Some deaf people will say, "No I didn't mean for you to ask right now." Maybe the teacher gets flustered or tries to ignore them. That's one situation. The interpreter is not interpreting what I call cultural information . . . it's just messy. And a lot of that is, in my opinion, because interpreters haven't learned to take a look at that as part of their role, and to integrate it well.

Unless the deaf person is really bilingual, how would they know? How could they know when to interject? . . . The intent is to interrupt but not to make a big scene.

I like using the analogy of the traffic cop: if there's no one in charge of the signals, the cars'll be going back and forth. Accidents are bound to happen.

Continuing the analogy of "traffic cop," as suggested by the interpreter quoted above, having an interpreter in the situation ought to be "collision insurance." It does require judgment and careful reading of the speaker and signer's intent to know how to facilitate the interaction. Within the role described by the quoted interpreter, the interpreter would not begin to interpret to a deaf person who is still reading a document, even if the hearing person starts speaking. Interpreters need to recognize that they have options: they can ask the hearing person to wait one moment until the deaf person has finished reading; they can wait to begin interpreting, holding the speaker's message in memory; a gesture to the speaker might be enough to indicate the deaf person is not attending; or they can take the initiative to get the deaf person's attention. The interpreter quoted above really is objecting to blindly following some set of rules, rather than using good judgment and recognizing that as perhaps the only bilingual in the interaction, the interpreter has special knowledge and abilities.

If the assignment is an ongoing one, the interpreter may be able to impart some of that specialized knowledge to the hearing and deaf clients. A semester-long course affords more opportunity to work through some of the transfer of responsibility to the deaf and hearing people. Certainly there's more possibility in a regular meeting with the same participants than in a "one-shot" assignment in a doctor's examining room or lawyer's office.

Interpreters as human beings

One of the attributes that interpreters have overlooked is the ability to assert ourselves as human beings, and to acknowledge other people's recognition of our humanness. Interpreters need to take breaks for attending to personal needs, and need to have a comfortable way to help others with their discomfort in the interpreting setting.

Let's say we're at a large public meeting. A speaker who is not experienced in using interpreters is addressing the group, and admits that this is a first for him—being interpreted. At some point the speaker turns to the interpreter beside him and asks: "Am I speaking too fast for you?" Interpreters have avoided responding as themselves, instead simply interpreting the exact sentence. It is true that this particular sentence could be addressed to the group or to the interpreter, but we know from the speaker's eye gaze, adjustment of loudness and change in manner that this question was addressed to the interpreter. In our effort to become professional, we have sometimes been rigid about refusing to acknowledge ourselves as people when we are interpreting. Let's consider the consequences of either: a) responding as ourselves, or b) just interpreting.

The speaker appears to be expressing some discomfort or uncertainty about how he is handling the new situation. If the interpreter simply turns and says, "You're doing fine," he will probably be relieved and be able to get over his self-consciousness about being interpreted. On the other hand, it does disrupt the meeting and inserts the interpreter as another person in the setting.

Alternatively, if the interpreter simply interprets, the speaker may become more self-conscious and more uncomfortable with this new situation. The interpreter waits for someone, hearing or deaf, in the audience to tell the speaker that all is well, just go ahead; but what if no eager volunteer speaks up? The speaker who is trying so hard to please and adjust to this unfamiliar setting asks again, and again the interpreter simply interprets. We have not won a supporter for interpreters; in fact, we may have alienated a potential ally. Here's another situation where the interpreter felt the need to assert herself as a person (this passage is taken from a taped conversation of the interpreter talking about her experiences on the job):

> . . . I'm still also my own person: I had an experience this semester where I interpreted for an Animal Health class where it was all these diseases (so lots of spelling) and the professor talked really fast, and one time the teacher came over and touched me. I kind of froze. I mean, he was approaching me at the end of a long thing, and sometimes I would just let him know he needs to put a word on the board by tilting my head toward him, or just looking in that direction briefly. He's been really cooperative about that—putting the spelling on the board, but he kind of squeezed my shoulder. I didn't say it, but I must have mouthed it: "Don't touch me." I'm sure the whole class saw it. Now that's not great behavior. Then a few days later, after class, the deaf student

stayed after to ask some questions. It was really interesting too, because a student interpreter was there that time. There were a few students left in class, and he was just behind me or next to me, and at one point he touched my shoulder, so I turned to him and said, "Please don't touch me." Now, that's kind of extreme, but I feel I'm myself first and then an interpreter. So that was something personal that I needed to take care of.

There are really two stories in this passage. One, of how the interpreter reacted as a person to the instructor's touch, how she felt the physical contact was inappropriate and yet had to wait for an opening at the right time to assert herself. She chose to mouth her message the first time, during the class, and criticized herself for less than exemplary behavior. Later she found the right opportunity in the after-class session, where the pressure of continuity was not so great, and the formal structure of classtime was partially suspended. The decision to speak up is certainly an assertion of the interpreter's personhood; the desire not to be physically interfered with is a legitimate one in the work setting.

But there's another hint of the many ways that interpreters communicate with the people around them in this story. The interpreter and the teacher have developed a system for her to signal which words are unfamiliar and need to be written out on the board. Since this subject matter is not her area of specialization, both she and the students need the support of seeing the written word to spell it. And it is not only the deaf students who benefit from the interpreter's signal. The hearing students can confirm or simply learn the technical terminology. The negative aspect is that deaf or even hearing students will come to depend on the interpreter taking the initiative to ask for spelling. The sort of head tilt, probably with eye gaze shift, that she refers to is not a verbal request, but it is a realistic sort of accommodation to the particular setting she found herself in. This interpreter's story could equally well fit under the heading "Interpersonal skills."

Public speaking

Interpreters need to control several registers, as was mentioned above under the heading "Language competencies." Joos (1967) gives an early and entertaining introduction to the notion of register; many others have since elaborated on this idea. He offers a five-level scale of intimacy-to-formality, and suggests that the participants in the communication, the setting, and the topics under discussion will help to determine which level will be appropriately chosen.

Interpreters may find themselves in any level, depending on the situation. A phone call between husband and wife can become very intimate, assuming both parties trust the interpreter (as they should be able to do). At the other extreme, the interpreter with the Pope who recites part of the liturgy will be in the most formal of communication settings. The interpreter needs to have full control of language skills to express the appropriate nuances for all communication settings.

Public speaking skills, including poise, appropriate breath control, varieties of intonation, volume, and vocal quality are of great value to the interpreter. Comparable abilities in adjusting sign language delivery for large or small audiences, formal and informal gatherings are demanded of interpreters, as well.

Cross-cultural communication

As we acknowledge the sign languages of various deaf communities as legitimate languages in their own right, independent of spoken languages, we also come to appreciate that deaf people who make up those communities share certain beliefs, values, experiences and behaviors. Padden (in Baker and Battison, 1980) defines the terms "deaf community" and "deaf culture." Hearing-impaired people from non-signing backgrounds share some of these behaviors, and also participate in another set of values and experiences. Interpreters need to be familiar with the cultures of deaf and hearing-impaired people, as well as with the culture of the spoken language community.

More than just familiarity, the interpreter is expected to be adept at making the interpretation of ideas and messages cross the boundaries of cultural difference. Cokely (1984a) reminds us of the inadequacy of literal translations at rendering the full connotation of signs or words. A word or phrase which may have positive connotations for the signer may have no deeper sense or even a negative sense for the hearing addressee. Cokely's example is the sign STATE-SCHOOL: "institute, state school for deaf people, residential school." Similarly, examples from spoken language can easily be found which give quite different connotations when signed.

While single words or signs may be easy to identify, we can also begin to notice particular communication-related behaviors that are appropriate to one culture but not the other. Turn-taking in spoken and signed languages is an obvious and immediate example, where the behaviors differ markedly. Signers permit a greater overlap from one person's turn to the next than do speakers, and claim the right to next turn by size of signs and withdrawal of eye gaze. Speakers may compete for the floor using rising pitch and volume, with some overlap of vocal message. The striking differences between the methods of turn exchange in the two modalities (vocal-auditory and gestural-visual) lead to another type of turn exchange in interpreted communication events. Cokely cites the false starts, silences, and awkwardness felt by both types of participants in interpreted phone calls, where the usual cues for turn exchange are not available. He argues for interpreters who are competent in both cultures and aware of how to mediate communication through the accommodation of another set of norms, those of the interpreted interaction.

Advocacy

Last, but not least, interpreters must be advocates for interpreting. We need to understand the economic and legal aspects of interpreting to promote the continued inclusion of interpreters wherever appropriate. We need to feel confidence in our colleagues in order to encourage our clients to avail themselves of interpreting services. Of course, the ideal situation is one where the deaf and hearing people will be able to communicate directly.

4 Research on Interpreting and Interpreters

In the past twenty years in the U.S., there have been several directions to the research on interpreting, dictated primarily by the interests of the investigators. The task of determining what directions would be useful to a national community of consumers was not addressed in an organized way until 1980. At that time, the U.S. Departments of Health and Human Services (HHR) and of Education, in conjunction with the National Academy of Gallaudet College, sponsored a meeting aimed at specifying the most important national research goals for this decade. Participants at the conference, "Interpreting Research: Targets for the '80's," held in Tucson, Arizona, ranged from within interpreting, for example, instructors of interpreting for deaf people and practitioners of interpreting, to research scientists in testing and measurement, language structure, deafness demographics, educational psychology, and also included staff members from several government agencies. The priorities for research defined at that meeting will be reviewed at the end of this chapter.

The following themes continue to appear in the published and unpublished research on interpreting:

—Who will be a successful interpreter? How can we predict success before putting a person through a full educational program? What personality factors, cognitive skills, or motor strengths are associated with accomplishment in the field of interpretation?

—What processes are involved in the act of interpretation? How do each of these factors affect the interpreter's performance: input message, background information, output message, environment? Can we create a model of the mental processes that the interpreter goes through? Can such a model aid in the development of curricula for education or improvement of interpreting skills?

—Can we objectively evaluate an interpreter's performance? Are the evaluation instruments we use reliable and valid? What is minimum competence for professional status? What does the deaf audience understand of the signing interpreter's rendition of a spoken text? How does the understanding of interpretation compare with other possible renderings of the same text (e.g., written)? How well do interpreters perform sign-to-voice interpretation? What is the hearing audience's understanding of the spoken rendering of a signed text?

Predicting interpreter proficiency

Since interpreting requires a period of devoted study followed by professional apprenticeship, and since most programs providing instruction in the early 1970's were subsidized or supported by the federal government, it was seen as desirable to screen potential applicants to interpreter education programs. The number of applicants who could be accepted was limited and, therefore, researchers sought to determine through objective testing who would become a good interpreter and who would not.

Two studies can be cited which demonstrate the difficulty of predicting proficiency only on the basis of test instruments designed for other purposes. Schein (1974) administered a battery of psychological tests to twenty sign language interpreters. Each of the subjects also interpreted two selections (one easy, fourth grade level, and one hard, twelfth grade level). Six judges rated the interpreters' performances, and Schein correlated those judgments with the results of the tests and with the interpreters' self-evaluation of proficiency with different deaf audiences. The correlations suggested that the successful interpreter "desires to be the center of attention, and to be independent, is not overly anxious, does not seek sympathy for self, and is not rigid" (Schein, 1974:42).

We can identify difficulties with the study that lead us to accept its findings with some uncertainty. For example, Schein himself notes that the judges do not correlate consistently on the easy and hard passages, implying that the criteria each uses in judging may not be identical for the two levels. The personality characteristics that appear to be significant come from a very small sample: only thirty-four interpreters from Connecticut and New York were tested. That sample may be systematically different from the potential candidates for education programs in interpretation. While Schein does not discuss this, we know that most people who were working as interpreters prior to 1974 had had no formal instruction in interpreting; they had picked up sign language skills at home or in work settings. We might understand the significant personality characteristics identified to be descriptive of people who would choose to enter a new profession, as much as who would be successful students in an interpreter education program. The whole structure of the marketplace in interpreting at that time may have had a strong effect on who happened to stay with interpreting before a national certification program was in effect and before interpreter education was generally available.

Shortly thereafter, Frishberg and Enders (1974) attempted to determine what factors could be used to predict success of student and community students in an interpreter education program. The same personality test used by Schein was administered to thirty students along with several other tests involving cognitive, language and manual motor skills. One judge rated each student on one voice-to-sign performance sample at the end of the eight-week instructional program. This performance task was correlated with the several other tests. None of the cognitive, language or motor skills tests achieved statistical significance in predicting success in the interpreting performance. Six of the personality characteristics did, however. The profile of the successful student is a person who would accept responsibilities, would like change, who is not especially analytical, does not feel a need to help others less fortunate, is not rigid, and has a low need for independence. Of these factors only the lack of rigidity matches the previous study of interpreters in the field; in fact, successful students show the opposite trend in independence from the Schein sample of working interpreters.

	Schein (1974)		Frishberg & Enders (1974)	
Subjects:	[34 working interpreters]		[29 interpreter students]	
	Exhibition	+	Change	+
	Autonomy	+	Deference	+
	Succorance	−	Autonomy	−
	Abasement	−	Intraception	−
	Endurance	−	Nurturance	−
			Endurance	−

Edward Personality Preference Schedule (EPPS) scales correlated positively (+) or negatively (−) with successful interpreting performance in two studies

Can we reconcile the personality variables in the second study with our understanding of those required for the job of interpreter? Or do they equally well fit the job of interpreter student? Again, this study can be

35

faulted for having a small and relatively homogeneous group. A high proportion of the subjects were students majoring in one of a few related fields (Art, Design, Communications) and it may be that the correlations actually showed the personality variables of people in those majors. Both studies are flawed by a lack of clarity about what is meant by good performance in interpreting. Neither specified which language variety subjects were asked to perform, did perform, nor how successfully subjects could stay with interpretation into a requested variety. Both studies tested only voice-to-sign performance, rather than sign-to-voice. The second study looked only at a single performance and that as judged by a single judge. Since that performance was taken from the end of the instructional period, and no comparison existed from the beginning of the instruction, no measure of the contribution of instruction to the performance was made.

Thus, so far, no objective tools have been found to predict who will succeed in the profession of interpreting. The factor of motivation of the student has never been added to the basic components of intelligence, personality, and linguistic and motor skills. The profession remains open to those who find it attractive. Each education program sets its own screening mechanism and performance standards.

Interpreting processes in spoken languages

Goldman-Eisler (1968) described the tasks of the simultaneous interpreter, whom she calls 'the translator,' quite neatly:

> The translator's task is to transform the verbal expression while maintaining the content, i.e., to transform it into as faithful a version as he can manage. He is under total semantic constraint in the area of content and meaning. As he operates under conditions of considerable stress which are inherent in the situation of simultaneous translation, he has priorities to observe. He must not lose the thread of the source text—in other words there are certain limits set by his immediate memory span to the lag he may permit himself—and he must transpose the content of the original passage. If the task is to translate faithfully, as distinct from an assignment to summarize. . .he is relieved of content decisions and his lexical and syntactic decisions are free only within the given limits of the text and its content. . . .
>
> (1968:77)

In looking at the performance of professional conference interpreters, the investigator was concerned with the "transposing" process as she calls it: how is the source language sentence structured? does the interpreter accept it as structured? if not, how does the interpreter change the structure? Looking at fifteen texts of about ten sentences each (four source texts and the corresponding sentences in eleven translations), the investigator analyzed them in two ways. One way looked at pause time as a ratio of speaking time. From previous studies of spontaneous speech, pausing or hesitating time is taken to be an indication of planning in spontaneous output. The other measure considered the syntactic complexity of each sentence, as judged by how many subordinate clauses each had. The pausing time ratios found in all fifteen texts were not correlated to the complexity index. Sentences rated less complex were unlikely to be differently constructed than the source language. Sentences rated more complex were structurally changed by the interpreters about half the time. With only one exception, the changes were in the direction of simplification. Because these two measures were found to be unrelated, Goldman-Eisler concludes that the syntactic operations of interpreters are a skill and not a planned or volitional activity. The pauses did correlate with changes in the syntactic structure, even if those changes did not always mean a simplification (1968:78-80).

The study also addresses the problem of effect of input rate on temporal rhythm in the interpreter's output. Speech rate, she notes, is actually a function of pause time: the more speech per unit time, the less time remaining for silence. The spoken language interpreter values the silence, since the more output that fits during silence, the less it is necessary to listen while speaking. (The sign language interpreter does not have exactly the same problem here, since input mode and output mode are not competing signals.)

Only texts with relatively greater pause times (more than thirty per cent) showed rhythmic alternation of hesitant and fluent periods in the interpreter's output. There was no relation between temporal rhythm in the input and the interpreter's temporal rhythm. However, for those texts with greater pause times, those where the interpreter introduced more pause time showed rhythmic interplay of speech and silence. Those where the interpreter shortened the pause time from the input text showed no rhythmic structure. Goldman-Eisler takes these results to mean that there is a cognitive rhythm for planning (pause) and production (speech).

Gerver (1976) gives two studies that may argue against this idea of cognitive rhythm. Gerver reviews a number of studies of the performance in simultaneous interpretation. These are all experiments where the interpreter performs in a laboratory, rather than in a natural setting. In studies of Ear-Voice Span (EVS), that is, the time lag between hearing the message and producing spoken output, interpreting shows a longer lag than shadowing. The shadower's output—a repetition of same input message in the same language—decreases in accuracy at faster speech input rates; the interpreter's output increases in accuracy as the input rate increases (from about 90 words per minute up to 160 wpm).

Gerver reviews the possible adjustment techniques open to the interpreter as the text speeds up or difficulties increase. These include *omission* (including possibly systematic omission of less important material, such as grammatical fillers, transitional phrases), *approximation* or less precise output, *holding back* some material until there is time to catch up later, *errors* and *cutting off input.*

Barik (1975) also discusses time lag in relation to errors in interpreter output. He notes that when the interpreter makes the lag too short, false starts and other errors occur. When the lag is too long, omissions become more prevalent.

Amateurs in Barik's study showed less accuracy when interpreting from their weak language to their dominant language. He suggests that more attention is devoted to comprehension of the incoming message or to the task of re-encoding the message, leaving less attention for short memory stores.

Goldman-Eisler (1972) has measured the interpreter's performance in another way. She looked at the relation between speaker-generated "chunks" of language between pausing and the interpreter's corresponding units or chunks. "Interpreters tended to ignore the input chunkings and imposed their own segmentation on the text" (136). She found that only in eleven per cent of the cases were the interpreter's chunks identical to the speaker's. Roughly half the time the interpreter broke the speaker's structural unit into smaller pieces *(fission)*, by beginning to interpret before the speaker paused. In the remainder of cases, the interpreters waited for several speaker chunks before beginning the interpretation *(fusion)*. The position of the verb in the source language was found to be a good predictor of the interpreter's behavior. It appeared that the interpreters would wait for a main verb to begin production. In languages where the verb appears late in the clause, interpreters showed more fusion.

Research on interpreting processes in sign language

We cannot assume that we can apply the results of research on spoken language interpreters' processing of language material to make predictions about how we expect sign language interpreters to behave. The structure of sign languages (at least American Sign Language) is sufficiently different, especially with respect to factors such as pausing and signing time, to warrant caution in applying findings directly. (See for example, Lane and Grosjean, 1980, for summaries of several experiments about pausing and signing time.) Still, the mental processes for interpreting, no matter what modalities are involved, seem to make similar requirements on the interpreter.

If we construe "interpreting processes" in the broadest possible sense, then we should include some older research on the accuracy of the translation and back-translation process (a process by which an interpreted discourse or text is interpreted back into the source language, to assist in determining accuracy of the original interpretation) in our discussion of interpreting research. Tweney and Hoemann (1976) summarize the results of several older studies involving the evaluation of the capacity of sign languages for transmitting meaning. Their own work on back-translation showed that meaning is largely unchanged when English sentences are translated into ASL, and then translated back into English. Like the subjects in Goldman-Eisler's work discussed above, the subjects in the back-translation studies involving sign language did change the grammatical structure of the sentences. The investigators conclude that sign languages "present no inherently unsolvable problems for translation theory" and "have unique properties that must be taken into account in translation activity" (156).

Llewellyn-Jones (1981) looked at the time lag between voice and hands in three native and three non-native interpreters in England. After checking each interpretation for comprehension by a deaf audience (reviewed below), he tried to relate patterns of time lag to more effective interpretation (high comprehension) and less effective interpretation (lower comprehension). He was surprised to find both relatively short time lags and extremely long ones even among effective interpretations. From the analysis of individual cases, it became clear that the interpreters were able to accommodate viewers' needs for an understandable Target Language message with several varieties of interpreting.

Effective interpretations included those in which the interpreter restructured the information for the presumed viewer, whether by reorganizing spoken English as signed English, or by taking the spoken English and producing British Sign Language messages. He relates lack of effectiveness to three factors: the interpreters' inability to analyze the in-coming message sufficiently deeply, their inappropriate choices about Target Language (given an audience who cannot be assumed to be competent in the spoken Source Language), and their lack of competence in the Target Language grammar and lexicon. In this study, the subjective ratings of "easy-to-understand" or "terrible signer" could be separated from how comprehensible the message was.

How well do interpreters voice-interpret (from signs to speech)? Hurwitz (1980a) compares two groups of interpreters. One group, HI, had a great deal of experience with both signing and classroom interpreting. The LO group correspondingly had much shorter experience. Included in the HI group were several individuals who had grown up signing. The interpreters in the HI group consistently performed better in accurately voicing for the selected texts. They also performed better on PSE texts than on ASL texts.

His experimental results confirm the intuition of many deaf clients and a large proportion of interpreters that, in general, sign language interpreters are weaker in voicing for ASL texts than for PSE, and that interpreters who did not grow up with the language have a more difficult time voicing.

We do not yet have good studies of the quantitative and temporal aspects of sign language interpreting, such as the relationship between pause time and either speaking or signing time. We have only hints, but no experimental results concerning typology of errors in interpreter performance. What sort of Ear-Hand Span will we find? What about Eye-Voice Span? How do these rates relate to Ear-Voice Span (as above) or Eye-Voice Span (as for reading aloud from printed text)? The field of research in interpreter performance has barely begun to be explored.

Evaluating interpreters

Culton (1981, 1982) took a different tack in research on interpreting. He found that the examination for certifying sign language interpreters in the U.S. had never been validated or checked for reliability. He did not know if the test looked at factors in interpreting that were consistent across different judges and different occasions of testing. He tried to find out by looking at California evaluators as compared to the national pool of evaluators, and by re-testing some previously certified interpreters to see how current Boards scored them.

Culton's analysis compared scoring patterns of California evaluators (for California candidates) with patterns of an equal number of randomly selected evaluators from across the U.S. (for their respective candidates). His study looked only at those candidates' scores who succeeded in passing the test at the Comprehensive Skills certificate level (the highest passing scores), and only at the performance section of the test, not the interview section. His analysis can only be considered a limited test of reliability since it assumed, rather than tested, equivalence between the several forms of the certification examination, it did not match deaf and hearing evaluators in the two samples, it did not look at patterns of scoring for evaluations other than CSC holders, and it did not look at patterns of scoring for candidates who failed to achieve certification at any level. Nonetheless, he found significant differences between the patterns of scoring by the California evaluators and the randomly selected national group of evaluators in three of the four sub-tests and also in the overall performance score. Only in the sub-test for Expressive Interpreting were California evaluators similar in pattern of scoring to the national group. Culton's work suggests that the certification examination as administered prior to 1981 may not have been a reliable test.

In the re-test of twelve volunteer CSC holders from California, a panel of evaluators (composed as a usual evaluation team would be) viewed the videotaped performances of the volunteers for re-test on the regular evaluation materials. The fact that the judges saw candidates on videotape rather than live is different from the original conditions of testing. Culton does not mention what the judges were told about the candidates: were they aware that all had already been awarded CSC's? Again, the analysis focused on the comparisons between original sub-test scores and re-test sub-test scores. Only on one sub-test (Reverse Interpreting) was there a high positive correlation, which could be considered an indication of the validity of the sub-test. On all other sub-tests and the Overall Performance rating, the test and re-test scores had low correlations, implying that candidates would not score the same way twice on the same evaluation.

There are some difficulties with the second part of this study, comparing the interpreters' performance from one occasion of testing to another. Culton did not control for the length of time between the original examination and the re-test. Some volunteers may have only recently been passed, while other may have passed long before. The evaluation is only a test of minimum competence; thus, great improvements in performance since the time the volunteer originally took the evaluation would result in higher scores at the later evaluation. No indication is given about the percentage of higher scores on re-testing, or any relationship between the time interval since original test and re-test, or between amount of interpreting work and continuing interpreting education undertaken in that interval. Also, since the first part of the study does not indicate California evaluators to be like the national group in pattern of scoring, the fact that the re-test team of evaluators appears to have been composed of judges from outside California implies that we could not have expected a positive correlation.

Still, irrespective of any problems in the study, the R.I.D. certification evaluation performance sections have still not been determined to be reliable or valid as test instruments. The factors which might lead to such a determination are discussed in greater detail in Chapter Eight.

Comprehending the interpreter

One of the important questions to ask is how well the deaf viewer will understand the interpreter. Naturally, the colleges and universities with large deaf or hearing-impaired student populations have been most interested in this question. Murphy and Fleischer (1977) review a study in which an interpreter rehearsed two passages, each in two distinct varieties of signing. Deaf students were divided into groups for viewing either ASL or "Siglish" (from the description it appears to be what today would be called PSE). Half the group seeing the ASL lecture reported preferring ASL to Siglish and half preferred ASL. The group viewing the Siglish version was similarly split in preference. They found no significant difference in deaf students' results on a multiple-choice test of lecture material. In fact, it made no difference what variety of signing the student reported preference for; each group did about equally well in recalling the lecture material. The authors conclude that these deaf college students are bilingual and can function equally well in either language.

Jacobs (1978) compared deaf and hearing students in good academic standing on their recall of lecture information. The deaf students performed a bit worse. They answered about eighty-four per cent as many questions correctly as the hearing students did. Jacobs suggests that this result means that interpreting is at least eighty-four per cent efficient in conveying information.

In both these studies, the student's ability to recall in English is being tested. How would the results differ if the testing task involved signing (that is, the input mode)? Would the deaf students perform better if the indicator of understanding the lecture material was an activity or other evaluation tool that did not depend on English skills?

In an attempt to measure the effectiveness of the interpreter, Llewellyn-Jones (1981) asked a group of experienced sign language users to interpret on videotape several passages into a form of language they would use with profoundly, prelingually deaf adults. He measured the comprehension of hearing listeners for the audiotaped version of the passages and used this standard to compare comprehension by deaf viewers of the videotapes. He found that deaf panels achieved better comprehension in passages signed by hearing native signers than for passages signed by hearing non-native signers (social workers with at least seven years' interpreting experience). He offers two possible explanations of the discrepancies in comprehension by the deaf panelists: either difficulties of experimental design or procedure, or differences of efficiency and skill of particular interpreters. He reports that the interpreters found the task artificial when the specific deaf audience was not present. His results and the interpreters' feedback suggest that the several target language varieties (representing features of the spoken source language, to greater or lesser extent) are determined in usage through feedback to the interpreter of audience comprehension. The work to measure the effects of audience feedback on interpreter effectiveness has not been completed.

Future of interpreting research

As mentioned at the beginning of the chapter, few efforts have been made to create a unified program of research on interpreting for sign languages. The priorities in this area defined at the conference "Interpreter Research: Targets for the '80's" fall into five general areas, and are listed below in the order that they were ranked by the conference participants.

1. *Profile of the competent interpreter:* Research is needed to identify factors in the interpreter's background, input message, and processing which lead to identification of successful interpretation. The research findings must then be transferred into aptitude tests, skills tests, and job satisfaction definitions.

2. *Evaluation/certification:* Research energies need to be directed into evaluation and certification in both the short and long term. Immediate issues concern consistent application of materials in the various evaluation boards, and the quality and content of the materials. Longer term issues relate to reliability and validity of the certification process.

3. *Entrance and exit criteria for interpreter students:* Research is needed to determine the aptitudes and skills at entry that lead to educating good interpreters efficiently (in terms of instructional personnel involved, time and money expended).

4. *Labor market analysis:* Research on factors relating to employment of interpreters is needed to plan for adequate services and educational facilities. Questions relate to who employs interpreters and where they are located, communication preferences of deaf consumers, and turnover anticipated in the interpreter pool. In addition, work requirements of the interpreting assignments (hours per day, days per week and year, compensation, and working conditions) will help to accurately project the needs of the market.

5. *Curriculum and materials:* The determination of what length an interpreting program should be and what must be taught in the core curriculum is a matter of debate currently. Research on instructional courses or practicum experiences can be conducted to learn which of the possible arrangements of curricula and materials incorporated into an educational program will lead to the preparation of competent interpreters.

In order to implement the ambitious research program outlined above, the meeting recommended a federally-funded research center concentrating on interpreting research. As of 1985, no funds have been allotted to realize this recommendation.

5   Texts and Translation

If we assume that the interpreter has the competencies discussed in Chapter Three, how can we describe the task of the interpreter in any particular assignment? The interpreter's task is to take a text, an utterance or series of utterances, and extract the meaning. Having isolated the meaning, the interpreter must then immediately (or with some relatively short delay) reproduce that meaning fully in another language, preserving the original speaker's intent. The discussion which follows looks at what we mean by meaning, expands on this process of translation, and considers difficulties in the task of translation. The adequacy of the interpretation depends on a number of factors, some of which will be considered below.

Settings vs. texts

Let us make a distinction between settings and texts. Settings (also known as situations) can be defined generally, by a topic such as "postsecondary education," or can be more narrowly specified, as particular occasions on which interpreting takes place, such as a college course lecture, a graduation ceremony, a student's tutorial session, or a student's meeting to discuss a project the group must complete for the course. These more specific settings can be further identified as to number of participants and the role each is expected to play. The instructor would be expected to have the lion's share of the textual material in the lecture; the university president and a few invited speakers would be prominent in the graduation. Tutor and student might have more equal shares in the communication, as would the various students in the group project discussion.

Texts, on the other hand, are the substance of what each person says in the setting. Texts, and the utterances within them, have purposes, can be categorized by register (degree of formality), and constitute the substance of the interpreter's work. For interpreters, the purposes of each text are often as important as the specific word meanings to consider in choosing appropriate translations.

Functions of a text

What might we mean by purposes of a text? Several different schemas for describing the functions of different texts have been offered by Casagrande (1954), Jakobson (1960) and Halliday (1970). While each differs from the others, they all seek to categorize communication acts according to the function the communication fulfills.

To take just one typology, Jakobson, in his closing remarks at a conference on style in language, attempts to focus on the poetic function of language by distinguishing it from several other functions. He analyzes each communication act as taking place between an *addresser* who sends a *message* and the *addressee* who receives it. The whole of the communication act is set in a *context* (providing some reference for the interaction), and assumes that the two participants share a *code* (a language or communication system, in his usage) and can make *contact* (through physical channels and with psychological connection). Each of these six factors in Jakobson's analysis "determines a different function," although few messages fulfill only one function (353).

Emotive utterances focus on the addresser, conveying either genuine or pretended emotions. Jakobson suggests that the purest form of emotive functioning is given by interjections, some of which are not even words. In his example, tongue clicking (as used by English speakers)—"tsk, tsk"—shows the speaker's emotional state. The actor's exercise of imbuing a seemingly neutral phrase such as "this evening" with a succession of distinct emotional overlays also highlights the emotive function of language.

Conative utterances are oriented to the addressee, whether present or not. The pure form of conative language use in the vocative or imperative, calling the attention of the addressee or commanding the addressee to action. "Let it rain" (addressed to God, nature or the television weathercaster) and "Now open your test booklets" are both examples of conative language use.

Referential utterances orient to the context, and constitute the pri-

46

mary task of many messages. Most of the text of this book can be classified as primarily referential.

Phatic utterances are oriented to the contact between addresser and addressee. Clearing the throat to get someone's attention (for hearing addressees) would be classified as a phatic communication act, even though it is not strictly a language act. Phatic utterances seek to initiate, continue, prolong, or discontinue communication, or check the channel. On the telephone, "Are you still there?" following static on the line would be phatic in function.

Metalingual utterances focus on the code, that is, clarify the communication. "What do you mean by 'verbal'?" "I mean any linguistic act whether spoken, written or signed." Such an exchange can be classed as *metalingual*.

Poetic utterances focus on the message itself. Jakobson does not restrict himself to textual material that would be called poetry by the author or audience. He includes all the aspects of language use which call attention to the form of the message. For example, the fact that English speakers prefer the phrase "meat and potatoes" to the reverse, "potatoes and meat," relates to this poetic function, according to Jakobson. Klima and Bellugi (1979:236) describe similar phenomena in ASL expressions for category levels, where a compound of RING-NECKLACE-BRACELET-EARRINGS-ETC. yields an unacceptable order of elements for the sense "jewelry"; but RING-BRACELET-NECKLACE-EARRINGS-ETC. or EARRINGS-NECKLACE-BRACELET-RING-ETC. are both acceptable compounds for the superordinate "jewelry." Klima and Bellugi also give descriptions of more narrowly poetic utterances in Chapter 14 of the same volume.

Jakobson's analysis assumes direct communication between addresser and addressee. In order to preserve the sense and the intent, an interpreter between the two will need to convey all the functions of the message. He reminds us, though, that few messages can be categorized by only one function. Wilss (1982) draws attention to the contrast between monolingual communication (within a single language) and interlingual communication (within spoken or written languages). We can augment his diagram by adding the dimension of intermodal communication (across spoken/written and signed modalities):

	Monolingual Communication	Interlingual Communication	Intermodal Communication
addresser	1	2	2
addressee	1	2	2
message	1	1	1
channel	1	1[?2]	2
code	1	2	2[?1]
context	1	1	1

[after Wilss, p.56]

Language Functions in One and Two Languages

For interlingual communication, transfer occurs in a single channel, either oral-aural for interpretation, or through written channels for translation. The possibility of two channels, represented by the bracketed number two, occurs in sight translation where written material is rendered orally. In intermodal communication, two channels are by definition involved: the vocal-auditory and the gestural-visual. Interlingual communication and intermodal communication in the usual sense involve two codes; the fact that the sender and receiver do not share a code is the motivation for involving a translator or interpreter. However, in the case of the expert lipreader who knows the source language fluently, perhaps only one code is involved. The bracketed number one represents this exceptional case of oral transmission in which the transfer is made only in the channel of communication.

Halliday's (1970) analysis of function in language names the categories differently, but divides the universe of possible functions somewhat similarly. He defines seven categories of function: Instrumental, Regulatory, Representational, Interactional, Personal, Heuristic, Imaginative. Whichever analysis one accepts, the conclusion remains the same: the interpreter is not simply translating the words or signs of the addressee, but is expected to respond to the message in several ways at once.

The process of interpreting

In seeking to understand the process of interpreting, we can look at several different stages of transformation from a form that the addresser utters (the source language) to the form that the addressee can understand (the target language). Herbert, in his seminal *Handbook,* gives a simple three-part process to describe the interpreter's task. Seleskovitch takes the process apart into nine steps.

Herbert (1968) gives *understanding, conversion,* and *delivery* as the three main steps in conference interpretation. He includes within the heading *understanding* the interpreter's ability to perceive the original message, the interpreter's intimate knowledge of the language used, the culture of the speaker, the specific usage within that country, the interpreter's background in both general education and the specifics of the topic. *Conversion* to the target language does not mean a literal translation of the words, but rather the speech patterns of a good public speaker, and includes the ability to handle special difficulties which may arise in learned or diplomatic addresses. Herbert (1968:24-29) cites six categories of such problems: proverbs and metaphors, allusion to literary works, jokes or stories, speaker errors, obscure or ambiguous material, and inserted excerpts of readings from documents that the interpreter does not have. The interpreter's *delivery* must include good control of the articulatory organs (for Herbert, the breath and voice exclusively), inconspicuous use of gestures and accent, and in general good instruction as a public speaker.

Seleskovitch's (1978) analysis of the interpreting process can be summarized in a similar way. In Roy's adaptation for sign language interpreters (1980:58), the interpreter must:

1. receive auditory/visual message;

2. already possess fluency in two languages;
3. be conversant with subject matter and refer to pre-existing knowledge;
4. comprehend message (source);
5. analyze the message thoroughly;
   identify interrelationships within message;
   recognize other meaningful elements, such as: gestures, facial expression, style of delivery, changes in volume, intensity, body language, etc.;
6. discard wording; but at the same time,
7. retain non-verbal thought through a process of visualization, seek equivalents;
8. recreate message in target language; and
9. produce oral/gestural-motoric message.

Seleskovitch encourages interpreters to form opinions about the source language material as it is received (1978:53-54). In her view, such opinions are solely for the purpose of helping the interpreter retain the speaker's point of view, and thus represent it accurately.

The interpreter's analysis and the reasons for his agreement or disagreement will not show through in his translation, because the more conscious the interpreter is of what has been said, the more aware he is of the difference between his own point of view and that of the speaker . . . in interpretation, an interpreter can never remain neutral with respect to an argument, for if he did, he might forget or distort it. (54)

Her thorough and thoughtful discussion of the interpreting process is worth careful study and discussion by all students of interpreting, even though she intended it specifically for conference interpreters. Much applies to other types of interpreting assignments, and her many examples from European languages trigger the recollection of similar examples from sign language-spoken language encounters.

The adequacy of interpretation

Interpreters working with deaf clients and sign language have often categorized their work by the sort of settings in which they work, but rarely have talked about the characteristics of texts as determining the nature of the work. Spoken language interpreters and translators, even more often, think of their work in terms of the topics that they must deal with, and the background preparation that readies them for accepting different tasks.

In order to approach any interpretation assignment, the interpreter must be aware of the alternatives that may arise, and the choices that will have to be made with split-second timing.

What will the assignment be about? Who will be speaking? Who will be listening? What is the context, setting, locale? How is each person participating? What are their styles? their moods? Why is this encounter happening? Knowing the answers to such questions will help the interpreter feel confident about entering the interaction.

Translation

Among the concerns which are shared by translators and interpreters is the desire that the translation be equivalent to the original message in as many dimensions as possible. (In this section, I will use the term "translation" in its most general sense, including work involving writing, speech and signs. The examples will be drawn from interpretation unless otherwise noted.)

Equivalence

Wilss summarizes several seemingly contradictory requirements for translation equivalence:

1. A translation must reproduce the words of the Source Language Text [SLT].
2. A translation must reproduce the ideas (meaning) of the SLT.
3. A translation should read like an original.
4. A translation should read like a translation.
5. A translation should retain the style of the SLT.
6. A translation should mirror the style of the translator.
7. A translation should retain the historical stylistic dimension of the SLT.
8. A translation should read as a contemporary piece of literature.
9. In a translation, a translator must never add or leave out anything.
10. In a translation, a translator may, if need be, add or leave out something.

(1982:134)

This set of principles of equivalence appears to allow anything to constitute an adequate translation, since for each guiding principle, its opposite can also be found. However, as Wilss explains, for literary translations especially, each of these will be appropriate in particular situations. Of some interest for those of us working in fields other than literary translation is the comparison between 1) and 2) above. The first promotes *literal* or *word-for-word* translation, while the second supports *free* translation. In examining any particular pair of languages, numerous examples can be constructed or found from actual language use which point out the inadequacy of *literal* translation. The English-speaking sociologist discusses the issues involved in the implementation of the death penalty: "Society takes the life of an individual . . . ." The sign language interpreter in this setting spontaneously produces the sequence, "SOCIETY TAKE-AWAY THE LIFE OF A INDIVIDUAL," (using initialized signs for "the" and "individual," spelling out the short items "of" and "a"). Of most interest at this point is the sign translating English "takes." The sign uses the grasping shapes of the hands, one over the other, but moves the upper (right) hand away from the center of the signing space toward the right side. That is, the sign TAKE or GET, in its dictionary citation

50

form simply closes the hands in the center of the signing space. The interpreter here has understood the sense intended by the speaker in this context and has expanded on the actual spoken word to its equivalent paraphrase, performing the actual translation on the expansion.

Consider another interpreter's solution in a different situation: the speaker continually uses the English "man" to mean generic human being. The interpreter chooses to spell M-A-N rather than use either of the signs for male person; she conveys her understanding that the sense the speaker intends is not specified for male. There is nothing in the pronunciation of the word "man" which would give the listener a clear indication of which meaning it is the speaker wishes to convey, human or male. It is the interpreter's judgment that the ASL sign MAN does not have the generic semantic extension that the English word man has; she has borrowed the English form (spelling) to convey the meaning. We must also assume her viewing audience understands this borrowing from English. (Moulton (1981:124f) argues that the English terms "he," "man," and so on, are not genuinely gender-neutral; however, the interpreter here accepts that the speaker is using the terms as though they are.)

A translator, working on translating a novel for a foreign audience, has the challenge not only of re-telling the story and recreating the author's style, but also of reproducing humor, word play and other aspects of the language which are too easily "lost in the translation." In *World According to Garp,* John Irving writes of how the child misunderstands his mother's warning at the seaside. She tells him to be careful of the undertow that can pull him out to sea. The boy imagines that a creature under the water might reach for him and remains apprehensive about the Undertoad until many years later.

In the Swedish translation of the book, the translator has managed to recreate the word play within Swedish where *underströmmen* "undertow" is taken by the child as *underst-hummem* "under-est-lobster." The translator has duplicated both the sound similarity, and the child-like construction of the name of the imaginary marine being. (Many thanks to Brita Bergman and Inger Ahlgren of the University of Stockholm for bringing this example to my attention.) Examples like this one give us the sense that equivalence of style and of meaning can be reproduced in the target language. But can the interpreter, working within more immediate time constraints than a translator of written language, produce similar results?

Mehta (1971) describes the work of simultaneous interpreters through his vivid portrait of the life of interpreters at the U.N., focusing on one remarkable individual, George Sherry. In the passage excerpted below, a particularly outstanding display of equivalence is recalled.

> "The great triumph of George-Porgie," Fagan said, his hand nervously playing with the microphone switch, "was when he translated Vishisky's allusion to Pushkin's 'Boris Godunov' by a quote from 'Macbeth.' A great virtuoso, my boothmate, a great virtuoso."
>
> "It was nothing," Sherry said earnestly. "You see, around

1950 there was guerrilla fighting between Greece, on the one hand, and Bulgaria and Albania, on the other. Vishinsky, while making a speech on the subject, shouted, 'The boys'—of the West, that is—'have bloodied themselves in front of our very eyes, and can say in the words of the poet, "I mal'chiki krovavye v glazakj!"' I remembered the complete verse of Pushkin, so I naturally recognized this as an allusion to Boris's being haunted by the vision of Ivan the Terrible's sons, whom he had done to death so that he himself could sit on the throne. Nevertheless, I knew I was in the middle of a split-second linguistic crisis—you have one of them every ten minutes with a good speaker who knows his literature and has a fondness for metaphor. What flashed before my eyes was the face of Richard III, whose life paralleled that of Boris, but the words that rolled instantly off my tongue belonged to Macbeth, I found myself shouting into the microphone:
'Will all great Neptune's ocean wash this blood
Clean from my hands? No, this my hand will rather
The multitudinous sea incarnadine . . .'"

[Mehta, 1971:16-17]

Obviously, Sherry's boothmate and Mehta both approve of this feat. It demonstrates the interpreter's very thorough command of both English and Russian, not simply language, but literature and social context. And we cannot help but admire the seemingly automatic, spontaneous manner in which the Shakespearean passage replaced the Pushkin. Sherry's behavior demonstrates the speed of processes like recognition, search, associate/analogize, encode to name only a few. Anyone who has worked with computers understands what a phenomenal and singular performance this interpretation was. It was noteworthy then, as demonstrated by the fact that both Sherry and his boothmate remembered it.

Herbert (1968) gives two types of advice which might be applied in this case, but with contradictory results. His suggestion for handling proverbs and metaphors encourages the interpreter to look for equivalent expressions in the TL, rather than trying to interpret very literally, so that sense of familiarity and "homely" truth are not lost (24–25). Following this suggestion, Sherry would get approval from Herbert, who also said literal translation is not acceptable. The interpreter's output should match in style, grammar, and usage a good public speaker of the target language (23–24).

Quite another recommendation can be found just a few pages later, where Herbert advises that when a reference is made to a well-known author, the interpreter's best recourse is to add the citation of the author by name, even when the speaker has not done it, and give a translation that is "likely to be understood" (25–26). Herbert seems in this passage to want Sherry to stay with the words of Pushkin rather than the equivalence of sentiment. Should it look like the translation in a book?

For the strictly tutored inexperienced interpreter, can the change from Pushkin to Shakespeare be reconciled with one's sense of the meaning of the RID Code of Ethics injunction to interpret faithfully? Sign language interpreters have been sensitized to the issue of preserving the original sense and wording, depending on the audience. Sherry's audi- is the English-speaking diplomatic corps of various national governments; he can legitimately assume they've all studied Shakespeare to some extent, even if they cannot, as he can, identify the play from which the reference comes. Likewise he knows that an educated Russian speaker would recognize the Pushkin excerpt as a literary reference. We may say he has faithfully interpreted, but what shall we say about the issue of finding an equally familiar literary reference when the TL does not have a written tradition, as sign languages do not? Traditional literature in sign language is not so universally known in the whole signing community. It is not taught in schools for deaf people, nor in most courses for interpreters. The solution, therefore, to the interpreter's dilemma cannot be decided by rule out of a particular context. For the Russian-to-English case with a diplomatic corps audience we can explain and defend the Pushkin-to-Shakespeare substitution easily. For another language pair we might not find the same solution or even a satisfying solution.

Translation difficulties

A few of Herbert's recommendations for handling problem areas are worth repeating here, since the same issues come up often for sign language interpreters as well. For example, he suggests that metaphors in one language may not work in the other, and thus the interpreter needs to look for equivalent expressions rather than trying to hold tight to a particular image. In the case of literary allusion, he permits the interpreter to add the citation of author or work, especially where it might not be well known to speakers of another language.

Where the interpreter is certain that the speaker has made an error, he would permit the interpreter to correct it. However, if there is any doubt, Herbert would have the interpreter follow the speaker's lead. He does offer some subtle suggestions about how to cue the speaker that an error may have occurred; for example, lowering the voice and slowing down might work well between two spoken languages, when the interpreter is audible to the speaker. Alternatively, the interpreter might ask for a repetition of the material in question, as though having not caught it the first time. Sign language interpreters have similar mechanisms, such as slowing the translation and turning gaze from audience to speaker, or asking for repetition, to cue in voice-to-sign situations. Facial expression adjustment might be sufficient for sign-to-voice interpreters, depending on the distance and angle of signer and speaker from one another. Herbert judges as risky the interpreter's changing an obscure, vague or ambiguous message to a clear one. He suggests that the interpreter would be more appropriate assuming that the speaker intended the message to be ambiguous and thus leaving it that way would match the speaker's intention.

Preparation

In defining interpreting as a task, we must consider whether the interpretation is spontaneous, fixed or prepared. A few examples will help to define and distinguish these three cases.

A *spontaneous* interpretation is the type we most often think of: it is performed on the spot, with no previous expectations or warning about what the speaker will be saying. The bulk of our work is spontaneous interpreting: the doctor's appointment, the job interview, the orientation to accounting procedures, the arraignment in criminal court are all examples where the interpreter can expect to perform spontaneously.

Of course, one's expectations about the setting, one's familiarity with specific participants or nearly identical situations lead to an interpretation that is not totally improvised. If one interpreter is involved with several deaf individuals all applying for the same job position, the interpreter will become familiar with the types of questions the interviewer will ask, and may be able to anticipate the types of answers the candidates will give. Still, there may be many surprises and the interpreter cannot assume very much about the nature of direction of the discussion. This would still be considered spontaneous, in contrast with the term fixed.

A *fixed* interpretation is much like a translation in writing. For example, the well-grounded interpreter will probably have learned a standard, set translation for the "Star Spangled Banner," "The Lord's Prayer," and other well-known and well-used texts. Each time it is said, the Lord's Prayer is recited with the same words, nearly the same phrasing, and in all major respects is essentially the same. The function of such a text is not communicative, or even instrumental. The Lord's Prayer has symbolic, religious and aesthetic functions. Deaf signers will be likely to recognize it and will appreciate its use for these functions when the interpretation looks fluent, rhythmic, and identical to the last time the text appeared.

One might think that the Miranda warnings would also require a fixed interpretation. Certainly, the use of the warnings in contexts outside of actual courts of law has given the warnings, even down to the exact wording in English, familiarity to the hearing television audience, at least. Many in that audience can recite all four points without prompting; others, if given the first line, would be able to complete the set. (You have the right to remain silent. Anything you say may be used against you in a court of law. You have the right to representation by an attorney. If you cannot afford an attorney, one will be appointed for you by the court.) The goal of saying these four warnings is to make sure the accused person understands the meaning and acts in his or her own best interest using that understanding. The interpreter who merely recites a fixed interpretation is not satisfying the goal of the communication. Still, the Miranda warnings are important enough so that interpreters would be well-advised to think about possible translations and possible audiences before actually being called upon to render the Miranda warnings into ASL.

A *prepared* translation or interpretation lies somewhere between spontaneous and fixed. The interpreter is familiar with the text material before the assignment actually begins. The amount of preparation necessary varies with the requirements of each assignment. It may be brief or extensive.

For example, the interpreter for the Speech and Hearing Association's annual awards meeting might ask for and receive a copy of the script for the presentation earlier in the week, read through the major addresses and become familiar with the names of award presenters and recipients, and arrive a bit early on the day of the occasion to check that there have been no major deletions or insertions on the program. But the interpretation that comes forth is not fixed; the interpreter has little idea which speaker will use what phrasing, who is an effective speaker and who sounds less polished, or how much anyone will stray from the scripted program. Rather the interpreter will remain alert to follow any spontaneous changes which occur, when a line is left out, when additional people are thanked, when topical stories are inserted into the presentation. The interpreter has prepared briefly, but not settled on exact translations ahead of time.

More preparation will help the interpreter working at a lengthy conference where technical papers will be read. Knowing the schedule ahead and being assigned particular papers will permit greater preparation. If the presenter cannot make that specific paper available to the interpreter, perhaps another paper by the same author has already been published. In that way, the interpreter will be familiar with the subject matter to be covered, the point of view of the presenter, and the technical vocabulary that might be used. Still, the interpreter cannot prepare for the style of delivery, accent, or use of visual aids and demonstration materials (slides, handouts, blackboard, and so forth).

Still more preparation would be expected where the interpreter is part of a team of two or more whose assignment is to perform a signed interpretation of a play. One would hesitate to accept an assignment where the actors were rehearsed, but the interpreters had had no opportunity to work together in rehearsal, to agree on translation of unison or coordinated material, to see the actors in rehearsal or performance several times, and analyze the script in the light of the actors' interpretations. Part of the negotiations for assignments requiring preparation is reaching agreement about the compensation for appropriate amounts of rehearsal or preparation time. (Also see the sections on working conditions and budgeting for interpreting assignments.)

Anticipating the audience

Another dimension to consider in interpreting is the number and communicative activity of the participants.

The character of an interpreting event is largely determined by the number of people one interpreter (or an interpreting team) must interpret for. One-to-one, small group and large group settings are quite different for the interpreter.

In a one-to-one encounter, one deaf person and one hearing person are relying on an interpreter to convey their messages through appropriate interpretation.

In a small group of three to ten or twelve people, the interpreter's functioning will depend in part on how many people sign for themselves, how many people speak for themselves. Is there a single deaf person in a group of hearing people? The interpreter's position and functioning will differ. Nonetheless, small groups where multidirectional communication is expected may be among the most taxing for the interpreter, who often has the task of not only conveying the messages, but also identifying who is talking, and trying to be aware of cultural mismatches in communication.

In large groups, of more than ten people, the interpreter needs to know what the format of interaction will be. Is there a single presenter and the rest of the group as audience? Will the group mix informally, and the interpreter move from dyad to dyad? Will this be a panel discussion? A formal banquet with after-dinner speaker and awards?

Every interpreting encounter is potentially interactive, but in fact some do not realize this potential. Consider the following three possible interaction complexes:

1) One-way communication: The interpreter is expected only to render messages from one language to the other and will not have need to transmit in the opposite direction. One example of such one-way encounters is: interpreting for a film or a play where all the action is on the screen or stage, without audience participation. (The source language might be a sign language if the play is performed by signing actors; the expected production would then be from signs to voice.) A number of other encounters that can be categorized as more formal also will probably involve only one-way communication: the prepared program at the graduation ceremony (but not the reception following), television interpreting where the interpreter appears in a corner insert, public rallies, and political addresses.

2) Two-way communication: The interpreter is expected to render messages between people who do not share a language, and thus must perform in both languages. Most one-to-one encounters will qualify as interactive: the deaf lawyer interviewing a hearing witness, the deaf parent meeting with the hearing teacher at the public school open house, the deaf rehabilitation client learning procedures at the new job during orientation with an interpreter. In each of these examples, and many more that each reader can think of, the interpreter has some options about the timing of the exchanges between the people. In one-to-one encounters, the interpreter's choice of consecutive method can probably be accepted by all parties easily. But contrast that with:

3) Multi-directional communication: The interpreter is responsible for translating between several people any of whom may be taking a turn at any time. The lecture portion of the class appears to be 'one-way,' but when the teacher starts calling on students, and the students vie to join the discussion, the interaction changes to multi-directional. A group therapy session, a task force meeting, a museum tour with both deaf and hearing audience are all examples where the interpreter must be ready for translation instantly from signs to speech and speech to signs.

Consider the following three deaf individuals' perspectives on their own participation in groups predominantly made up of hearing people.

The system fails deaf workers not once but twice. They get less education than the hearing, and they don't get jobs that fully exploit the schooling they have.... Part of the problem is pure prejudice, but communication can also present very genuine obstacles to advancement. Supervisory and executive positions, as well as many professional and technical posts, require constant conversation and frequent meetings. Although a skilled speechreader can hold his own in discussion with one hearing person, groups of hearing people present an almost insuperable challenge to even the hard-of-hearing. E. Latham Breunig, for example, suffered a profound loss at age seven, but went on to earn a Ph.D. from Johns Hopkins and pursue a successful career as a scientist and statistician with the Eli Lilley Company. He retains an easily understandable voice even in his late sixties.... But even this dedicated oralist ... readily admits that throughout his career he found that "committee meetings are impossible, unless you're the chairman and can control the agenda."

(Benderly, 1980:17)

Betty Broecker ... spoke of her plans to return to her home town for the thirtieth reunion of the Vineland High School class of 1949, where she finished in the top third. But this time she's taking an interpreter. Deaf since age eight, she says, "I am looking forward to engaging in conversation with my former school friends, and for the first time I will be able to understand what they are saying to me." [from Lamendola, 1979]

(Benderly, 1980:251)

Roslyn Rosen ... says, "I'm mainstreaming myself in a doctoral program at Catholic University. I go with an interpreter. Even so, my degree of participation there isn't nearly what it is here on this campus [Gallaudet College]. When discussion bounces around the room I lose contact. Who is saying what? I don't even know when there's a pause. I wait and wait and when I do speak I'm interrupting. I feel silly, and here I am, a person with all the skills and capabilities for mainstreaming. I don't interact with other students. Maybe it's not necessary, but it's lonely. What about kids at a young age? It's hard for them even to express that feeling." [from Thomson, 1978]

(Benderly, 1980:253)

Interpreters thus have a special challenge in aiding deaf people participating in verbally active groups, such as business meetings, social events and educational pursuits, as described by Breunig, Broecker, and Rosen.

Summary

This very sketchy description of texts and translation looked at two views of the function of a text, and two descriptions of the process of interpretation. From spoken and written language translation work, we can define the factors which make a translation adequate and acceptable.

The notion of equivalence between two languages, rather than identity, has been touched on. We have defined several sorts of translation difficulties, kinds of preparation which are possible, and factors relating to the size and participation of the audience which influence the interpreter's choices. Not surprisingly, the biggest challenge is presented by the mixed language group where many members are expected to participate.

6   Role, Ethics, and Etiquette of Interpreting

The role of an interpreter is familiar to the general public from films such as "Fail-Safe" and "Judgment at Nuremberg," to name only two examples. Such treatments in the media, however, do not give the full scope of an interpreter's responsibilities, nor can they show the boundaries and gray areas for interpreters. This section will begin to delimit the specifics of an interpreter's role and will mention the issues of ethics and protocol which come up frequently.

Images of the interpreter

The interpreter's role has been compared to a machine, a window, a bridge, and a telephone line among other metaphors. All of these are in part apt, and at the same time all of them ignore the essential fact that the interpreter is a human being.

The interpreter-as-machine is a convenient reminder that the interpreter will, all things being equal, reproduce the message from one participant to another faithfully, accurately, and without emotional distortion or personal bias entering into the interpretation. The flaw in this metaphor is that the interpreter's human needs may be neglected. For example, a machine might be expected to give consistent performance over many hours of operation, while a human interpreter needs periodic pauses to refresh mental and physical alertness.

The interpreter-as-window metaphor again emphasizes the clarity and fidelity of the interpretation. The interpreter-as-bridge and interpreter-as-phone-connection likewise point to the distances or barriers between the participants who do not share the same language or communication system. The interpretation makes it possible to transport information from one to the other. All of these images still deny the animacy and human qualities of an interpreter.

The role of Fair Witness in Robert Heinlein's novel *Stranger in a Strange Land* in some respects is like the role of an interpreter. A Fair Witness is supposed to be an objective and complete human presence in a meeting or event. The character of a Witness is like an interpreter in that recollection must be complete, and the Witness must not give opinions about what was seen and heard. Clientele of a Witness are not, in the fictional future world, to discuss what the Witness might see or hear on a case pending before the Witness. The Witness's instruction includes specialized memory development and excellent recall. The Witness dons a white cloak as an emblem when on duty, to distinguish from traveling to or from an assignment or off duty. Witnesses are specifically required not to participate, rather to serve as Witness only. The Witness is unlike an interpreter in that the Witness might be asked to remember much later what had happened in the observed situation, and could be called upon to testify ("witness") in court of law. One example should suffice to demonstrate the comparison.

> ... Jubal called out, "That house on the hilltop--can you see what color they've painted it?"
> Anne looked, then answered, "It's white on this side."
> Jubal went on to Jill, "You see. It doesn't occur to Anne to infer that the other side is white, too. All the King's horses couldn't force her to commit herself ... unless she went there and looked—and even then she wouldn't assume that it stayed white after she left."
> "*Anne* is a Fair Witness?"
> "Graduate, unlimited license, admitted to testify before the High Court." (1972:98)

The fictional character of Fair Witness idealizes the traits of accurate memory, careful observation, and objective point of view, leaving the tasks of deduction, forming opinions, and influencing action to others. All of these traits are equally desirable in an interpreter. Like the Fair Witness, the interpreter may set himself or herself apart from the proceedings by dress. Unlike the Fair Witness, however, the interpreter is not held responsible for remembering the communication transmitted until the indefinite future. Unlike the Fair Witness, the interpreter cannot assume that the clientele are all equally familiar with appropriate procedures and protocol. The interpreter often finds it necessary to educate the clients about the responsibilities and limits of the interpreter's function. We will elaborate on these several similarities and differences below.

It is interesting to consider how the current conventions about ethics and etiquette have developed. Hearing children of deaf parents, as we saw in a preceding chapter, were the first interpreters. Lauritsen (1973) sets down a few of the common experiences of hearing offspring in a household with deaf parents. Walker (in press) recalls her own experiences in the light of contemporary standards of behavior. Grosjean (1982:200-201), in a larger work on bilingualism, mentions the responsibilities of a bilingual child in a household where the language used is not that of the society at large. The child's role as dependent and subordinate to the parents potentially conflicts with the child's function as interpreter for the parents. The parents, naturally enough, are expecting to be represented as adults. The child may not be able to separate out feelings directed at the addressee through the interpreter from feelings directed at the interpreter, or may be uncomfortable expressing culturally appropriate expressions from the source language, if they are inappropriate in the target language. The constant here seems to be early reliance on the child as intermediary in the communication setting. Thus, hearing children of deaf parents sometimes take on more responsibility than would normally be expected for their age, and sometimes feel the need to protect their parents from misunderstanding. We find as interpreting has become recognized as a profession both by the practitioner and the consumer, that a formal distance between consumer and interpreter has developed. This distance is unlike the relationship described by these several authors between bilingual child and monolingual parent.

For a contemporary audience, Fink (1982) provides a good introduction to the interpreter's role for consumers of interpreting services. She emphasizes that the interpreter will work best when least noticed by the participants. The illusion that the consumers are talking directly with each other is easiest to maintain when neither party tries to draw the interpreter into the conversation.

Ethics

When the decision is made to involve an interpreter, the clients enter into an act of trust. They trust that the interpreter will be accurate and that the interpreter will admit or acknowledge when the situation requires skills, background, or preparation that he or she does not have. They trust that the interpreter will not become emotionally involved in the issues to the detriment of the interpretation. They trust that the interpreter will be discreet about the knowledge acquired during the interpretation or as a result of the interpreting situation.

People who perform interpretation and who violate the trust placed in them do a disservice not only to themselves but to the whole of this growing profession. Since the profession is relatively young, and most of the occasions for people meeting an interpreter on the job are not in the public eye, a single interpreting assignment is an opportunity for enhancing the lay person's view of interpreters and interpretation.

The Code of Ethics drawn up by the Registry of Interpreters for the Deaf, Inc. simply serves as a reminder of this trust, and as an encouragement for professional treatment of professional behavior. Appendix A gives the Code of Ethics, along with the guidelines for understanding it in use.

Discreet

By arriving in good time, dressing appropriately, and maintaining a low profile on the job, an interpreter will lay the groundwork for a process that will be remembered little. As Fink has aptly put it: "Being ignored can be bliss!" When everything is working best, the interpreter is unobtrusive and the fiction maintained by the interpreter and the clients that the clients are directly interacting is comfortable for all. The trust involved includes certainty about the interpreter's prior and subsequent ability to maintain confidentiality.

Confidential

It is obvious that during interpreting assignments, one gains access to much information that would never otherwise be learned. What exactly might be confidential? Anything might be, and everything could be. But confidential for whom? It is confidential for the interpreter. Even after things become public, the interpreter still is obligated to remain mum. The only exception is where a participant formally waives confidentiality, and the prudent interpreter would still want to ensure that the client(s) understood exactly what information is to be released.

Confidentiality is sufficiently central to the interpreter's ethical stance that we should elaborate with several examples. The interpreter who assists with communication during a doctor's examination is bound by the rule of confidentiality not to reveal who was examined or what was discussed. Even such seemingly inconsequential information as how long the appointment lasted and what laboratory procedures were conducted are the business of the patient and the doctor, and are not the interpreter's to reveal. The interpreter who meets a friend outside the doctor's office can safely respond to inquiry that he or she was working, on an interpreting assignment, or had business at the office. The interpreter who is accosted by a relative of the deaf person and asked what happened at the doctor's office must respond diplomatically: "I'd prefer not to answer for your son; please ask him about his visit to the doctor," or "Your mother can give you all the details, I'm sure; I don't trust my memory." The plea of memory lapse is handy, if not completely truthful. One can also explain the interpreter's code of ethics if all else fails. The doctor's office example is a pointed one, if perhaps extreme: the interpreter is not responsible for the outcome or consequences of the communication, only for its accurate transmission at the time of the interpretation. The interpreter who keeps confidences will be saved much ambiguity and awkwardness in the long run, whatever the short term discomfort.

Even good news is confidential. The deaf job applicant wants the pleasure of informing friends and colleagues when the new position is secured. This person also wants to choose who gets to know and who will find out on the grapevine, or who doesn't need to know. The interpreter needs to appreciate the equal importance of confidentiality in cases such as this one.

> Marianne Quackenbush [not her real name] is an interpreter in our community. She has had a lot of opportunity to interpret in theatrical settings in the city. I was astounded at her lack of discretion a few weeks ago, when I heard her in discussion with a group of new sign language students and supporters of interpreting. They asked her about what problems she had had working with the different theater staffs. She didn't even hesitate as she commented on how wonderful everyone had been to her except the stage manager at one theater. Someone asked which show that had been. And can you believe? She actually named the theater and the show!

This interpreter, in attempting to be accommodating and open with the community, has violated the trust placed in her. Even though she may choose not to work with that theater or stage manager again, she need not discredit them in public. Despite the fact that she has revealed no specifics, she has nonetheless violated the confidentiality of the working relationship she had with those people and that organization.

Let's consider another example: In September, 1983, the National Association of the Deaf sponsored demonstrations in front of CBS offices and affiliates around the country. At one of these demonstrations, the following exchange between a reporter and a deaf performer took place:
Reporter:
"What special problems did you encounter as a deaf performer when you were acting in 'Children of a Lesser God' downtown?"
Performer:
"I'm here as a deaf citizen to let people know that I want CBS to fulfill their responsibilities to all hearing-impaired people by making their programs accessible through the use of captioning, open or closed. I'm not here as an artist today."

This is a wonderful demonstration of how an experienced public figure can identify priorities and not let someone else's agenda sidetrack the real issue. And watching a deaf performer do it in sign language is truly thrilling.

The problem with this story is that I learned about it later, in a meeting with the "interpreter," who is a native signer and professional in a deafness field, but not a certified interpreter. Instead the "interpreter" tells me that he was the interpreter and then relates the event. Is this a breach of confidentiality?

Since it was an encounter intended for public display, one might argue that the story can be repeated, even by the interpreter. Nonetheless, strict adherence to the confidentiality rule of conduct would argue against the interpreter even repeating comments intended for the general public. If this was edited out of any news coverage of the demonstration, then it was in fact never heard by the public, but only by the performer, the interviewer, and the interpreter. Confidentiality is not intended only to limit the spread of information which may be detrimental to someone. Confidentiality is not intended only to prevent sensitive communication from getting out.

I would have believed that this individual was at the demonstration for his own purposes. If one adheres to the argument that the comment was intended for public consumption, the story could have been told, "I saw our mutual friend [names deaf performer] being interviewed by the media. . . ." The irony of this example is that the "interpreter" told the story after reminding me that the contents of the meeting, just ended, were highly sensitive, and of course confidential. In explaining my role to an outside facilitator, the "interpreter"—now the meeting planner for quite a different group said:

"She is prevented by the code of confidentiality from discussing what went on here today with her colleagues."

Probably, my colleagues—other interpreters—would be only mildly interested in the events of the meeting. But the "interpreter's" staff and parallel staff at other organizations might be very interested in learning what had gone on at this confidential meeting.

What information is the interpreter able to communicate and to whom, without violation of confidentiality? To the person or agency responsible for hiring the interpreter, the time of arrival at the job site, the length of assignment and any subsequent meeting of the parties (where an interpreter will need to be assigned) are all relevant to the payment and scheduling of interpreters. Such logistical information has generally been accepted under the heading of what can be revealed.

Much more problematic is a second type of information. Arts organizations (museums and the like) may ask the interpreter to indicate how many hearing-impaired people attended a particular interpreted lecture or workshop. The interpreter can generally offer an estimate or decline to estimate on the grounds that no one was asked to identify themselves. More difficult is the role of "interpreter-as-enforcer." Many schools, for example, ask the interpreter to report if a student is absent, tardy or if there are problems that arise (such as incomplete homework or inappropriate behavior). The interpreter should understand this condition and agree to it before accepting an assignment with an organization that makes this requirement. Some interpreters would find such conditions a violation of confidentiality, and would argue that a deaf student has every right to be absent or tardy occasionally, just as hearing students do, and furthermore that it is the faculty who can be called upon to report student absences and any difficulties. Fritsch Rudser (1980) elaborates on this and similar examples, bringing such conflicts between an ethical behavior and accepted practice into focus.

Are the participants also bound by confidentiality? Recently, hearing people who are learning about interpreters' ethical boundaries have been applying similar standards to themselves about encounters where an interpreter was present. But it is not those people who need hold back; on the contrary, if they have had successful interpreting experiences, let them advertise it! The clients can describe their own experiences freely or with restraint as they choose. The idea is that the interpreter will not be the information broker.

Accurate

What does accuracy mean? Accuracy means that the interpreter will have made an assessment of the audience, will share each speaker's understanding of the intention of the message, and will be able to render a message from the speaker's language into the listener's language. When sign language is one of the languages, then we can re-phrase the task to rendering a message from the sender's language into the addressee's language, or from the source to the target language.

Accuracy does not mean that there will always be an equivalence between a word in one language and a word in the other. Nonetheless the myth of word-for-word translation survives in the public view. Volumes have been written and will be written about the difficulties of matching meanings from one language to another. Of no little concern here is the rendering of words with specialized or heightened meaning in one language into the other. Messages that are fraught with idiomatic phrases or proper names (of products, of places, of official roles) often have many built-in cultural assumptions. Thus, accuracy means that the interpreter says as much as the sender of the message, but no more. Accuracy also means giving the receiver the complete message, including the part carried by pauses, hesitations, or other silent or non-verbal signals. The interpreter transmits the full message, not merely the words.

Proficient

Proficiency means that the interpreter will accept only those assignments which are within his or her capacity to perform. One of the difficult areas in the ethics of interpreting involves saying "no." Several quite distinct situations would make it likely that an interpreter would have to refuse an assignment. An assignment which is beyond a particular individual's present ability, where the interpreter cannot understand one or more of the individuals involved, certainly would be such an occasion. For example, someone with limited sign language skills might be able to make a phone call with a deaf person where the two are well-acquainted, and thus familiar with each other's foibles. But the same person, offered an opportunity to interpret in court, would wisely decline.

Sometimes an assignment demands more preparation than the interpreter can accomplish in the time available. A certified interpreter who has previously undertaken theater interpreting may choose not to accept the task of interpreting for the Broadway roadshow company of a hit play before a large deaf and hearing audience, given only one day to prepare. This interpreter, by refusing the assignment, is maintaining high standards and saying in effect that this particular task demands the same level of care from the interpreter that the actors and technical people have put into it.

Impartial

Impartiality implies that the interpreter will not attempt to advise or lead either party, will resist being sought for advice, and will otherwise avoid expressing opinions about the content of the communication or procedures. An interpreter would also want to avoid assignments involving close personal friends or family members, since one's judgment and ability to remain impartial are then severely jeopardized. An interpreter who anticipates strong conflicting opinions from those of some of the participants may wish to bow out of an assignment, since again one's ability to remain neutral would be tested. Some people, however, might find the difference of opinion a challenge. It really would depend on what sort of feelings were aroused by the issue at hand. Each of these examples assumes that one has sufficient information to accept or decline an assignment when it is offered.

Interpreters can maintain their impartiality by staying strictly in role. They will say "no" during an assignment when the clients have requested that the interpreter perform some task outside of the role of interpreting. The interpreter in the classroom who is requested to distribute homework, the interpreter who is asked to run for coffee while the meeting is in recess, and the interpreter who is asked to express an opinion in the discussion session all will find it advantageous to say "no" tactfully. The interpreter can only be effective for hearing and hearing-impaired people when the interpreter fulfills one role only and functions to facilitate communication exclusively.

Anderson (1978) notes that in any translation situation there are at least three participants, of whom two can be assumed to be monolingual. The interpreter, being bilingual, thus has a privileged position in the communication. At the same time, by virtue of the role of interpreter, that person is presumed to have no special allegiance to either party. Anderson suggests that individual interpreters whose two languages are not completely equal in strength may be expected to identify more strongly with one language and culture than the other. Professional interpreters always attempt to be aware of and guard against possible bias. Anderson describes the interpreter's position as one of potential conflict, in which the interpreter must perform under pressures of time, mental strain, and possible fatigue, while making rapid judgments. The interpreter may wish to simply be an echo, but clients will try to draw him or her into the role of ally or advisor. The interpreter may try to prevent some of the overload problems by setting working conditions, with adequate breaks, obligatory turn-taking and so forth.

Anderson (1978) gives a number of examples where the public "face" of the interpreter (as an ethical professional) contrasts with the anecdotes told by individual interpreters about specific assignments, and with observations of interpreters on the job. He finds interpreters expressing strongly negative opinions about particular people or classes of clients, and wonders whether such opinions affect the interpretation. He notes that most interpretation occurs not in conferences where the interpreters are subject to careful scrutiny by both peers and other bilingual participants, but in places where no one present can monitor the interpreter's performance.

How might it happen that the interpreter is less than impartial? Interpreters are people; they have feelings about the messages and people they are involved with. These feelings may be the mundane ones of interest, anger, amusement, or boredom. The interpreter may feel that one party is attempting to defraud or mislead the other. Alternatively, the interpreter may have strong religious, political, or other beliefs that would lead to support for one person's ideas or to opposition with the other person. Seleskovitch reminds us that acknowledging these feelings is useful and positive in the interpreting process, since having clearly defined attitudes towards each party lets the interpreter give life to the interpretation. She warns interpreters to guard against allowing those personal feelings and attitudes to come out in the interpretation.

What are the negative consequences of the interpreter interjecting his or her own opinion, volunteering information, or attempting to influence deaf or hearing people's decisions? At least three undesired outcomes are more likely when the interpreter participates, and less likely when we remain impartial.

First, the interpreter becomes responsible for the outcome of the interaction by virtue of having entered in as an ally or advisor. The hearing-impaired student may ask the interpreter to recall the homework assignment without being willing to make the same request of the instructor or another student. If the interpreter believes that he or she can recall the pages, problem numbers or study questions perfectly, fine; perhaps this interpreter worked with same instructor in the same course during the previous semester. But if there is an error or misunderstanding, the student will blame the interpreter, and with just cause. So the first difficulty is that the interpreter assumes partial or complete responsibility for the outcome of the interaction. In the example, the interpreter in effect is taking responsibility for the student doing the correct assignment.

Secondly, by the interpreter entering into the interaction, he or she encourages the deaf and hearing people to become dependent on the interpreter. Instead of facilitating independent communication, the interpreter who participates and advises appears to be a resource of vital importance. This sort of participation can lead to continued dependency, especially on the part of the deaf or hearing-impaired person, and has often been related to an attitude of paternalism on the part of the interpreter or other service provider.

Thirdly, and directly following from the situations described above, the next interpreter may not be so well informed, or so desirous of involvement. The clients will have an altogether inconsistent or incorrect notion of what an interpreter's role and function are if the professionals do not hold to a firm policy of non-involvement and impartiality. For example, in a phone conversation, a hearing job interviewer may recommend a particular bus for the deaf applicant to take to the interview site.

The interpreter for this phone conversation may be very familiar with public transportation and realize that the interviewer has left out the step of transferring between two different buses. Another interpreter who prefers to drive everywhere might not know about the bus system, and legitimately could plead ignorance when the deaf person complains about having arrived late because of confusion with transportation. The interpreter who presumes to know about buses would nonetheless be better off to stay out of the business of giving corrected directions for all three reasons: the interpreter will not be responsible for the outcome, the client is not encouraged to become dependent on interpreters' specialized knowledge, and any interpreter would have done the same under the same circumstances.

There is another aspect to impartiality. The interpreter does not make a judgment about what needs to be interpreted and what does not. It seems unnecessary to say it, but since there have been occasions when it was not obvious, let us say clearly that the interpreter interprets everything. This means when the hearing participant is interrupted by a telephone call, the interpreter translates the audible portion of the call. When someone other than the deaf participant is addressed, the interpreter still translates. When the deaf students are having a bit of gossip during the lecture, the interpreter voices their side comments.

The classic dilemma for the interpreter has been what to do when one party in the interaction (especially one in authority) says, "Now don't interpret this. . . ." This situation is one of the most awkward; the interpreter needs to communicate that everything heard and seen will be translated, and at the same time has an obligation to maintain the dignity of the communication setting. Even when the interpreter has begun the interaction with a brief introduction to how to proceed using an interpreter and what can be expected, the dilemma may still come up. Deaf people sometimes interject comments to the interpreter which are not intended for public consumption. These clients also deserve reminders that the interpreter will transmit all messages, and that the interpreter is not a party to the interaction.

Requesting compensation

While the request for compensation may seem at first to be exclusively a business concern, it is also an ethical issue. Interpreters have an obligation to the profession and to clients to inform clients of the fees for service when the arrangements for service are made. Interpreters often find that both hearing and deaf people are unaware that in many cases this service is not supported from any outside agency or organization. And at the same time, provision of interpreting services may be required by laws of the state or federal government.

The appropriate amount to charge cannot be determined at the national level for both legal and practical reasons. Nationally determined fee scales might be construed as price-fixing, a practice which is prohibited by law. More to the point are the practical concerns. Some local agencies set the amounts they will pay, and the interpreter may need to agree to those amounts in order to work for those agencies. There will be times when the compensation for interpreting service takes a form other than monetary. Such occasions are left to the individual interpreter's judgment and choice.

Smith (1983) draws our attention to the possible conflict in values between hearing and deaf cultures which affects interpreters and interpreter education programs. Each culture can be defined by its beliefs, behaviors, and values, deaf culture no less than others. In a cultural milieu where resources are scarce, reciprocity of services or other community goods may be offered or available and such reciprocity will be expected to be acceptable. Where we have developed our stance as professional interpreters, we have embraced a different set of values within a payment-for-services economy. Interpreters are earning a living from what was previously a service available within the resources of the community. As we promote professional distance as a positive value, we are influencing and jarring the traditional view of exchange within the deaf community. Smith urges us to be aware of the potential conflict between such traditional values of the smaller community and the accepted values and practices of the majority culture, and to take this conflict into account as we interact sensitively in the deaf community.

Etiquette

In simultaneous interpretation in general, whether between spoken languages or between spoken and signed languages, the interpreter is expected to interpret everything that is said. Summaries, simplification, and explanations are not the same as interpretation. Of course, in practice, it is often a matter of judgment whether a particular rendering of a text has passed beyond the acceptable limits of interpretation into one of these other forms.

Interpreting everything

Everything that is spoken in the presence of an interpreter and a deaf person must be interpreted into the client's preferred form of communication. During an interpreting assignment, interpreting everything means interrupting conversations (the secretary buzzes to let the hearing interviewer know of the next appointment), telephone calls (despite the fact that only half of the conversation is audible), public address system announcements (e.g. "a blue Chevy, license number 123 ABC, has its lights on in the north parking lot"), outside noises (sirens, film soundtrack from the next room), and the like.

The opposite is true as well, of course: things that are signed in the presence of an interpreter and a hearing (non-signing) client must be interpreted into spoken language. Again, remaining true to the interpretation and the communication, common sense should dictate which messages are part of the stream of dialogue and which are not. On occasion, and if deemed appropriate to the dialogue, an interpreted "comment" between deaf people may at first be found to be disconcerting to deaf people when they realize that their formerly private talk is now public, but they will appreciate the reciprocal access to communication that interpreting affords.

This guideline may extend to coffee breaks, informal receptions, standing in line and so on. Of course, an interpreter is permitted the personal time necessary to go to the bathroom, rest for a few minutes, and get refreshed at agreed-upon breaks. It's important that the interpreter assert his or her need for that break, and not get drawn into interpreting a conversation during the supposed "break." If the interpreter is part of a team, it is assumed that the time that the partner is working will be used for attending to one's personal needs.

Introductions

Making the proper introduction of oneself as interpreter, or having someone else do this, can make the whole assignment proceed smoothly. For example, one can say:

"Hello, I'm _____. I will be the interpreter today. When you talk, I will sign everything you say, and when Ms. Jones signs I will say everything she signs. You can speak directly to her in your usual way, and if I have any problem keeping up or understanding you, I'll let you know. I'd like to sit/stand here, where Ms. Jones can see me easily and you and I can hear each other."

A deaf person who has some experience in using interpreters can make the introduction equally as well:

"Hello, I'm _____, and this is our interpreter for today's meeting _____. She will assist us in communicating, since I've found that people who are not familiar with my speech often have a rocky time understanding me. The interpreter will let me know everything you're saying and will act as my voice as well. If there are no objections, I'd like the interpreter to sit/stand here where she'll be in the best position to see and hear our conversation."

Interpreters are often asked about the deaf participants' abilities to lipread and speak. The appropriate response is to direct the questions to the deaf people themselves. The interpreter is not responsible for reporting personal information about clients, their communication skills or background. Despite the fact that some interpreters do have knowledge in issues of deafness or sign language, while on an interpreting assignment this expertise is generally not available for discussion. The interpreter in orienting consumers to the interpreting environment would do well to encourage the participants to address such questions to each other directly.

Arriving early enough at the place where interpreting will happen permits such introductions to occur before the actual meeting, interview, course, or other communication begins. Over the telephone, such introductions may need to be repeated. Arriving early also permits explanations or adjustments of the interpreter's placement. A speaker who will be standing may prefer that the interpreter remain seated and slightly behind. Assuming the interpreter can still be seen by the viewing audience, such requests are not unreasonable.

First person or third person?

There have been debates from time to time about whether it is better to interpret taking on the role of each speaker, using the first person, or whether to represent each person as third person. The currently accepted practice among both spoken language interpreters and sign language interpreters is to use the first person. There are two reasons for adopting this habit. First, it avoids many possible misunderstandings. The interpreter is less likely to get confused between the client as "he" and the person the client refers to as "he." Only those ambiguities introduced by the client will remain, when one person is "I" to the other person. Secondly, as mentioned above, the practice of first person address permits the illusion that the parties who do not share the same language can speak to each other directly. It helps to accustom them to speak to each other and not to address the interpreter.

Maintaining a low profile

Herbert, among others, recommends that the interpreter maintain a low profile. In practice, a low profile includes restraining one's emotional reaction of surprise, sympathy, disgust, or joy. The interpreter, by referring to himself or herself in the third person, while referring to the participants in the first person, again promotes this low profile.

A low profile means dressing somewhat less formally than the most formally dressed participant, but certainly more formally than the most informal participant. For signing interpreters, the dress code can be specified even more explicitly. Wearing any but the simplest jewelry can draw both auditory and visual attention to the interpreter, and can obstruct the viewer's ease of reception. Similarly, loud patterns or colors may strain the eyes or distract the vision of the deaf viewer. For female interpreters, a low profile means a simple make-up scheme. For male interpreters, a low profile implies that facial hair will be well trimmed to permit easy viewing of lip and lower face movements.

Some educational programs, organizations, and schools have promoted the use of a colored smock to signal the interpreter's role. Smocks can be worn over ordinary clothes by both men and women, and have usually been offered in colors which contrast well with all skin tones (medium blues, greens). In these institutions, the clients learn to recognize an interpreter on duty, as one who has his or her smock buttoned up. An interpreter on the way to an assignment may be wearing a smock that is open. An interpreter who is off-duty and can be approached will have taken his or her smock off. While this is a convenient signal system, some clients have complained that it is overdone. In school, where students are still learning the appropriate ways to approach interpreters, or where there are likely to be many interpreters known in the community, it may work well. But these clients ask why the interpreters continue to practice this stylized signaling system off-campus in the community. They object to an interpreter appearing at a formal event such as a wedding or funeral in the "uniform." When an interpreter accompanies a deaf family with a real estate inquiry or to the accountant's office, the use of the smock may call attention to the interpreter, rather than letting the interpreter simply remain in the background. The use of smocks can be useful, but needs to be evaluated in light of community standards, where the community includes clients as well as interpreters.

In regard to physical arrangements of participants, the interpreter must seek to keep a low profile. For the spoken language conference interpreters in the booth, the physical position at some distance helps to maintain that profile. Interpreters are expected not to mix with the assembly. For sign language interpreters the situation may not be so simple. The interpreter needs to find a position from which the target audience can see clearly. The position must not obstruct the view of any other participant insofar as it is possible, while still performing the task of interpreting adequately.

Simultaneous speech and sign

Roy (1980:115) gives a few hints of etiquette for interpreters and others in the presence of deaf persons. She suggests interpreters should sign at all times that a deaf person is in the area, when deaf participants are coming into and going from a room, and while on the phone. Rather than chat using voice only, she advises signing at all times in large mixed gatherings. This prevents having to "catch up" when a deaf person joins the group. Earwood (1983) concurs, admonishing those who have the skills to sign and speak to use them.

Summary

Ethical considerations of interpreting codify the interpreter's respect for all participants in an interpreting situation. People who rely on us for conveying their communication count on us as trustworthy, accurate and impartial. In addition, we sometimes serve to introduce one or more participants to a new culture or a new communication encounter.

Carlson (1984) has presented a neat package of her interpretations of the current Code of Ethics. She summarizes the approach to ethical behavior in four points:

1. the interpreter needs to focus on the function for which he or she has been hired, rather than the feelings that arise;
2. the interpreter will be more successful who avoids "owning" other people's emotions and decisions;
3. the interpreter's primary responsibility is to facilitate the communication of others;
4. each interpreter needs to identify his or her own set of standards or requirements, what Carlson calls our "should" lists.

In this respect, she acknowledges the primacy of ethical behaviors such as confidentiality, impartiality, accuracy, and the others, by focusing on a method for carrying out the Code of Ethics.

Reading through the RID Code of Ethics (Appendix A) and discussing it with others will offer additional insights, since the guidelines that elaborate each item in the Code spell out the standards from another perspective. For comparison and contrast, we also offer the Code of Professional Conduct and Practice of the AIIC, the International Association of Conference Interpreters (which goes by its initials in French). *[Because AIIC is revising its Code, we only include part of it. See Appendix B.-Editor]*

7 The Marketplace and Working Conditions

Where do interpreters work? How do they find work? Who hires an interpreter? What is the job market like for interpreters?

Demand for interpreting

The number of potential hours of interpreting work for sign language interpreters in a particular locale depends on the number of deaf people and on their interaction with the larger community around them. The national office of the RID (1983:2-3) took a hypothetical example of a state with 1,000 deaf residents, where each deaf person is provided with one hour of interpreting per month. In this imaginary state, there will be 12,000 hours of interpreting annually. How many interpreters are needed to meet this demand for interpreting services? Assuming that one interpreter can function effectively working between twenty and twenty-five hours per week, the interpreter will be working between 1,040 and 1,300 hours. Between nine and twelve full-time interpreters would be needed to meet the one hour per month per resident estimate of interpreting service. We might revise this figure upward when we realize that these full-time interpreters will each need two weeks' vacation time. The figure also would need revision depending on scheduling: if two requests are received for the same time slot, more interpreters will be needed; if two requests are received for the same event, one interpreter might be able to cover it. And of course, we cannot forget the original hypothesis: each deaf person will receive only one hour of interpreting per month, only twelve hours each year.

If fact, many deaf people currently receive no interpreting services. They hold down jobs, raise families, meet their obligations to the community and enjoy their independence. Others benefit from many hours in the process of gaining job training, or in the course of ordinary work and recreation. Still others receive interpreting services as a result of encounters with government agencies, schools, or the legal system. Because of the great variety of demand, it is difficult to estimate accurately the number of hours of interpreting per resident.

As more deaf adults are "mainstreamed" in their workplace, more innovative uses of interpreters will be seen. Deaf professionals can be found as legislative aides, actors, educational administrators, engineers, accountants, computer programmers, social workers, psychologists, and designers, as well as in the more familiar roles of teacher and rehabilitation worker. More deaf adults are becoming entrepreneurial, starting their own small businesses.

Factors within the market for interpreting

Interpreters' work circumstances can be predicted in part by knowing whether the work is happening in a large urban area or a more rural community, knowing whether the interpreter works full- or part-time, and knowing whether the interpreter is attached to a particular organization or institution or instead works freelance. Each of these dimensions will be discussed below.

Urban/rural

One factor which affects the market for interpreting services includes the urban vs. rural dimension. Urban areas can support more interpreters, because there are more deaf people interacting in a greater variety of activities. The larger the interpreter population, the more likely the group can organize themselves for better pay and working conditions. A few interpreters working in isolation, distant from major educational centers and without a "critical mass," may find it more difficult to come forth with new proposals for improved wages and working conditions.

A large city may need tens of thousands of interpreting hours in a single year. One or more schools for deaf people, as well as mainstreamed programs, will be in operation. Traffic violations, family court, civil court, criminal court and administrative hearings will each require interpreter services during the year. Job training, public assistance interviews, food stamp appeals, housing department applications, driver's license examinations, and many other mundane interactions will require an interpreter. Immigrants from Asia, Central America, and Eastern Europe may have settled in the metropolitan area and will need job training or re-training, as well as the administrative social services to help them with re-location adjustment. Area colleges and universities will enroll hearing-impaired students. Theaters, museums, and special cultural events provide interpreters under their accessibility programs. Religious institutions, hospitals, and mental health clinics will have need for interpreters. And let us not forget baptisms, bar mitzvahs, weddings, and funerals!

When the accounting department of a major urban bank changes its procedures or equipment, deaf staff members need re-training along with their hearing co-workers. When a new benefits package is explained to the employees at the national headquarters of a large corporation, the deaf employees may have a special briefing with interpretation. A large urban area will be the site of professional conferences, government and public service interests, national group meetings.

New York City, for example, has approximately 100 sign language interpreters; do not be misled by this figure. Of these, only a handful work as full-time staff members within a few institutions (two at a social service agency, one at a mental health facility, another at a hospital, less than a half dozen coordinators or referral personnel). Roughly two dozen more earn fifty per cent or more of their income from interpreting, and the remainder take on a few assignments a week, or a year.

In contrast, a rural area will have many of the same activities going on, but less frequently, therefore, it cannot support the number of interpreters. For example, the Mid-Hudson Valley, a short 100 miles north of New York City, includes five counties with a total deaf population of roughly 300 people. They are equally entitled to interpreting services. The high school includes some mainstreamed students; some young adults are involved in job training through state-sponsored educational facilities. The courts and businesses in the area occasionally have need for an interpreter. The cultural events where an interpreter might be hired do occur, but not so regularly that someone can depend on them to earn a living. As a practical matter, only the educational interpreters at the high school can afford to live on their interpreting wages.

The contrast between urban and rural settings portrayed above may be extreme, but it is worth exploring a bit more to see what other implications it carries. For example, the urban interpreter is less likely to be acquainted with the deaf person, and may never have another assignment with him or her. Many of the urban interpreter's clients—both deaf and hearing—will need orientation to using interpreters.

In the smaller population areas, even if the interpreter has never had a professional encounter with the deaf clients, it is quite likely they have met before. The issues of trust and prior reputation may have more of an influence in this encounter.

Freelance vs. in-house

There are many advantages to having an interpreting job at one institution. The policies will be laid out. The salary and job benefits can be determined when one is hired; one knows when a paycheck is coming and how much it will be. There are positive values in developing relationships with colleagues and clients within the institution. Many people are attracted to the security and the potential for long-term contribution that an in-house position offers. Some organizations support the interpreters on their staff who contribute to professional associations such as the state RID, national RID, or CIT, so that these interpreters gain credit toward promotion, bonus pay or other recognition within the organization.

Freelancers like the variety of work, the possibility of travel, and the ability to control their own schedules. Since they depend on the seasonal or sporadic availability of work, they risk going without regular work for a period of days or weeks. Therefore, freelancers may undertake more work than is desirable some weeks in order to guarantee income. At the same time, freelancers can take advantage of special short term assignments (one day, one week, one month) for which payment may exceed the usually quoted rates. Freelancers who contribute to their local, regional or national interpreters' organizations do so on their own time, without expectation of financial or other employment benefit.

Full-time vs. part-time

From the statistics that Cokely (1981a, 1981b) gives about earnings for interpreters, it appears that interpreting with deaf people is not yet a consistently well-paying job. Full-time educational interpreters in most communities still earn less than $10,000, and are often categorized as paraprofessionals. People who work part-time may earn less since they are often not eligible for benefits (vacation time, health insurance or pension). As more interpreters make known their qualifications, and as more deaf people reach positions of responsibility in business, government, and other arenas, we can expect interpreters' incomes to increase.

Perhaps the changes are already upon us. A recent announcement of a position vacancy offered an annual salary of between $17,604 and $20,102 for a full-time interpreting job. The variance in the range depended on certification held. The job came with benefits of medical insurance, annual leave, sick leave, and holidays. The announcement did not specify the maximum number of hours of interpreting as opposed to other duties (community outreach, training to clients and the general public, in-office phone support), but it did require the interpreter to accept up to two overtime assignments per week.

Demographics of interpreters in the United States

Who is interpreting in the U.S. today? Only one attempt has been made to survey a large sample of interpreters about their personal background, education, relationships with the deaf community, with spoken and signed languages, and socio-economic status. Cokely surveyed interpreters at the RID national convention in Cincinnati, Ohio in 1980. The results of that survey are reported in Cokely 1981a, 1981b.

Let's look at a few characteristics that he found, keeping in mind that the interpreters who attend a national convention may not be representative of the group of interpreters as a whole. For example, we might expect those in attendance at the RID convention to be among the top wage earners among interpreters, since they could afford the time and expense of the national meeting held for several days in a large hotel. Either they are having their way paid by an employer who values a professionally-affiliated interpreter, or they are pulling in an income which permits such an expense.

Among the group of 160 respondents, about three-quarters of them were female and one-quarter male. Very few Hispanic, Black or Asian interpreters were in the group. About half of the group surveyed was married, and about half have children. Nearly forty per cent have a deaf or hard-of-hearing mother, and an equal proportion a deaf or hard-of-hearing father. (Cokely does not report what percentage have two deaf parents.) A slightly smaller percentage, almost a third, report learning American Sign Language first as a child.

Women and interpreting

Many people have wondered, "Why are there so many more women in sign language interpreting than men?" Some people would claim that Cokely's 3:1 ratio actually underestimates the proportion of women to men. Here are several hypotheses about why women might be attracted to interpreting in larger numbers than men. No special meaning should be attributed to the order of hypotheses listed:

1) Helping professions: Women are more heavily represented among all of the helping professions—nursing, social work, personnel, counseling, etc. Work with deaf people is likely to be seen as similar to these other career choices. In fact, Cokely's data confirm this hypothesis as far as they go. Most of the active interpreters in his group have college degrees, and more than forty per cent are continuing in higher education. Upwards of ninety per cent of the surveyed group had chosen major fields in one of four broad areas: education (especially deaf education, special education, or elementary education), social sciences (psychology, sociology, social work, rehabilitation), particular languages and linguistics, and media or visual arts (photography, educational media) for their undergraduate or graduate work (or both). The first two categories, education and social sciences, make up about two-thirds of the undergraduate degrees and a greater proportion of the major fields for graduate work.

2) Language: Professions or fields of study that are related to language and verbal skills are more heavily represented by women in the general population. Girls test better than boys in verbal abilities. More women declare majors in foreign language study and the humanities. Again, the sample group looks like the general population.

3) Movement: Interpreting is a profession that requires one to display one's body movement in public. In this culture, women are encouraged in movement fields. Outside of professional sports, men are not.

Women choose cheerleading, pom-pom, drill team, baton twirling, modeling, and dance, all of which require coordination of fine body movements. Sign language may draw on some of the same physical capabilities or culturally endorsed proclivities. No demographic statistics are available on interpreters and their involvement with other movement systems.

4) Working conditions:

a) Salary: Pay rates for interpreting are not high. Cokely's survey shows that average annual income for all respondents is between three and four thousand dollars per year. Those who work as interpreters full-time earn a bit higher average (seven to ten thousand dollars). Only seventeen per cent of the group were full-time interpreters, though. About forty per cent of the respondents gave their primary occupational category as "educator," "educational administrator," "interpreter educator," "interpreter coordinator." (The frequency of these job titles supports the hypothesis mentioned earlier that the individuals are not truly representative of working interpreters nationally. The group may, however, fairly represent the interests of interpreters, since so many are actively involved in educational or administrative efforts related to interpreting.)

b) Part-time: Interpreting is a profession that at the present time permits part-time employment. In fact, many interpreters would argue that working a 35-40 hour week exclusively interpreting is not possible. A job advertised for full-time interpreting work may require forty hours per week, but the position may include community outreach, information and referral services, training to clients and the general public about the interpreting profession, and similar additional tasks adjunct to interpreting to make up a full-time schedule. Among Cokely's surveyed group, those with deaf parents reported working seventeen hours per week; those with hearing parents about twelve hours per week. The range of pay rates is quite wide, from $4.15 per hour up to $35 per hour. However, few of the respondents are earning near the high end of the range: average pay rates were approximately $10 per hour.

Standards

Interpreters find themselves working in a variety of different situations, for different lengths of time and under a number of different conditions. In this section we will consider some of the conditions that interpreters can specifiy when being hired.

Number of hours per day, hours per week

When interpreters consider the work week, only twenty to twenty-five hours can reasonably be spent in actual interpreting. Interpreters on the staff of an institution or organization will have additional related duties, such as were mentioned above. The education of the public about interpreting, coupled with information and referral efforts, make good use of the interpreter's knowledge without taxing the individual in the same way as interpreting. Freelance interpreters will either need to receive adequate pay for their limited time and energy devoted to interpreting, or will need to supplement interpreting work with other work. For comparison, U.N. interpreters are limited to four to five hours per day of interpreting, and likewise, a maximum per week of about twenty hours. They have additional duties in preparation, telephone consultation, and similar alternate tasks. The section on working conditions in the Code of Professional Conduct and Practice of AIIC specifies that member interpreters not work more than eight hours per day in teams of two (that is, four hours per person).

Pay per unit time

For interpreters who work full- or part-time on the staff of an organization, the rate of pay may be hourly, weekly, monthly or annually. Usually, a maximum number of work hours per day or week will be set, with some guidelines or policy concerning how many hours of actual interpreting would be expected.

For freelance interpreters, rates of pay may be hourly, per assignment, or per day. In some locations, interpreters earn only minimum wage, while in other parts of the U.S. they may earn $25 per hour or more. In determining what to charge (or alternatively, what to pay), consider a comparable employment group, the individual's background and preparation, and the market in the particular area. For example, an interpreter with no high school diploma or interpreting certificate may not qualify for highly technical interpreting work, but only can accept the least demanding assignments. Such an interpreter would not be likely to command a high rate of pay. In contrast, an interpreter with a graduate degree and interpreting certificates might be able to accept a wider variety of assignments. Such an interpreter would be unwilling to accept the lower wages.

Again, referring to the AIIC conditions for conference interpreters, payment is required for travel beyond the interpreter's home site (in AIIC terms "professional domicile"), and for rest days following such travel, rather than mileage. Where an assignment spans a public holiday, Sunday, or other non-working days, these days need to be compensated at the basic minimum rate. An interpreter who is quoting rates needs to include such days in figuring the cost to the conference or organization.

We might ask what other occupations are comparable to interpreting so that we could figure out what a reasonable hourly or annual wage is. In the past, interpreters have been rated with LPN's (licensed practical nurses) and court reporters. Neither of these occupations requires more than a high school diploma, with some additional technical education. Contrast that background with the 1983 RID demographic survey, in which three-quarters of the respondents hold at least two-year college degrees (A.A.'s, A.A.S.'s, etc.). Almost thirty per cent of the respondents have advanced degrees (master's level or higher). In some locales, the percentage of interpreters with both RID interpreting certificates and college degrees may be even higher than the national averages. Depending on the sort of settings where one can find the interpreting, more comparable occupations might be certified social worker or systems analyst.

Perhaps a better comparison for interpreters who work with deaf people is the situation of translators and other language specialists. Language specialists (interpreters and translators) who are employed fulltime by the federal government hold ratings of GS-5 up to GS-16. The lowest rated specialist had only a high school diploma with sufficiently high scores on the application exams. Salaries for these ratings range from $14,000-19,000 for the lowest rating, to between $59,000 and $66,400 for the highest level. The usual salary is somewhere between these extremes, with GS-12 paying between $30,000 and $40,000 per year. Specific agencies and departments have different ratings for language specialists and recognize language skills differently. For example, Crump (1984a:47) cites the Social Security Administration as one agency which underrates translators with two or more languages, whereas in the National Security Administration (NSA) a large number of translators are employed, and NSA offers an internship program and employment incentives for those who wish to seek full-time employment there.

Among the largest employers of language specialists in the federal government is the State Department. The following chart gives the State Department rates paid to freelance language specialists (as of January 1, 1984):

Conference Interpretation	$240.00 per day
Seminar Interpretation	190.00 per day
Escort Interpretation	95.00 per day "standard" range from $70-124
English Language Escort	85.00 per day "standard" range from $65-110
Miscellaneous Interpretation including Court, Immigration, Administrative Hearings	15.00 to 50.00 per day
Conference Translation	136.00 per day
Review	190.00 per day
Foreign Language Typing	80.00 per day
Freelance Translation	63.00 per K words general*
	68.00 per K words semitechnical
	73.00 per K words technical
Freelance Review	42.00 per K words general
	47.00 per K words semitechnical
Typing	13.00 per K words Roman alphabet text
	17.00 per K words non-Roman alphabet text
Proofreading of Foreign Language Texts	6.50 per K words

*Translation work is paid in 1000 words units (K words). (Crump, 1984a)

These rates give the values currently assigned to the variety of different tasks involving language specialization for which the federal government hires. It is not obvious from this chart whether travel expenses or other costs to the interpreter are paid over the listed rates.

Volunteering

Despite the professional nature of the work and the serious effort that interpreters expend in meeting the communication needs of people from diverse backgrounds, interpreters are still often asked to volunteer their services. There are at least two good arguments against using volunteers.

First, one has no check on the quality of the performance when the interpreter is a volunteer. Someone might agree to volunteer "just to help out," but what can be done when it is found that the volunteer is not qualified to do the job? A volunteer may or may not know and understand the Code of Ethics, accepted professional practice and procedures, and may or may not follow these practices and procedures. It is not always the case that any interpreter is better than no interpreter, and in fact the deaf person may be better off without an interpreter than with an unqualified one.

The second argument against volunteering is that interpreting is a legitimate service, mandated in many instances by law. Other services which were previously provided on a volunteer basis have now been converted to paid positions. In fact, the preponderance of women in the field of interpreting, coupled with the continuing expectation of volunteer service, leads one to suspect that there is systematic albeit possibly unconscious devaluation of this work. Interpreting requires specialized instruction and skills, and thus needs to be valued appropriately. Organizations which include deaf members need to budget appropriately to offer adequate access to those members in the organization's activities. In order for interpreters to remain in the marketplace, they must receive a living wage for their efforts.

There are occasional instances where volunteering one's service can be justified. Some interpreter programs offer this kind of service with their students who are in practicums. A qualified professional can make a contribution of service to an organization. It is inappropriate, however, for the organization to pressure professional interpreters into such volunteer service. Some people mistakenly believe that an interpreter who volunteers her or his time to a not-for-profit organization can deduct the amount equivalent to the hourly or daily pay at income tax time as a charitable contribution. Such a deduction is currently not allowed. Contributions of goods, but not services, are accepted by the IRS. If an interpreter wishes to make such a contribution to an organization, one way to do it is to have the organization pay the interpreter, and then have the interpreter pay the organization. The interpreter must declare the payment as income, but can deduct the contribution legitimately. The organization will have spent nothing more than bookkeeping expenses.

Similarly, a qualified interpreter may choose to donate services to individuals during off hours. Again, the decision to volunteer should be the interpreter's and not the client's. Interpreters may decide to volunteer as a way to introduce the service while an organization is considering it as a regular accompaniment to the program. This last sort of volunteering should be clearly stated as a "one-time special offer."

Finally, students who are studying interpreting under the supervision of an instructor or mentor may feel it inappropriate to charge for services before they are fully trained or certified.

Benefits

Benefits which are usually part of a staff position can include health insurance, retirement, paid vacation time, paid sick leave, personal days, moving expenses, and F.I.C.A. A freelance interpreter who acts as an independent contractor with respect to one or several agencies and organizations will want to clarify whether any of these benefits are available to him or her. For example, it is sometimes possible to join the group medical plan, pay the premium to the organization, and receive the same or better health coverage than one can get not being a member of a group.

Freelancers who make their living interpreting need to be careful to pay the appropriate amount of Social Security Insurance, and to file quarterly estimated income tax, if no taxes are taken out of their paychecks.

Travel compensation

Interpreters who are on the staff of an agency or institution may be expected to interpret in several different sites. If the interpreter uses his or her own car, will the agency pick up the cost of travel? Each agency will probably have a standard reimbursement rate for mileage; the interpreter will need to keep track of tolls and parking expenses, as well as miles. If the interpreter uses public transportation and the agency does reimburse for car use, then similar records of the travel expenses should be submitted for reimbursement.

Interpreters who are hired as independent contractors (freelancers) need to find out whether travel time or travel expenses are reimbursed. The time to determine whether travel expenses will be paid for is at the time the assignment is offered and accepted.

Cancellation policy

Let's say the interpreter has been hired, the rate of pay has been agreed on, and the responsibility for expenses involved has been decided. It may happen that the event is postponed, the deaf person must bow out, or the interpreter learns of a schedule conflict. There are actually two sorts of cancellation policies that need to be determined. One is the policy regarding how much notice the hiring organization must give the interpreter to cancel an assignment without paying. The other is the policy about what the organization wants to do if the interpreter needs to cancel.

The interpreter's cancellation policy may specify a number of hours or days prior to the beginning of the assignment that the interpreter must be notified in order not to bill. For example, some freelance interpreters ask for forty-eight hours' notice for ordinary assignments. In that way, the interpreter has an opportunity to look for and possibly find other work to replace the hours scheduled and lost. With no cancellation policy, an interpreter may believe his or her week is fully scheduled only to find as each day occurs that cancelled assignments result in no income for the week. An interpreter who accepts a longer assignment, such as a semester's work, may request compensation for the full semester or a lesser period such as a week or two, if the assignment be re-scheduled or dropped after the commitment by the interpreter has been made. Such compensation would normally only be paid in the case that the same time slot cannot be filled with other work in that location. An interpreter, in another example, accepts an assignment requiring preparation, such as a performance where attendance at rehearsals is part of the work involved, although the actual interpreting would occur only at the end of the preparation period. In the process of negotiating the conditions of the assignment, the interpreter would probably want to specify the pay as part for rehearsal fee and part for a performance fee.

It may happen that after an interpreter accepts an assignment in good faith, he or she will need to cancel. Cancellation by the interpreter might occur for any number of unavoidable and legitimate reasons. Whose responsibility is it to find a replacement? If the hiring organization is experienced in hiring interpreters and has a large deaf population, they may wish to find an acceptable replacement themselves; the coordinator knows which clients prefer which interpreters, or knows which interpreters are likely to be available at the particular time. The interpreter may offer to find a substitute or suggest names of possible substitutes. The manner in which the interpreter's cancellation is handled will differ from one organization or assignment to another, but should be clearly determined before the assignment is accepted. It is generally not appropriate to cancel because one is offered an alternate assignment at a higher rate of pay, although the interpreter may find a discreet way to handle even this marginal case.

Supervision

Who is the interpreter's supervisor? In many cases, there is no obvious supervisor, especially for a freelance interpreter. In other cases, the supervisor, that is, person who has the hiring and firing responsibility, is not the same as the person responsible for the determination of specific schedule, or procedures undertaken at the event or interaction. The clerk of the court may be the person responsible for hiring an interpreter, but the interpreter will be required to follow procedures in the courtroom defined by the judge. A private agency may hire an interpreter for a client's conference, but the conference planners will set up the workshop schedule, break times, and specific working conditions (lighting, seating arrangements, and so forth).

A recent newspaper article highlights the difficulties of having a supervisor who is not on site, and a job which has no clear description. Lowe, a columnist for "Newsday," a Long Island (NY) newspaper, reports a case in which an interpreter in a high school setting was actually hired by the Board of Cooperative Educational Services (BOCES) and not by the principal of the school. Neither the principal nor the interpreter realized that the interpreter's hours were regulated by BOCES and not by the school. The interpreter accepted a Saturday assignment on the principal's request, when the deaf student took her SAT's, and submitted the time sheet in the usual way. Apparently because these Saturday hours (and irregular hours on several other occasions) were not previously approved by BOCES, the interpreter was not re-hired (Lowe, 1984). This example underscores the importance of having clearly defined conditions of work, a contract or letter of agreement that specifics rates of pay, payment intervals, cancellation policies, and all other aspects of the assignment. Without reference to a written contract or letter, later discussions about overtime hours, benefits, cancellations and other aspects of the work situation are difficult if not impossible to resolve to the benefit of the interpreter.

Evaluation

The person who supervises the interpreter may or may not be the same person who is responsible for evaluating the interpreter's performance on the job. In some cases, the interpreter will be evaluated by the clients. In other cases, a professional peer will observe and offer feedback. In order to make evaluation a beneficial experience for the interpreter and the evaluator, the criteria by which the interpreter will be evaluated need to be stated in advance of the evaluation. Interpreters need to be advised that they will be evaluated periodically, and given timely feedback. Where continued employment or rate of pay is contingent on successful evaluation, a predetermined system offering opportunities for improving performance needs to be available to all interpreters equally.

Liability insurance

Interpreters may not realize it at first, but they may be held legally accountable for the interpretations they provide. While it has not happened to our knowledge, the possibility exists that an interpreter could be sued for wrongful or false interpretation. Unlike translators who have written evidence of what was the original text and what their output product is, the interpreter's output is as ephemeral as the original message. Translators are encouraged to purchase "error and omission" insurance. Interpreters who are on the staff of an organization may be covered under the liability insurance of the organization. Freelance interpreters may want to be covered by malpractice liability insurance. Such insurance premiums would probably be deductible as a business expense.

Checklist for hiring interpreters

The following checklist gives ten points to be covered at the time an interpreter is hired. It has been adapted and expanded from the Long Island RID Directory of Members (1984).

1. Date of assignment
2. Time of assignment
3. Duration of assignment
4. Number of hearing-impaired participants
5. Number of hearing participants
6. Names of participants, where applicable

7. Contact person's name and telephone number
8. Nature of assignment
9. Languages/modalities preferred by hearing-impaired participants
10. Procedures for payment

Summary

Professional practices and standards are as much a part of a profession as is evaluation and certification. Interpreters must, through their national, state and local associations, develop and actively follow conditions and practices that enable them to provide quality interpretation. In pursuing an ever-increasing amount of interpreting services, for all deaf and hearing people, interpreters and clients alike must recognize the value in developing and maintaining a market for interpreters that allows them a fair wage, a living wage comparable to the amount of the service provided. Interpreters who are able to remain "gainfully employed" are better able to increase the availability of interpreting services in their respective communities.

8 Education and Evaluation

Interpreter education is a topic worthy of a whole volume on its own, as is evaluation. This chapter will look briefly at the development of instruction for interpreters working with deaf people. U.S. programs and contemporary issues are the focus. Spoken language interpretation instruction and evaluation are only briefly mentioned.

Why do interpreters need instruction or evaluation? For many years, children of deaf parents fulfilled the role of the interpreter without benefit of formal instructional programs; neighbors or charitable individuals with personal acquaintances in the deaf community also filed in as "helpers" to meet the communication needs of deaf people. While some of these people performed adequately or even superlatively, others did not. Deaf people had no way to account for the variation in proficiency, and often were dismayed by the departures from the strict ethical role of the interpreter. For deaf and hearing people to have confidence in the accuracy and impartiality of the interpreter's performance, standard instruction and uniform evaluation must be available to all professional interpreters.

Education

Spoken language interpreter programs are growing in universities, although not necessarily the same ones where sign language interpreter education takes place. State University of New York at Binghamton, Georgetown University, Georgia State University, and the University of Ottawa are a few of the North American institutions of higher learning where one can study translation and interpretation.

Interpreter instruction for sign language interpreters today consists of anything from private tutoring by an experienced, certified interpreter, workshops sponsored by local chapters of the Registry of Interpreters for the Deaf or community agencies, courses given one or two evenings a week by community colleges, up to degree-granting college level programs of two to four years' duration. The student may enter with no background in sign language and deafness, or may be screened for minimal competency in spoken and signed languages.

Federal support for interpreter education

The first national effort at interpreter instruction began with the National Interpreter Training Consortium (NITC) in the early 1970's. This five-year effort to establish regionally based, standardized instruction was renewed for several more years of support by the federal government. NITC programs offered basic interpreter instruction in different length programs, and supplemented existing interpreters' skills with special workshops or seminars in areas of interest or need. Articles in the January 1974 issue of the *Journal of Rehabilitation of the Deaf* summarize several programs offered during the early 1970's some of which were part of the NITC-funded group (Carter and Lauritsen, 1974; Nowell and Stuckless, 1974; Sternberg, 1974; Riekehof, 1974; Fant, 1974). Each of these programs existed in an institution of higher eduation where deaf students were also enrolled. Thus, the immediate need of each of these instructional programs was to provide classroom interpreters for postsecondary institutions. Each institution made some effort to acknowledge the larger deaf population who had interpreting needs outside of the classroom.

Depending on which institution housed the NITC program, interpreter instruction became a regular part of the curriculum or continued as an adjunct to formal coursework. Ending in 1980, NITC has been succeeded by federally-sponsored instructional programs in ten institutions around the U.S., matching the ten federally-serviced regions defined within the Department of Health and Human Services. In the meantime, many other colleges, universities and community agencies have set up instructional programs. Some of these offer degree programs, and others simply provide short-term instruction. At the present time, there is no universally accepted standard of what constitutes an adequate instructional program.

One attempt to pin down interpreter instruction is contained in the report of the conference sponsored by the National Academy (Gallaudet College). "Interpreter Training: The State of the Art" (Yoken, 1980) covers issues relating to the interpreter, the instructor, policies and administration of an instructional program, research and materials for instruction. Of some interest is the categorization of materials, since this beginning of organization of diverse bibliographic and media resources suggests the outline of a curriculum. Language skills are emphasized heavily in the materials available. Special settings for interpreting and special populations for interpreters to be aware of likewise receive much attention. Psychosocial aspects of deafness and role and ethics make up the remaining two major categories of materials in instruction.

Student selection and length of education

A national conference of researchers, educators, and government policy-makers selected the topic of "identification of entry and exit criteria for interpreter training programs" as one of the top five problems facing researchers in the field of interpreting during the 1980's (Per-Lee, 1980). Selection of students may depend on criteria such as above-average literacy, demonstrated interest in social service work, maturity, flexibility, and active interest in pursuing interpreting as a career. Knowledge of deafness (whether from academic study or family relationship) is generally deemed not essential for entry to interpreter instruction. Should sign language proficiency be required of students at entry? Some programs now require minimum proficiency in American Sign Language and English for students to be admitted (see for example, program brochures from the National Technical Institute for the Deaf (Rochester, NY) and Portland (OR) Community College for two-year degree programs). Other programs will admit students with no previous sign language background (for example, Maryville (TN) College, University of New Mexico, Madonna College (MI) for four-year programs).

The issue of what length an educational program must be is currently in debate among educators. Some believe that interpreter instruction can occur simultaneously with acquisition of sign language skills, so that at the end of two years of full-time study, students will be ready for interpreting in some settings (one-to-one encounters, well-managed small groups), and will benefit from further development through short-term workshops or specialized intense instruction while in the field. Others argue that interpreter instruction cannot proceed until both languages are well-mastered, and that a four-year course is the minimum needed for adequate preparation of individuals without sign language fluency at entry. The debate will only be decided if research is undertaken comparing graduates of each type of program to see, for example, how long it takes them to become certified as interpreters. There may be more than one appropriate answer, since some communities may afford graduates with little experience more opportunities for work with substantial supervision. Other communities may only offer work to whose who do not require supervision.

For comparison, consider the instructional programs for conference interpreters in spoken languages: for these, there is no question that language skills must be firmly in place before interpreter instruction can proceed. These courses all assume that admitted students have completed undergraduate degrees and possess a breadth of general knowledge usually not expected in sign language interpreter courses. After one or two academic years, those who successfully complete the programs are ready to participate as full professionals in high-level international meetings and negotiations (New Yorker, 1984; Keiser, 1978; Longley, 1968, 1978; Arjona, 1978). An important distinction here is that all of these programs intend to educate conference interpreters only, whereas programs for sign language interpreters consider conference work an infrequent placement, not recommended for the novice. Of equal importance in the sign language field is the ability to handle small groups and one-to-one interaction.

Perhaps a more apt comparison would be the instructional program at Vancouver (BC) Community College, where 180 hours taken over two semesters prepares court interpreters (Repa, 1981). In the first two years, nine different languages were represented as the students' non-English fluency, including sign language.

Curricular components

To continue the above comparison, spoken language interpreting courses assume that entering students have at least two and often three languages. Students prepare addresses for one another to interpret, join in mock diplomatic proceedings, and traditionally learn translation as well as interpretation. The incorporation of laboratory practice in both simultaneous and consecutive translation, as well as in public speaking, all give the students many opportunities to use their A, B, and even C languages in an environment as close to the actual work situation as possible. Many programs eschew lecture classes, opting for sessions of practice with immediate feedback. Programs divide course content by several methods, such as languages used (e.g., a laboratory section only for students with a French-Arabic combination), topics of texts practiced (commercial and financial, scientific and technical), or type of interpreting expected (simultaneous, sight, consecutive, as well as combinations of these types).

NITC programs described in the special issue of the *Journal of Rehabilitation of the Deaf* (mentioned above) emphasized development of sign language skills, especially the ability to read and voice (then called "reverse interpret") for signing, and the effective use of non-manual components of signing by interpreters. They also frequently refer to preparing interpreting students for the various settings where interpreting work would be found. Depending on the community and college needs, the early curricula were oriented more toward rehabilitation and social service settings, or else toward educational settings. All of the programs spent much more time on cultivating students' ethical behavior.

More recently, descriptions of programs at several institutions show refreshing views on how to organize an instructional program. Cogen (1982) describes Northeastern University's interpreter instructional program in terms of courses, topics covered, and skills and sensitivities to be developed. She focuses on participants' development of human relations skills, ability to handle physical and mental stress, cultivation of good judgment, tact and respect for others, and cross-cultural views of interpreter-consumer relations. Roy (1982) proposes a program for the

Southwest Collegiate Institute for the Deaf modeled on a discourse view of linguistic interaction. Text types (conversational, political, scientific, aesthetic) are the focus of instruction after introductory level courses. The SWCID program assumes fluency in ASL and English, and at least one year of work experience in a work setting with hearing and deaf people, prior to entry.

Kanda and Alcorn (1984) propose a model of an interpreter instructional program inspired by the Monterey (CA) Institute for International Studies program. Under their plan, students would complete two years of academic work with three options for a career path, interpreting constituting only one of those options. All students would undertake the same first year of coursework, heavily oriented to acquisition of sign language skills, and would be assessed at the end of that year. Students who had not achieved sufficient proficiency in ASL to begin interpreter instruction would be encouraged to continue coursework for service careers in deafness-related areas, where communication skills in sign language are still important. Those whose interests or talents lay in the areas of linguistics, comparative literature, or cultural studies could opt for the specialization in American Sign Language Studies.

At least a few interpreter programs in two-year colleges offer specialization in a particular subfield of interpreting. The St. Mary's Junior College Health Care Interpreter Program (Minneapolis, MN) assumes that students will have completed a basic interpreter instructional program and are interested in pursuing more intense study where interpreting skills and ethical and interpersonal skills can be honed in the health care setting. North Central Technical Institute (Wausau, WI) graduates educational interpreters, who will function as part of a deaf education team (presumably in primary and secondary schools). Vancouver (BC) Community College, mentioned above, requires applicants to pass proficiency tests in English and one other language before acceptance into the program for court interpreters. Three areas are stressed in the curriculum: the practice of interpretation, the legal system, and communication.

Students completing such programs would be expected to have skills relating to language use, assessment of clients' language preferences and arranging interpreting situations for their own and clients' comfort. They would also be expected to demonstrate knowledge of principles of interpreting, role of interpreters, aspects of interpersonal and group process. Traditionally, programs to educate interpreters for deaf and hearing people — housed within departments of special education, hearing and speech, or deaf education — have brought in much information about hearing aids, audiology, speech pathology, and education of hearing-impaired people. Interpreters who were students of these programs have a good orientation to hearing loss. More recently, interpreter programs have become independent academic units, or are relating to psychology, modern languages, and cross-disciplinary studies, and have emphasized language and culture issues. Students of these programs approach the interpreting assignment as an experience in cross-cultural communication.

Practicum

Many programs advocate the practicum or internship as a bridge between formal instruction and professional employment; however, few make explicit what constitutes an adequate practicum experience for the student. Earwood (1984) provides us with a comprehensive view of the interpreting practicum experience. He details the faculty members' roles as practicum supervisor and seminar leader (which in some programs are held by a single person), the student's perspective, and the outside mentor's role. He makes clear the impact of both deaf and hearing consumers on the student undertaking a practicum.

The practicum may include students' observation of professionals working in interpreting, as well as supervised and unsupervised experience in the field. Regularly scheduled meetings between the mentor (outside supervisor) and student can help to evaluate work performance and handle dilemmas that arise on particular assignments. Seminars with classmates and a faculty member will put students' new experiences in perspective, and teach novice interpreters how to criticize their own work in constructive ways, how to offer supportive feedback without being negative or competitive, and in general how to articulate issues from interpreting assignments while maintaining confidentiality, and otherwise conforming to ethical professional standards.

Earwood emphasizes that the practicum course should not be seen as another occasion for study and book-learning. While academic institutions generally require some evaluative mark be given at the end of the term, he recommends that this mark be based on completion of contracted assignments, attendance and participation, and a student's own growth as reflected in documents such as a journal, field notes, or progress reports. In addition, mentors are encouraged to offer written evaluations.

Acevedo (1981) notes several activities which should not be on the intern's agenda, such as office work, filing, making phone calls (except for telephone interpreting), and providing transportation for clients or mentor. Interns should feel free to accept or reject unrelated or inappropriate activities (such as those named above), without fear that the decision will negatively affect their grades.

In addition, mentors may require compensation for making professional time available to student interns. Freelance interpreters, for example, who agree to supervise a practicum student, make a commitment to regular meeting times with the intern and to offering feedback to the intern and the program. This commitment constitutes work, and thus needs to be recognized as such by the instructional program. Salaried interpreters may be able to include supervision of interns as part of their regular job, but should clarify this question before accepting the role of mentor.

Perceived educational needs

Interpreters, clients and researchers in related fields have all contributed ideas about what gaps currently exist in interpreter programs. The following several paragraphs give a sampling of the wide range of possible directions which can be followed in educational programs, in-service sessions and professional development workshops.

Colonomos (1982) reminds us that too few interpreters have truly adequate skills. Lack of awareness of the full range of at least two languages limits the competence of many interpreters. Listening skills, attention to variation in geographically and socially determined features, and to register are all part of the set of proficiencies which the accomplished interpreter brings to the task. Colonomos challenges programs to incorporate such elements into the curriculum.

Heath and Lee (1982) report the complaint of many deaf viewers that interpreters are "boring monotones." They respond with an analysis of the function of facial expression in sign languages as an overt signal of sentence boundaries, and suggest several ways that interpreters can improve their communication of phrasing, emphasis and sentence types through the increased use of appropriate facial gestures.

Woodward (1977) points out that the structure of the relationship between the deaf and hearing communities limits the opportunities that most hearing interpreters have for learning vocabulary related to sexuality. While many hearing professionals who work with deaf people claim that American Sign Language does not have signs for sexual behavior, Woodward disproves this claim through his own direct investigations with deaf signers. Since this part of the lexicon varies greatly based on factors such as region, sex of signer, ethnic background and age, he advocates local research and instruction for signs relating to sexuality and sexual behavior. Legal, medical, mental health and educational settings may all require the use of this part of the language. Woodward has offered two slim volumes with a sampling of signs in the areas of sexuality and drug use (1979, 1980).

Stawasz (1983), responding to the increasing numbers of interpreters being hired in primary and secondary school settings, proposes course work specifically on interpersonal and group dynamics for the interpreter. Some of the course content introduces the interpreting student to general ideas about the communication process and group dynamics. Later, the course deals with particulars of classroom dynamics and the interpreter's role, emotional fallout, ethical dilemmas, and interaction both in and out of the classroom.

Conference of Interpreter Trainers (CIT)

If interpreter instruction is relatively new to academia, instructors and instruction as professionals and profession, respectively, are even newer. It was only in 1979 that the first Conference of Interpreter Trainers (CIT) meeting was held. Since then, annual meetings have provided a forum for exchange of materials, methods, and approaches to instruction. The proceedings of the CIT meetings show a gradual turning outward, as the formal presentations include more addresses from speakers outside of sign language and interpreting for deaf people (see especially McIntire, 1984, for interchange between spoken language and sign language interpreting instructors).

Anderson (1982) surveyed 150 interpreter instructors who are affiliated with CIT. Nearly eighty per cent responded to the survey, which asked them to rank-order twenty possible areas of expertise for interpreter instructors. Respondents agreed that sign language fluency, interpreting skill and knowledge of research (including research on the topic of linguistic structure of American Sign Language) were among the most important areas of preparation or development for interpreter instructors. Interpreter instructors see their role as distinct from language instructors, however, judging from the low ratings of the importance of certification as sign language instructors, and ability to use foreign language instructional methods in educating interpreters. Respondents felt teaching background was relevant, but rated the study of deaf education low in importance.

Accreditation

Currently, no professional organization takes responsibility for accrediting programs for interpreter education. The Conference of Interpreter Trainers has convened a committee which offered a suggested set of standards for accreditation of programs. Both institutional requirements and specific expectations of the particular program were listed. Among the institutional requirements suggested are that the institution itself be accredited (thus limiting accreditation to academic institutions, and excluding community or social service agencies); and that the program be supported financially from a firm base and with appropriate support services to students and faculty. The suggestions for program composition include no fewer than two full-time faculty positions, specific requirements relating to student selection, curriculum components, administrative support, and class size.

In addition to defining the dimensions that an accrediting committee would look at in evaluating programs, these dimensions need further expansion. For example, if we say that a program should have an audiovisual lab available, how do we decide if a particular lab meets the criterion? If the college has a lab where instructors can make video or audiotapes for classroom use, but not one for students to use independently, would this still satisfy the requirement? How many of the requirements in the list must a program have to achieve accreditation? Will some requirements be weighted more than others? As can be seen from these questions, much work remains before accreditation can be implemented. Assuming that interpreter education continues to grow and become firmly established in more colleges and universities, however, we can predict accreditation of programs will be in place within the next five years.

Evaluation

Evaluation of individual interpreters takes place in several ways. During instructional programs, periodic opportunities for evaluation by teaching staff, community members, peers and one's self sensitize interpreters to their own strengths and weaknesses. As the interpreter enters the job market, evaluation may come directly through the reaction of hearing and deaf people to the interpreter's performance on each assignment. Of course, we would do well to keep in mind the comment of one university instructor of conference interpreters when she said:

> Only when interpreters make errors, or are otherwise inept,
> are they noticed. If they are very good in their profession,
> they achieve an absolute anonymity . . .
>
> [New Yorker, 1984]

For spoken language conference interpreters working in a booth out of the direct view of the participants, this is particularly true. Still, the interpreter who is "ignored" has a good sense of the effectiveness of the interpretation.

In more formal ways, interpreters are often screened or assessed before being accepted for the roster of particular referral services or for a regular staff interpreting position in an organization. In many organizations which hire or contract with large numbers of interpreters, periodic evaluation of individual performance will assure quality to clients and assure interpreters of regular and systematic feedback. Evaluation on the job, then, may consist of spot observation by an interpreter-coordinator, or may include written comments from deaf and hearing participants.

Several sorts of objective testing for interpreters exist. Arjona (1984b) describes the procedures which were developed for certifying federal court interpreters. While the Court Interpreters Act of 1978 mandated that all non-English speaking litigants be provided with certified interpreters, Spanish was the first language for which an examination was developed. The certification test included a written screening instrument and an oral examination of how the interpreter would function in a court setting. Arjona also gives details of the competencies covered in this test, and of the scoring system.

Another objective test is the Registry of Interpreters for the Deaf's national certification. The procedures involved in RID certification and administration are explained thoroughly below. In addition, some locales depend on a quality assurance assessment to rate interpreters in their region who have not taken or passed the national test. Licensing is the ultimate form of evaluation at the state level.

RID Certification

One of the first formal tasks which the Registry of Interpreters for the Deaf set out for itself in 1964 was the design and implementation of a national certification system to test the skills, ethics and professional behavior of interpreters. Since 1972, this national "performance-based" evaluation has been used to certify sign language interpreters. In 1989 a major revision of the certification process was implemented. Under the new system, two general certificates are awarded:

1. *Certificate of Interpretation* (CI): ability to interpret between American Sign Language and spoken English in both sign-to-voice and voice-to-sign.

2. *Certificate of Transliteration* (CT): ability to transliterate between signed English and spoken English in both sign-to-voice and voice-to-sign.

If a person wishes to stand for evaluation, he or she completes an application and pays specified fees which are used to pay for rater services and adminstrative costs. Applicants need not be members of RID. Tests are given at 26 regional sites. There are practice videotapes and a study guide available to help applicants prepare for the evaluation including sample questions, interpreting vignettes, and a suggested reading/viewing list.

Test Components

There are two parts of the evaluation: the written test and the performance test. The written test consists of two sections:

a. *Ethical Standards:* This section is a series of dramatized vignettes lasting from thirty seconds to several minutes. Each scene depicts interpreters interacting with deaf and/or hearing consumers. Questions relate to whether or not the depicted behavior conforms to generally accepted RID ethical practices. The applicant answers each of the forty (40) questions in a test booklet.

b. *Knowledge:* This section consists of 125 multiple-choice questions on the subjects of ASL, Deaf Culture, the role and function of interpreters, the RID Code of Ethics and Bylaws, and the history of the RID and the NAD.

There are separate performance tests for each of the two different RID certifications (CT and CI). Each performance test consists of the following:

a. *Sign-to-voice segment:* Each candidate will view a platform presentation in American Sign Language (for the CI test) or in English-like signing (for the CT test) by a deaf person and be asked to simultaneously interpret or transliterate into spoken English.

b. *Voice-to-sign segment:* Each candidate will see/hear a lecture in spoken English by a hearing person and be asked to simultaneously interpret the text into ASL (for the CI test) or transliterate it into English-like signing (for the CT test).

c. *One-to-one segment:* Candidates will be asked to simultaneously interpret or transliterate in both sign-to-voice and voice-to-sign for this interactive segment.

All stimulus materials are unscripted. Every person is authentically a doctor, lawyer, teacher, insurance broker, or whatever role he or she depicts in the videotape. This adds realism and validity to the test — by capturing natural, spontaneous signs/speech.

Test Results

Once completed, the written test is corrected by a Scantron machine in the National RID office. Applicants passing both portions of the written test are then considered "Candidates for Certification" and are eligible to take one or both of the performance tests. At least one performance test must be completed within five years or the individual is required to retake the written exam.

The performance tests are evaluated by three raters (one deaf, one hearing layperson and one interpreter) who compare the performance they are viewing with the performance standard set by the certified members of RID in 1987. If the candidate's performance does not meet or exceed the acceptable level, certification is not awarded.

The RID Certification System: 1972-1987

Under the former certification system, the RID recognized two types of full certification for sign language interpreters:

Comprehensive Skills Certificate (CSC): ability to interpret between American Sign Language and English and to transliterate between English and an English-like signing.

Reverse Skills Certificate (RSC): ability to interpret between American Sign Language and English or transliterate between English and an English-like signing. This certificate was awarded to deaf or hard-of-hearing people only.

These certificates indicate that the holder was tested before July 31, 1988, and demonstrated a satisfactory level of performance in both interpreting and transliterating at that time. These certificates were issued for five-year periods and will no longer be recognized as valid after 1995.

Prior to 1988, RID also granted the following partial certificates to sign language interpreters:

Transliteration Certificate (TC): ability to transliterate between English and an English-like signing.

Interpretation Certificate (IC): ability to interpret between American Sign Language and English.

Holders of these certificates have demonstrated a level of performance in the categories tested at a percentage lower than that required to earn the CSC. These certificates will no longer be recognized as valid after 1995.

Between 1975 and 1978, specialist certificates were available to persons holding full certification. These specialist certificates indicate that the holder has completed specialized training and has demonstrated a satisfactory level of performance in the specific area tested. Prior to 1988, the following specialist certificates were available:

Specialist Certificate: Legal (SC: L)

Specialist Certificate: Performing Arts (SC: PA)

Beginning in 1979, RID recognized the skills involved in making spoken language visible to deaf or hard-of-hearing persons who prefer speechreading as their mode of reception, and acknowledged that not all of such persons have speech which is intelligible to naive listeners. Three certificates were granted in interpreting for oral deaf persons from 1979 to the mid-eighties:

Oral Interpreter Certificate: Spoken-to-visible (OIC:S/V): indicates the ability to paraphrase and transliterate a spoken message from a hearing person to a deaf or hard-of-hearing person.

Oral Interpreter Certificate: Visible-to-spoken (OIC:V/S): indicates the ability to understand the speech and silent mouth movements of a deaf or hard-of-hearing person, and to repeat the message for a hearing person in spoken English.

Oral Interpreter Certificate: Comprehensive (OIC:C): indicates the ability to paraphrase and transliterate a spoken message from a hearing person to a deaf or hard-of-hearing person, and the ability to understand and repeat the message and intent of the speech and mouth movements of the deaf or hard-of-hearing person.

Like the certificates described previously, oral interpreter certificates demonstrate minimal competency in each of the areas tested. These certificates will no longer be recognized as valid after 1995. More information about oral transmission can be found in Chapter Ten.

RID National Certification Board and National Testing Board

The National Certification Board (NCB) and the National Testing Board (NTB) of the RID are the committees which regulate the certification system. The NCB, composed of five certified members and one liaison member from the Board of Directors, are appointed by the Board of Directors. The NCB has the authority to set standards and procedures, hear appeals, and award and revoke certificates. The NTB designs, administers, and revises the evaluation materials with the help of the National Testing System (NTS) coordinator in the home office. The NTB also administers evaluator training and approves evaluators.

Quality Assurance Programs

The demand for interpreters is greater than the number of certified interpreters currently available. People without certificates have been and continue to be employed as interpreters. The goal of quality assurance programs was to provide a way to test levels of lesser skill than RID certification demands. Individual RID chapters are prohibited from creating or administering these programs although RID members are free to participate in any such screening. Cooperation between vocational rehabilitation agencies and interpreter referral services, two of the largest employers of interpreters, often result in state-wide assessment programs. The screenings and levels awarded vary from state to state and anyone interested will want to look carefully and cautiously at the standards set and the validity of the instrument used.

Licensing

At the present writing, no license for interpreters is offered anywhere in the U.S. Licensing systems are regulated by individual states for practice of professionals such as teachers, psychologists, doctors, physical therapists, and landscape architects. The advantage of a licensing system is that people who do not possess a state license cannot call themselves psychologists, physicians, or architects. The licensing system can prevent harm to the public from unethical or unqualified practitioners. The state can invoke its authority to sanction those who misuse the professional title, and those who do not conform to the accepted standard of conduct or quality of performance.

States are more willing to institute licensing for occupational groups for which professional education in universities exists, since such education indicates that applied, specialized knowledge is required for the occupation. In addition, the practitioners must be autonomous, rather than primarily employees of an institution. The occupational group that wants state licensing must demonstrate that it tries to regulate practitioners' conduct, through codes of ethics or by promoting high standards, but that further regulation is required. States are generally unwilling to institute licensure, the most strict form of regulation, unless self-monitoring has proven unsuccessful and can be demonstrated to result in harm to the public health, welfare or safety. States also will not support licensure when it will result in a monopoly on services.

The disadvantage of a licensing system is that it inserts another layer of bureaucracy between the individual and the practice of the profession. Undoubtedly, it will require the individual practitioner to pay additional fees to the state to gain entry to the profession initially and to maintain the license. The practitioner would probably need to pass on these additional expenses in higher fees to the public. There is also no guarantee that licensing would increase the number of professionals available, and in fact might further limit the number available. The composition of the licensing board, as authorized under the legislation providing for licensure, must be scrutinized carefully at the time the legislation is passed. Would it include practitioners of interpreting? Experts in related fields? Consumers? What instruction would be recognized as necessary or sufficient to be accepted for licensing? Would instruction in a college or university be the only preparation permitted or would other educational endeavors be recognized? In short, licensure cannot be approached as a panacea to difficulties in making a workable evaluation system.

9 Settings for Interpretation

The settings for interpreting we will describe here make up only a partial list of the possible settings in which interpreting occurs. The eight categories that are discussed could probably be supplemented by eight additional categories; we have not touched on interpreting with travel tours, for example. Some readers will argue that what we have called a single category is actually two different ones conflated; we have combined elementary, secondary and post-secondary education where many people would call these two or even three separate setting types. Other readers might prefer lumping two categories together; medical and mental health settings often share features relating to physical facilities, training of the professional personnel, anxieties of the client. Certainly, all experienced practitioners will agree that none of these treatments does justice to the complexity of dilemmas that working interpreters face on the job. Most settings deserve a whole book to themselves!

Indeed, readers should take care in examining these sub-sections: we have given only cursory attention to some of the most frequent settings that novice interpreters will face. For example, in this chapter, rehabilitation and social services is among the shorter sub-sections, but is among the most common placements for interpreting students as interns, and for recent graduates of interpretation. The fact that it appears here only briefly means that limitations of the author's time prevented giving a more intensive discussion. What a wonderful opportunity for less experienced interpreters to directly inquire of more experienced people in the community, both deaf and hearing!

The educational, legal, and medical settings have been updated in this revised edition. The only sub-section that has been more extensively developed is the performing arts setting.

Interpreting in Educational Settings

Introduction

Interpreting in educational settings has been one of the fastest growing areas within the profession of interpreting where deaf people are concerned. This setting was not even mentioned in the earlier manual for sign language interpreters, *Interpreting for Deaf People* (Quigley and Youngs, 1965), probably because the practice was so limited at that time. According to the Report of the National Task Force on Educational Interpreting, *Educational Interpreting for Deaf Students,* the number of interpreters working with deaf students at all levels almost certainly exceeds 4,000 (Stuckless, Avery, Hurwitz, 1989). Two causes for this growth can be cited. First, beginning in the late 1960's, many more opportunities have become available for deaf people to attend postsecondary institutions. Secondly, Public Law 94-142 has influenced school districts to include deaf children in public schools, often with the support of an interpreter.

Cokely (1981a, 1981b) reports on demographic characteristics of 160 interpreters who responded to a survey distributed at the 1980 convention of RID. For this group, educational or classroom settings were the most frequently listed paid interpreting situation, cited by nearly half the respondents as the source of all or part of their interpreting income. In 1989 the membership of the RID special interest group EdITOR (Educational Interpreters and Transliterators of the RID) was surveyed and 147 responses were tabulated and analyzed. These data showed that approximately 59% of these self-described educational interpreters depended on their earnings from interpreting in educational settings as their sole source of income. Additionally, 49% of these interpreters held a bachelor's degree (McLachlan, 1989).

Mainstreaming, the integration of disabled students, has been a strong trend in educational policy since the early 1970's. Legal support for mainstreaming has come from Section 504 of the Rehabilitation Act of 1973 and from Public Law 94-142, also known as the Education for All Handicapped Children Act. These laws and the regulations implementing them have mandated that all handicapped children receive a "free and appropriate" public education. This education must be specially designed to meet the child's needs, supported by related services, and must take place in the "least restrictive environment." Chapter Three of the book *Legal Rights of Hearing-Impaired People* (DuBow, *et al*, 1982) gives an overview of the issues around educational opportunities under these laws. Greenberg and Doolittle (1977) examined several sides of the educational and psychological impact of mainstreaming versus state school education for deaf children. Further discussion of these issues can be found in *Toward Equality,* the 1988 report to the President and Commission on Education of the Deaf (Bowe, *et al.,* 1988).

Interpreters, then, have become part of the support services that may be provided to deaf students in elementary school, junior high school, high school and postsecondary settings. As the National Task Force on Educational Interpreting points out, however, several problems became evident as interpreters began to work in educational settings. These problems included:

—Local educational agencies and postsecondary institutions did not generally have policies and guidelines outlining the roles and responsibilities of interpreters in the educational system. Further, interpreters and educators often had differing views on these issues.

—Traditional interpreting credentials alone did not automatically accord interpreters the status, remuneration or working conditions of other professional staff in the educational milieu.

—Having been developed based on the relationship between the interpreter and the deaf adult client, the RID Code of Ethics did not seem to be immediately applicable to the relationship between the interpreter and the deaf child in a school setting.

—Interpreters often had little or no special preparation or experience in working with deaf children or knowledge of child development or pedagogy.

—Interpreting at the postsecondary level and in technical settings often called for a knowledge of content areas for which interpreters had no background and for which a standard sign vocabulary was not readily available (Stuckless, Avery, Hurwitz, 1989).

Elementary and secondary school settings

The role of the interpreter at the elementary through secondary levels is in some ways more problematic than in other settings, simply because one is working with children. The elementary school interpreter must have excellent interpreting skills plus the common sense and caring heart to be an adult in a child's world and still adhere to the interpreter role. A hug for a kindergartner having a sliver removed by the nurse may be in order at the same time one is voicing, "I don't want it out!"

The traditional models for interpreting, as well as the RID Code of Ethics, were developed on the assumption that the clients involved would be adults. In this setting, the deaf clients in question are almost always children. Not only are there unique legal constraints operating in the educational setting where school personnel function *in loco parentis,* but deaf children are most typically language learners as well as language users. Both of these factors require some modification of traditional interpreting protocol, such as the practice whereby the interpreter matches his sign language to the language the deaf client uses or states a preference for. Child language learners may not be in a position to state a sign language preference. Additionally, some school programs mandate the use of a particular sign system or language that may or may not be what is used by the deaf students.

Educational programs are generally designed with the goal of moving students toward increasingly greater degrees of intellectual, emotional, and social maturity. This developmental continuum may necessitate differing roles and responsibilities for all members of the educational team, including the interpreter, at different levels and with different individual students. An example of this would be when an interpreter in an elementary school is called upon to tutor as a way of introducing children to both the mainstream classroom and the interpreter function. In a first grade math

Figure 9-1
Library story hour

104

classroom, the interpreter may interpret the general directions and then tutor the student through the activity. The interpreter/tutor may choose to be available to the other students as well so as not to isolate the deaf students. This first experience will shape the deaf student's understanding of the role and function of an interpreter. This understanding will need to evolve as the child progresses through school.

In addition, the interpreter may be the only person (or one of the few people) in the school who can talk directly with the child. The other children may have had no contact with deafness or deaf people, and the teachers may be less prepared to manage the situation than either they or the interpreter would prefer. Moreover, the deaf child in a classroom with an interpreter may be the only deaf child in the grade level, or even in the school. The interpreter will be looked to by the deaf student, the hearing students, and possibly the teachers and administrators for guidance and orientation. It is critical to remember that much of this guidance and orientation takes place in subtle and indirect ways through the interpreter's day-to-day interactions with the students and staff.

In some school settings, the interpreter will be working with only one deaf student and may be the only staff member in the building familiar with deafness on a daily basis. In other settings, the school may house a program staff of teachers, special counselors and a number of other support personnel including interpreters. Some educational interpreters serve students at several schools and commute daily to more than one site. In some settings, the same interpreter may be working for part of each day at the elementary level and for part of each day at the secondary level. Even in the same school an interpreter may go from a first grade social studies class to a sixth grade English class to a fourth grade physical education class in the same day. Each of these various arrangements, as well as many other possibilities, presents its own challenges. Clearly interpreters in educational settings must be flexible and possess a wide range of skills and depth of knowledge.

Equally important, the interpreter must have a clear understanding of the role and responsibilities in each setting. The importance of clearly defining the expectations of the interpreter, the classroom teacher, and the deaf student in each setting cannot be overemphasized. Public Law 94-142 requires that each deaf student have an Individual Education Plan (IEP) that specifies support services the student will need to benefit from the particular educational placement. Students may be placed in classrooms or take part in curricular and co-curricular activities with the support of interpreters for a wide variety of reasons. It is essential that all parties in the decision-making and service-delivery process be clear about the goals of the placement and the activities in question. These goals should help define the responsibilities of the interpreter in each situation.

The process of interpreting is limited by certain physical constraints. Only one speaker can be adequately interpreted at a time. Deaf students cannot visually attend to the interpreter and read text material or visual aids simultaneously as hearing students are often asked to do. Interpreting involves a necessary "lag time" between when the speaker (or signer) speaks and the interpreter processes the content and reproduces it in the second language or mode. This processing is most evident during rapid-fire discussions or question-answer sessions. A sophisticated understanding on the part of the classroom teacher of the process of interpreting and the needs of visual learners is required. Only when the teacher and the interpreter work as a team can a truly accessible educational environment be created. A clear understanding of the goals of this placement and activity are crucial if the most appropriate decision is to be made. An example of this type of dilemma might be the high school classroom wherein a free-flowing general classroom discussion includes a good number of "extraneous" comments by students. If the exclusive goal of this deaf student's placement in this class is mastery of the course content, the interpreter may elect to follow the topic-relevant comments and include only those "extraneous" comments as can be comfortably included. Conversely, if one goal of the deaf student's placement in this class is to develop age-appropriate social skills, the interpreter may elect to balance the topic-relevant comments with the "extraneous" comments providing a more complete model of the social skills demonstrated by the hearing students in the class.

The need for interpreters to protect the privacy rights of their clients is central in the ethical guidelines under which interpreters generally work. This focus on confidentiality is equally important in educational settings, although from a different perspective. In elementary and secondary educational settings the deaf client is almost always a minor whose right to privacy may necessarily be balanced against the responsibility of school personnel to protect the student's welfare and provide appropriate services. Interpreters are often employees of the local educational agency and, as such, agents of the school functioning *in loco parentis*. Clear guidelines concerning the interpreter's role is critical here, as is the need to communicate these guidelines to all involved parties, including parents and students. To illustrate, an interpreter in a public school may be expected to report any instances of cheating and may therefore be expected to report to a school authority a hearing student who asks (via the interpreter) to copy a deaf student's work. This same dilemma would most likely not arise in a postsecondary setting.

Postsecondary settings

Technical-vocational schools, community and junior colleges, as well as four-year colleges and universities with graduate programs have also opened their doors to deaf students. Those which have maintained enrollment over time are often those that provide high quality support services, including counseling, note-taking, tutoring and interpreting, along with instruction.

Many institutions have a special office to coordinate support services to disabled students, sometimes specifically to deaf students. A coordinator (or similarly titled individual) may schedule and supervise the interpreting staff. This person may also function as the deaf students' counselor or may work closely with such a counselor. This office or staff person will often provide orientation for faculty who have not previously had hearing-impaired students and interpreters in their classrooms. The same person may also be in charge of orienting deaf students to their rights and responsibilities in working with an interpreter, as well as the particular policies of that institution. The interpreter cannot hope to interpret successfully and take the time to do in-depth consumer education during the same class period. Such an orientation to interpreting in general and specific institutional policies, prior to the beginning of class, will do much to ensure the success of the interpreter/student relationship.

In contrast to the elementary and secondary settings, students at this level are typically adults with established language preferences. The traditional interpreting model that assumes the interpreter will adapt to the linguistic preference of the deaf client is generally accepted. Typically, postsecondary training programs are structured to accommodate easily the need for separating the roles of the interpreter, tutor, and notetaker. When

Figure 9-2
Classroom

the need arises for a single person to function as both interpreter and tutor for a particular class, this can be accomplished by having the tutoring occur in a different setting than the interpreted class itself.

One dilemma that interpreters in postsecondary settings face more often than their peers at lower educational levels is that often these interpreters are part-time contractors who do not work consistently with the same institution. This dilemma is exacerbated in situations where the

107

institution does not have any full-time or regular staff charged with coordinating interpreting services. This may mean that there is no one directly connected with the educational institution to provide orientation/consumer education to faculty members and/or students. In these situations the interpreter may be faced with the need to provide this consumer education as part of the interpreting duties. As is true in other interpreting settings, this task should be accomplished as much as possible by including both deaf and hearing clients together (in this case, the student[s] and teacher).

Considerations in the workplace

While job titles and descriptions may vary greatly across educational levels and settings, there are many elements common to all. As is true in interpreting in general, practitioners must be sensitive to both the environmental and human aspects of the work environment.

Dress and grooming should reflect an understanding of the need to present a comfortable contrast with one's skin tone while avoiding visual distractions. Some classroom interpreters wear plain colored smocks. Such uniforms not only provide the requisite solid color background for the interpreter's hands but also serve to identify the interpreter. In some (often postsecondary) settings, the sheer size of classes and/or the staff makes it difficult for faculty and students to always be familiar with all of the interpreters, and it is easier for everyone simply to look for the uniform. In settings where interpreters have multiple roles, such uniforms may help all concerned remember when an individual is functioning in the interpreting role — a junior high interpreter/aide may wear the smock while interpreting in the science class and not wear it during the math class when working as a tutor. Dress should also be considered from a more human perspective. Interpreters should strive to dress in a manner that aligns them visually with other professional staff in the classroom. Both kindergarten teacher and interpreter may find slacks appropriate as they work at eye level with small children. In a lecture classroom both teacher and interpreter may be in business suits or the like. A vocational shop or lab may require that both instructor and interpreter wear overalls and safety glasses.

Placement is a major consideration when interpreting in educational settings. Naturally the primary objective is to ensure that the deaf students have a clear sightline to the interpreter. As much as is possible this sightline should also include the primary area of visual focus for the class — the speaker in a lecture setting or the blackboard or screen for projected images. Because many teachers use multiple visual aids and a wide variety of teaching techniques, it is often not possible for the interpreter to assume that any one placement will be standard or permanent. The classic example of a classroom with the teacher standing front and center and the interpreter standing or seated slightly to one side is only one possible arrangement. The interpreter may need to stand at the side of the screen or the blackboard. In some classrooms where discussion is a primary teaching tool, the deaf students may prefer to sit with the interpreter in the back of

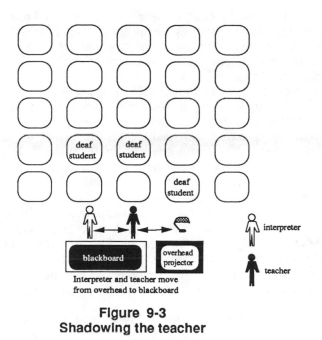

Figure 9-3
Shadowing the teacher

the room or to one side so they can easily look past the interpreter to identify changing speakers. In one classroom it may be best for the interpreter to move along the blackboard with the teacher as a series of problems is explained. (See Figure 9.3.) In another classroom the same interpreter may find it more successful to remain seated on one side while only the teacher moves across the board. An occasional change in placement on the part of the interpreter may allow the deaf students to comfortably attend visually to the signed message and the speaker, blackboard, film, etc. However, too much movement by the interpreter can be visually fatiguing or distracting. Some trial and error may be necessary until the right pattern is found in each classroom. The teaching strategies and visual aids used, the personality and preferences of the teacher, and the preferences of the deaf students all must be taken into consideration.

This is one reason why interpreters in educational settings need well-developed interpersonal skills. Teachers are typically unaccustomed to "sharing the stage" with another person. At the same time, it is the interpreter's responsibility to ensure that the special needs of visual language users are accommodated. When this concern can be clearly communicated and demonstrated by the interpreter, all the participants in the educational setting are best served. Teachers may be confused to find that what was comfortable and successful with a deaf student in one class is not ideal for a different student or in a different class. Teachers may not readily understand that deaf students cannot attend to both the interpreter and printed text or a second visual message simultaneously. In postsecondary settings, much of the responsibility for this kind of "in-service training" of the teachers may rest with the deaf students. With children in elementary and secondary classrooms, much of the responsibility will rest with the interpreter.

A unique feature of educational settings is that in most cases the interpreter has the opportunity to work with the same group of people on a regular, sometimes daily, basis for an extended period of time. This allows for relationships to be established and for the interpreter to increase effectiveness through the careful analysis of the various types of feedback received. Just as interpreter and student placements can be "tried out" until the ideal arrangement in this situation is achieved, the interpreter can work with the teacher and students (in age-appropriate ways) to discover the most effective ways to make the class experience truly accessible for the deaf student. It is not uncommon to see interpreters in classrooms using the blackboard, usually by pointing to previously written items, to reinforce specific English vocabulary that might otherwise use a non-standard sign for or fingerspell. For the interpreter who enjoys analyzing situations, educational settings provide unparalleled opportunities for creativity and satisfaction.

Scheduling of interpreters in educational settings is an area of real concern. Many educational interpreters have developed physical problems related to the overuse of certain joints, tendons and muscle groups. While settings (both educational and other) that involve extended lectures or similar non-stop spoken language have traditionally allowed for two interpreters to "spell" each other at regular intervals, the average class of 45 to 90 minutes (depending on the level) is often not long enough to warrant assigning two interpreters — nor could most educational agencies afford to do so. While it is true that often classes do not involve continuous spoken language for the full period, it is equally true that in a high school setting, for example, an interpreter may be assigned to four 50-minute classes in a row with only five-minute breaks dividing them. Should even two or three of these consecutive classes require non-stop interpreting, physical fatigue and the concomitant lowered performance (if not physical damage) are a real threat. The demands on the interpreter are further complicated by the fact that activities that reduce the amount of "teacher talk" may not reduce the interpreter's workload. Non-captioned movies, videotapes, or discussion groups and similar non-lecture teaching strategies are often very demanding for the interpreter. Conversely, an interpreter may be assigned to a class that requires almost no actual interpreting on a given day. Students may be involved in individual seat-work or lab activities that require minimal spoken language. Field trips or other activities may totally change the interpreting needs for a given day. Interpreters and the administrators responsible for scheduling them are thus faced with conflicting constraints. An individual interpreter cannot be expected to perform well for extended periods without rest time, and at the same time it is not economically prudent to have paid staff simply "available" but not needed for extended periods. Some schools are able to resolve the dilemma by creative scheduling and using interpreter pools where individual interpreters can float between settings with high and low demands. Other schools find the solution in hiring interpreter/tutors or interpreter/aides who balance their time between interpreting and other tasks to provide the physical down time the interpreters need. The possible solutions are many, and each school must design its job descriptions and staffing patterns to suit its unique needs.

One consideration that is sometimes overlooked is the interpreter's need for professional preparation time. Educational institutions typically build this into the schedules of their teaching staff but may overlook it for interpreters. Interpreters at all levels need time to prepare themselves adequately. The following list is only a sample of the kinds of activities that interpreters may need to engage in if they are to be maximally effective in the classroom: reading class texts; previewing films, videotapes, and other media; researching appropriate content-specific signs; previewing lecture notes and meeting with teachers regarding key concepts, target vocabulary or teaching strategies so that appropriate decisions can be made regarding interpreter placement.

Pre-employment expectations: Employers

Interpreters in educational settings need to understand the theoretical and historical basis of the field of interpreting and accepted professional practices. In addition they should possess a high degree of competence in both voice-to-sign and sign-to-voice interpreting and/or transliterating. Ideally this competence should be demonstrated using the language(s) and/or mode(s) specified by the hiring educational agency and with students of the target age group(s). At this writing no such standardized measure of competence is available that is specific to the educational setting. The traditional measure of interpreter competence, the RID's National Testing System, includes only adult language users in its stimulus materials.

The 1989 Report of the National Task Force on Educational Interpreting identified three general areas of preparation for interpreters in all educational settings: general studies, pre-professional, and professional (to include practicum training). The range of competencies in this report include (but are not limited to): proficiency in English at the college level; a broad "liberal arts" background in the humanities, social sciences, mathematics and science; skills in public speaking and interpersonal and group dynamics; an understanding of human development and the impact of hearing loss; a knowledge of the foundations of education and of special education (Stuckless, Avery, Hurwitz, 1989). Postsecondary institutions often find it ideal to employ interpreters with a college level background in the content area of the courses they will be expected to interpret.

Pre-employment expectations: Employees

— Who is the interpreter's supervisor? Is there someone who can act as the advocate for the interpreter? Is there a job description within the particular school or throughout the school district? How is the interpreter's pay rate determined? Are there certification or educational prerequisites for the position of interpreter? Is there a defined path to promotion, regular pay raises, opportunities for professional development which are appropriate for the position? Who are the interpreter's colleagues within the school or district?

— What hours constitute full- or part-time employment? For what benefits is the interpreter eligible? When should an interpreter take on additional duties, for example, in response to student involvement with extra-curricular activities? What additional compensation is available for such work? (These activities can be quite extensive, depending on how many deaf students are involved with the school, and what "extras" the school offers, e.g., club meetings, athletic teams, field trips, school plays, or outside theatrical experiences, just to name a few.)

— What are the policies regarding absences on the part of the student? How much notice must the freelance interpreter have in order not to bill for the time? How long must the interpreter wait before assuming that the student is not coming? What about absences on the part of the interpreter? Will substitutes be paid? Is the interpreter or coordinator responsible for finding a substitute? If a student drops a class or otherwise changes schedules after an interpreter has committed to the schedule, will the interpreter be compensated for loss of income? (In post-secondary settings, where part-time or freelance people are hired for each course, such a cancellation may constitute a serious loss of income. The interpreter may have refused other work assuming that these hours were filled for several months' time.)

Interpreting in Legal Settings

When we think of providing interpretation services in a legal context, we usually think of court. However, there are numerous other environments in which interpreters may provide service, including, but not limited to: police interrogations, attorney-client consultations, meetings in correctional institutions or with probation officers, and during the taking of depositions (in some states called "examinations before trial" or EBTs) and administrative hearings. Trial courts in which interpreters may appear include criminal, civil, municipal, family, surrogate, or appellate courts. Although states may have different names for courts, they are conceptually the same; for example, in New Jersey, the Family Court Division of the Superior Court hears matters involving juveniles, dissolutions (divorce) and domestic violence, among others. Other states may have separate courts for each type of matter, such as juvenile and matrimonial court.

Provision of interpreter service: Legal obligations

Each state differs in how broadly it authorizes the presence of interpreters in court and other legal settings (see *Legal Rights of Hearing-*

Impaired People, Chapter Nine, Dubow, *et al,* 1982). The United States Constitution, Amendment VI, guarantees criminal defendants the right to a fair trial, to confront witnesses against them, and to the assistance of counsel. Federal laws (e.g., the 1973 Rehabilitation Act, Section 504) protect the rights of deaf individuals to interpreter services in criminal proceedings. However, in municipal, civil, and administrative proceedings, the right to an interpreter may or may not be a provision of state statutes or case law. It is incumbent upon interpreters to familiarize themselves thoroughly with the laws that govern their state and to remain aware of any changes in state or federal legislation which affects their status in legal settings. See Appendix C for a summary of state statutes providing for interpreters for deaf persons.

Payment for interpreter services in non-criminal cases may be an issue. In some states the court is required by law to pay for services provided in any court or court-supported service (e.g. probation). In others, the issue of payment beyond criminal proceedings is not clearly defined and, as a result, interpreter services are sometimes assessed as part of court costs. Where state statutes are ambiguous, the decision is left to the discretion of the court.

Unless interpreters are being paid by a referral agency, it behooves interpreters to make contact with the court prior to the assignment to negotiate payment. There will be occasions when a written contract is advantageous, especially for an extended assignment, such as a lengthy trial. Interpreters who wait until the close of an assignment to negotiate or request payment may encounter resistance on a variety of payment issues, such as a travel-time fee in addition to mileage reimbursement, a fee for waiting time, reimbursement for tolls and parking, as well as the expected hourly fee. When negotiating the fee for services, interpreters should be sure to speak with someone who is authorized to approve or deny payment.

Legal language

For interpreters to be effective in the legal realm, they must possess not only a high level of competence in American Sign Language (and/or signed English) and spoken English, but they must understand English as it is spoken in legal contexts. That is, they must understand not only individual legal terms (e.g. the difference between *breaking and entering* and *burglary*) but the structure and purpose of legal language as well. For example, in order to interpret accurately both direct and cross examinations, interpreters must understand the rules for questioning witnesses. Questions posed by attorneys are often awkwardly constructed and purposefully vague; interpreters must be able to retain ambiguities to render faithful interpretations. Ramifications of incorrect interpretations are far reaching, and include the possibility of a mistrial.

Interpreters should begin preparing for their first court appearance long before they enter a courtroom to interpret. Observing court proceedings and paying strict attention to the content and style of courtroom discourse is one good way to begin preparing. Observing and working with experienced legal interpreters is another. Finally, taking criminal justice courses at a local college or university and participating in special RID approved courses on legal interpreting is an excellent way to gain insight into legal issues and court procedures.

A brief look at deaf litigants

As in other interpretation settings, deaf people from all walks of life appear in court for many reasons. Some of these individuals are highly skilled American Sign Language users and require — or prefer using — the services of an American Sign Language/English interpreter. Others use signed English or another manual code for English and require — or prefer using — the services of a qualified Signed English/spoken English transliterator.

Beyond deaf people with sophisticated ASL and/or English language skills, there is another group of deaf people who sometimes appear in court. These are individuals with minimal language competence (MLC). (See Chapter Ten.)

MLC deaf people require special consideration to enable them to communicate with and receive information or direction from the court. In most matters involving an MLC deaf person, interpreters can most ably assist the court by working in a team context of one deaf and one hearing interpreter. Even when special consideration is given, however, the MLC deaf person is often unable to access court proceedings or assist counsel to any meaningful degree given their limited understanding of the process or action.

Team interpreting in the legal realm

Deaf and hearing interpreters in a team interpreting context

Over the past few years, the theory and practice of working with relay interpreters has changed. There was a time when requesting a relay interpreter carried a negative stigma; it was assumed such a request indicated that the hearing interpreter was not qualified to complete the assignment alone. Fortunately, this viewpoint is no longer prevalent. With the increased need for relay interpreters, especially in the legal context, an awareness has developed regarding the vast amount of cultural and linguistic knowledge deaf interpreters bring to an interpreting situation.

When deaf and hearing interpreters are working together in a court matter, it is critical for both interpreters to meet with the judge and attorneys prior to the start of the case. A judge may have had one interpreter in his courtroom but is unlikely to have encountered two. Interpreters should be prepared to explain the need for both interpreters. Justification for the additional expenditure of court funds will likely be necessary. The previous section entitled "A brief look at deaf litigants" provides an analysis of situations requiring a relay interpreter.

Team interpreting trials: Two hearing interpreters

Because of the mental and physical fatigue and stress associated with interpreting in the legal realm, it is often advantageous to interpret lengthy matters with a team interpreter. Permission to do so must be granted by the court and payment negotiated prior to the assignment.

A team approach in this context can provide not only physical relief but also ensure the integrity of the interpretation. When two interpreters are working together during a trial, the teamwork begins the moment the interpreters arrive at court and ends at the close of the trial; when one interpreter is actively interpreting, the other interpreter monitors the interpretation rendered by his colleague and "feeds" missed information as necessary.

The interpreter who backs up the active interpreter is also in a good position to address the court if the interpreters have information they must bring to the attention of the court, such as the need for a break or other logistical information. This allows the active interpreter to continue interpreting.

Team interpreters provide support to one another. Having a colleague upon whom one can rely is especially important when the case is emotionally trying, as, for example, during a child abuse or rape case. The support of a team interpreter is indispensable when, regardless of an interpreter's impeccable credentials, there is hostility or distrust on the part of the attorneys, the court, or others in a given matter, and the interpreter's abilities are challenged.

Implications of legal interpreting

At first glance, an interpreting assignment may seem self-contained, that is, it may seem to have no future legal implications. However, interpreters must be aware of certain characteristics of an assignment which could lead to an arrest, a police investigation, or a court hearing.

Here is an example. An interpreter is contacted to interpret between the Department of Social Services (DSS) and a deaf mother who is alleging child abuse by the child's father. During the meeting between the DSS worker and the mother, the interpreter hears no specialized legal vocabulary and no attorneys are present. How could the matter have legal ramifications? In some states, if the mother's allegations are substantiated by the DSS, a district attorney, or (prosecuting) investigator is brought in to investigate filing criminal charges against the father, especially if the allegations involve sexual abuse. The mother may be advised to seek a restraining order from the court, barring the father from further contact with the mother or child. Once the case is activated in court, the DSS file and statements made by the mother through an interpreter would be available to the father's defense attorney. The qualifications of the interpreter and the fidelity of the interpretation could come under the attorney's, and perhaps eventually, the court's, scrutiny.

Here is another example. An interpreter is contacted by the staff at a hospital emergency room during the night and asked to interpret for a deaf woman in the emergency room. Upon arrival, the interpreter discovers the deaf woman has been raped and several tests will be administered. The doctor informs the interpreter that the police have been contacted and they will take a statement from the victim. A statement is a formal narrative of facts (H. Black, 1983). It may be spoken or signed and then is translated into written form. When a victim gives a statement to the police, it becomes part of the police record. If there are errors in the interpretation of the statement, when the case comes to court, discrepancies between live testimony and the police report could call into question not only the victim's testimony but the interpreter's qualifications as well. It could mean the difference between a conviction or an acquittal for the defendant.

Interpreters must always use discretion when accepting assignments, but they must be especially mindful of the potential ramifications of interpreting in legal or quasi-legal matters. For interpreters, the impact on one's professional credibility cannot be overstated.

Protocol

Protocol refers to the body of customs and regulations dealing with diplomatic formality, precedence, and etiquette. It dictates how and to whom interpreters address their concerns. Since protocol is at the heart of judicial procedure, understanding protocol is integral to the legal interpreter's effective involvement in judicial proceedings. In other words, interpreters must understand how to bring issues of import to the court in a way that maintains the demeanor and dignity of the court.

Here are a few issues interpreters may bring before the court which require a judicious approach:

1. Disclosing information which carries the appearance of impropriety — If, for example, an interpreter has previously interpreted for a litigant or an attorney involved in a current court matter, such information should be brought to the attention of the court. This is especially critical if the interpreter has been previously paid by the attorney for any work rendered.

2. Challenging the court when the court or attorney requests behavior of the interpreter which compels the interpreter to violate his code of ethics, such as asking the interpreter not to interpret certain information.

3. Providing information to the court on the interpretation task, the interpreter's qualifications, and the ability or inability to assist the court.

4. Making personal requests, such as a short break.

Observing court proceedings will aid interpreters in better understanding how to move comfortably through judicial proceedings. One should note the dress, vocabulary choices, and demeanor of attorneys as a key on how to proceed. However, an interpreter should not assume a demeanor or style of talk that is inconsistent with his professional image. By slowly assimilating behaviors that are observed in court, interpreters can emulate those behaviors which will assist them in better fitting the decorum of the courtroom.

Privileged communications

Privileged communications are statements made by persons protected by state law from "forced disclosure on the witness stand" (H. Black, 1983). Certain professionals, such as attorneys, clergy, and doctors (depending on the state) are protected by privilege (also called "cloak of confidentiality"). Interpreters, when in the presence of those protected by privilege, are also exempt from forced disclosure, unless all of those who hold the privilege request the interpreter to testify as to what was said during privileged communications. In this situation, the interpreter has no legal ground for refusing to testify. The RID Code of Ethics can and should be used as a basis for asking to be excused from testifying; however, the code holds no legal status and could be struck down.

In situations not covered by privilege (such as police interrogations), the interpreter may want to request that the interpretation be videotaped. The videotape then becomes the record of the interpretation. If later asked to testify, the interpreter could refer the requesting party (usually counsel) to the videotape. This strategy may save the interpreter from testifying.

Qualifications necessary for court interpreters

State statutes differ somewhat in the way interpreter qualifications are defined. Usually, however, interpreters are required to be "qualified," without any definition of what that means, or to hold RID certification. Regardless of how qualifications are defined, interpreters working in the legal realm need training and credentials which will support the interpreter's claim of being qualified to interpret legal matters.

A court may inquire as to the interpreter's qualifications prior to the start of a trial or court proceeding. The interpreter should be able to produce a resume, a copy of his national certification (or valid RID membership card with the current certification listed), and letters of recommendation, as well as to recite for the record the type of legal interpreter training he has taken, the number of years experience interpreting legal matters and other pertinent information.

Summary

This section on "Legal Settings" has described in brief a variety of issues professional interpreters face in legal settings, including statutory mandates for interpreters, payment to interpreters, deaf litigants, team interpreting, implications of legal interpreting, protocol, privileged communication, and interpreter qualifications. Because it is impossible to cover all facets of legal interpreting in this introductory text, interpreters interested in and serious about legal interpreting are encouraged to seek additional information.

Interpreting in legal settings presents special challenges and rewards including exposure to interesting environments and individuals and enhanced understanding of the underpinnings of the American judicial system.

Interpreting in Medical Settings

Interpreting in medical settings encompasses a variety of situations, from routine consultation with a physician to emergency procedures, from prepared childbirth classes to support for complex laboratory testing. Interpreters for deaf people in medical settings are not a luxury or nicety, but rather a service mandated by law. Chapter Five of the National Center for Law and the Deaf's book on *Legal Rights of Hearing-Impaired People* describes in some detail the supports (including, but not limited to, interpreting services) necessary for adequately meeting the needs of deaf patients in hospitals and other health care facilities.

Interpreters make it possible to obtain complete medical histories from deaf patients, to explain the purposes of test procedures, to prescribe a regimen with precision. Without interpreters, ordinary or well-known medical problems may go unattended or undetected, since a deaf person often finds communication with the physician and nurses difficult and uncertain, and since similarly, practitioners often assume that complete communication is impossible or unnecessary and information is minimized and instructions given without explanation. Schein and Delk (1974: 122) suggest that "even those conditions which may, by themselves, be innocuous can become severely disabling when occurring in combination with deafness." Reisman, Scanlan and Kemp (1977:2398) report that nearly fifty per cent of the patients seen at one mental health clinic specifically for deaf people had "additional long-standing problems that had not been diagnosed previously, even though the patient had been seen by a physician in the recent past *without* the use of an interpreter."

Attitudes toward interpreters in medical settings

An interpreter entering a medical setting may find inappropriate assumptions or attitudes about the interpreting role and the interpreter from the health care staff (doctors, nurses, laboratory technicians, or administrative personnel).

Medical personnel may assume that, because the interpreter has the ability to communicate with the deaf person, the interpreter is privy to all sorts of knowledge about this person, including their mental, emotional or physical status. Such assumptions may also be a holdover from the days when most medical interpreting was done by family members or friends. It may be an innocent assumption on the part of the medical person that the interpreter knows the deaf patient and that they will be involved in the patient's treatment in ways other than facilitating communication. Related to this, because the interpreter knows sign language and is familiar with deafness, medical personnel may assume that the interpreter is an expert on hearing loss. An interpreter who faces these assumptions will need to clarify the role of the interpreter and the relationship of the interpreter to the patient and the practitioner.

In contrast to the willingness of some health care personnel to attribute magical knowledge to the interpreter, others find this unfamiliar situation threatening. They assume that the interpreter will take over the role of the health care practitioner, or that the interpreter will be in the way of medical procedures. Some nursing staff or technical support people attempt to by-pass the interpreter on the mistaken belief that the additional professional will limit access to "their" patient. These assumptions or beliefs can interfere with the interpreter's successful delivery of communication services and with the deaf client's lawful right to interpreting services. Again, taking the time to explain the interpreter's role should help to reduce the "threat" and promote a smooth interaction. It is hoped this will also establish positive attitudes about working with interpreters in the future.

Medical terminology and procedures

The interpreter will find the medical setting easier if he has some familiarity with medical terminology and procedures. For example, a routine physical follows a series of steps that are reasonably standard within the U.S. and probably within all of Western medicine. Being familiar with these steps can help the interpreter to prepare and to anticipate. Medical terminology uses many of the same Latin and Greek roots and suffixes over and over. Knowing that -itis means an inflammation, -ectomy means something is going to be cut out, and -rhaphy means that something is going to be sutured, means that the interpreter can be conceptually accurate and timely in his interpretation. Practitioners sometimes assume that health care interpreters have complete knowledge of medical terminology and that it is the interpreter's responsibility to explain or clarify terms for the patient. This is incorrect. When the patient does not understand a word or concept, it is the responsibility of the practitioner to explain it. It is the interpreter's responsibility to understand the explanation and to be able to interpret it (Barnum & Siebert, 1987).

Patient privacy

Medical procedures are often intimate and require exposure of private body parts. There are several options available for sensitively handling these situations.

The first option is to have a same-sex interpreter for the patient. By determining in advance what the anticipated procedures are and what the gender of the patient is, the interpreter can make decisions about accepting or declining the job and can make recommendations to the referral agency about hiring a same-sex interpreter.

The second option is for interpreters to place themselves in such a way that the patient is afforded the utmost privacy. Usually this means

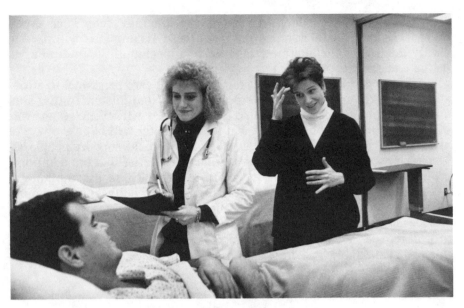

Figure 9-4
Medical examination

placing oneself at the level of the patient's shoulders while they are lying on the examining table. It also involves maintaining eye contact or looking at the wall past the deaf person or at the floor when not interpreting.

A third option is to leave the room. This requires making sure that all information/explanation and questions are interpreted and then stepping out of the examining room during the procedure. The interpreter should remain just outside the door so that he can reenter when needed. Using this option requires careful clarification of the interpreter's role to the medical personnel involved. They will need to understand clearly that they need to call the interpreter back in each time something new needs to be discussed or each time the patient has a question. It might be helpful to encourage the patient and the practitioner to establish a signal for the patient if he wishes to have the interpreter come back into the room. This option is especially viable when the interpreter and the patient are not the same gender.

Physical arrangement

Interpreters in medical settings will find that many of the usual teachings about physical placement of the interpreter do apply. But there are also some unique factors in medical settings that must be considered.

The first was discussed above — privacy. In most interpreting situations, the interpreter will stand next to the speaker so that the client can have the speaker and the interpreter in the same sightline. For a pelvic exam, this will not be appropriate. Again, the most appropriate placement in such situations seems to be at the patient's shoulders with careful attention to maintaining eye contact.

A second factor is the procedure itself. The interpreter needs to find a position which will not hinder the medical personnel's delivery of services. An example of this might be a physical therapy setting. Suppose a deaf patient is learning the use of crutches for the first time. The therapist and the patient will be working very closely with one another, and an interpreter who attempts to keep moving with the therapist may get in the way. Here the interpreter should involve the client and the practitioner in deciding the best place for the interpreter to stand.

Examples of interpreting in the radiology department can exemplify a third factor — safety. One concern in this area is moving equipment. For some procedures large machines quickly move back and forth. The interpreter may need to make sure all information and questions have been interpreted and then step back out of the way. A second concern is radiation. This can be resolved by wearing a lead apron or by stepping behind the protective shield with the x-ray technician. In the latter case, signals can be established to let the deaf patient know when it is time to hold his breath and when to start breathing again. Examples of simple ways to manage this can be found in more detailed manuals on medical interpreting (Barnum & Siebert, 1987).

Figure 9-4 suggests one possible arrangement of physician, patient, and interpreter.

Medicated patients

Interpreting for deaf patients who are under the influence of medication can require some modifications in the interpreting process and some understanding on the part of other medical personnel involved.

Since the eyes are a muscle, they are affected by drugs in ways that ears are not. A hearing person, even though heavily sedated, can hear and understand auditory input. A deaf person, on the other hand, must work to focus his eyes in order to understand the interpreter's signing. Sometimes it's as basic as needing to open one's eyes! It is important to point this out to medical personnel so that they will have reasonable expectations of the deaf person and of the interpreter. A good example of a medical situation where drugs can be an issue is surgery. Prior to surgery a patient is sedated, during surgery the patient may be under a local anesthetic but heavily sedated or under a general anesthetic, and in the recovery room, the patient may be coming out of general anesthetic.

During such times, the interpreter can modify what might be the normal style by being brief, extra clear, and avoiding fingerspelling. Explain to the recovery room nurse that you will be happy to interpret as soon as the patient's eyes are open!

Confidentiality foremost

As always, the interpreter has the responsibility to maintain absolute confidentiality about everything in the medical interpreting setting. The details of someone's medical history, current health situation, or prescribed treatment are private and personal. In the interest of keeping the particular client's trust and building awareness of and confidence in current interpreting practice, all interpreters will benefit from practicing confidentiality most conscientiously.

Expanding horizons

Not all medical interpreting situations will be for deaf people who are the recipients of health care services. More and more deaf people are entering the medical field. Nurses, medical technologists, medical records clerks, dentists, and doctors may be requesting interpreting services for participation in staff meetings, professional association activities, professional development, and meetings with their patients.

An interpreter may interpret in public health programs, wellness courses, genetic counseling, weight-loss groups, and academic courses such as anatomy and physiology. All of these settings will involve medical terminology.

Interpreting in Mental Health Settings

Interpreters may be found in a variety of contexts that all can be grouped under the heading "mental health." Perhaps a psychologist is evaluating a deaf individual who is about to receive vocational rehabilitation support. Perhaps a family including a hearing-impaired member is seeking counseling services. Perhaps a teenager has been placed in a psychiatric ward of a hospital for violent behavior, but later it is learned that the teenager was being abused at home and is kept for her own protection. Perhaps someone who previously was diagnosed as mentally retarded is now discovered to actually be hearing-impaired. Perhaps a deaf psychologist is working with a deaf patient, and the hearing supervisor needs an interpreter to observe the case through a one-way mirror.

In each of these cases, an interpreter can make an important contribution to the successful communication between parties. An interpreter who agrees to undertake assignments like those mentioned above must be aware of the possible psychological repercussions for self and with respect to the consumer/patient.

Psychological evaluation

In a psychological evaluation, an evaluator, generally a psychologist, administers one or more standardized tests to the clients. These may evaluate intelligence, reasoning, personality factors, aptitude, memory, neurological functioning, motor skills, and cognitive functioning. The tests may involve questions and verbal responses, timed performances, structured interviewing or paper and pencil tasks. The interpreter will function best if familiarized ahead of time with the purpose and procedures involved.

For example, in the draw-a-person test, the interviewer asks the client to draw a person. Usually people draw someone of their own sex first. Later the client is requested to draw a person of the opposite sex. One of the dangers of the translation in the first case is that the interpreter may choose to orient the sign PERSON close to the interpreter's own body. Then, client may misunderstand the instruction to be "Draw a person, like me (the interpreter)." If the client is male and the interpreter female, the client may respond with a female person first, an unexpected response. If this result comes from the interpretation, rather than the client's own understanding of an appropriate response, then the psychologist may draw some conclusions about the client wrongly.

Vernon and Ottinger (1981) describe some of the potential problems in testing deaf people. While they generally feel it is preferable to have the psychologist or other mental health professional communicate directly with the client, they state that few of those with the appropriate professional education have the requisite communication skills in American Sign Language.

Therapy and counseling

As with testing, the interpreter needs some background about the purpose and techniques in therapeutic treatment to be able to function most effectively. The interpreter may think that the professional stance dictating non-involvement protects him or her from being drawn into the process, but as the communication link the interpreter will be drawn in anyway. Stansfield (1981) reminds us that it happens whether intended or not. Even if the therapist and interpreter share an understanding about the interpreter's role, the client may have a different view.

Stansfield gives a number of examples for each of the three participants, therapist, client and interpreter, of typical feelings that may come up in the process of therapy. The therapist may feel intruded upon in his or her own turf, may be uncertain of how to behave with a deaf person (where to look, how to address the client), may feel left out or that rapport is difficult to gain. The client may be unfamiliar with therapy, and may bring feelings from past interpreted encounters to the therapy sessions. The issue of trust in relation to confidentiality and accuracy in translation is likely to be a live one for the client. The interpreter may feel put in an awkward position: on the one hand, the interpreter may have some understanding of deafness that the therapist does not, but may feel it is beyond the role to take the initiative to explain that understanding. In the interest of complete communication, the interpreter may wish to ask for clarification of something the client says; but the therapist may be deliberately choosing not to clarify.

Stansfield also emphasizes the implications of even the ideal seating arrangement. If the interpreter is seated slightly behind and to the side of the therapist, the client can see both the interpreter and the therapist, getting a verbal message from the interpreter at the same time as the therapist's tone, and mood. Also in this position the therapist is in front, encouraging the direct relationship between client and therapist. However, Stansfield reminds us that the client may feel that the interpreter and therapist are closer linked, or ganging up, because they are seated close together; the client may even feel reminded of feelings toward parents or other authority figures.

Other aspects of the interaction may be problematic. For example, therapists are accustomed to using eye contact as a cue or controlling device. The client, if cooperating, will be looking at the interpreter while the therapist is talking, thus throwing off the therapist's usual technique. Also, counselors often choose to remain silent waiting for the client to initiate communication. How best can the interpreter match the auditory effect of silence? Shall the interpreter remove eye gaze or maintain it?

Interpreters in therapy or counseling sessions must be ready to deal with a variety of sensitive and potentially unpleasant issues, such as suicide, incest, child abuse or spouse abuse, drug use, anger, grief, and hostility.

The therapist and interpreter have a responsibility to each other and to the client(s) to communicate with one another. Mutual trust and respect will grow as the therapist and interpreter work together as a team. The Code of Ethics requires that the interpreter maintain confidentiality. In this context, it means confidentiality from the community outside the setting. The interpreter should feel at ease discussing feelings that arise during sessions with the therapist in post-session de-briefings or before the subsequent session. Stansfield gives several examples of difficult feelings that the interpreter was able to work through with the assistance of the therapist (1981:25).

Seriously disturbed clients present an additional challenge for the interpreter who must take care not to normalize their disordered thoughts and language. One of the most difficult tasks in interpreting is to voice accurately for a psychotic deaf client, who makes no sense (to the interpreter) and whose affect may not match the signed message.

Group or family therapy

Many of the same issues that come to the fore in individual therapy also occur in group therapy. As with any group interaction, the roles and numbers of deaf and hearing people will make a difference in how the interaction goes. For example, is there a single deaf person in an on-going therapeutic group? Are all of the group members deaf? Is the therapist hearing or deaf? Answers to such questions help the interpreter anticipate how best to facilitate the communication.

If, for example, one family member is deaf and several hearing family members are present, a deaf therapist is at a disadvantage to (1) watch the signing of both the deaf patient and the interpreter, and (2) catch the non-verbal interchanges between other family members while talk is happening (Harris, 1981:238). Figure 9-5 shows a group discussion where several members are deaf with one hearing interpreter. The reader can begin to appreciate the difficulty of the task both for the interpreter and for the deaf professional.

As in other group situations, if more than one person talks at one time, a solo interpreter will have to make a choice of who to sign or voice

Figure 9-5
Group discussion

for. The negotiation of the turn-taking signals may be part of the group
process: will an overt signal, such as raising hands be used? The interpreter may want to refrain from bringing this up in the group, and wait
for the leader or a group member to address the issue. Of course, alerting
the leader beforehand that turn-taking may be a loaded issue would be
wise.

The deaf mental health professional: Education and practice

Deaf people are undertaking the graduate study and professional
education involved in becoming social workers, psychologists, and counselors. Interpreters are a valuable asset to them in pursuing these studies. Harris reports his own experiences (1981:238):

> As a result [of being funded for interpreting sevices], I could
> participate in all the programs of a regular internship—
> including taking seminars in child therapy, psychodiagnostic
> testing, family therapy, group therapy ... attending grand
> rounds and various colloquia, and receiving supervised practice
> in individual and group therapy.

With an interpreter in the observation room, Harris could observe his
supervisor interviewing a hearing patient through a one-way mirror.
Subsequently, the supervisor and graduate intern could review interviewing techniques and responses. Later, the deaf intern interviewed

deaf clients with the supervisor assisted by the interpreter looking through the one-way mirror, again with a subsequent discussion. As a result of those observations and the discussions, the intern could modify his techniques to interact more meaningfully with the patient.

In professional practice, the deaf mental health specialist will still rely on interpreter services at least part of the time. When working with families with both deaf and hearing members, interacting with professional peers in conferences, school or clinical settings, and similar encounters, the deaf psychologist or counselor needs expert translation and interpretation assistance.

Summary

Mental health settings can be extremely challenging and taxing. The interpreter who undertakes these assignments should be prepared. Course work in appropriate content areas (personality theory and treatment modalities) is important. Equally important is awareness of the emotional issues which may arise for the interpreter in the interaction. The interpreter will function best if calm and confident, despite the client's emotional disturbance.

Interpreting in Rehabilitation and Social Service Settings

The Vocational Rehabilitation Act of 1965 provided the impetus for government-supported interpreter education, since it recognized interpreting services as a legitimate case service for hearing-impaired clients. More recent legislation has required "reasonable accommodation" in employment for disabled people. This accommodation includes providing interpreters for instructional programs that are prerequisite to obtaining employment (DuBow, *et al.*, 1982).

The areas of rehabilitation and social services provide many diverse contexts for interpreting. Some of the skills and background that will prove useful overlap with those needed in education, medical, mental health, and business situations. Some deaf people seek communication assistance with public offices such as the Social Security Administration, food stamps, or the Department of Human Resources. Testing for vocational interest, aptitude, evaluating hearing, vision, or level of disability, and interviews with counselors or prospective employers all enter into the rehabilitation process. Of course, job training and orientation to the workplace are important steps in the rehabilitation of deaf adults. Rehabilitation may also cover the assistance provided to deaf people seeking post-secondary education. So the interpreter in the rehabilitation or social service setting cannot presume any particular language ability or level of functioning on the part of the deaf client.

Social service workers' concerns

Baker (1981) discusses the need for using interpreters in social work with immigrant and refugee populations, where insufficient numbers of native language users have been instructed in social work. While his comments about interpreting and interpreters developed out of contact with an Indochinese population, many of his observations hold for the deaf population as well. (Of course, among the deaf population resident in the U.S., there are also large numbers of immigrants and refugees from Eastern Europe, Indochina, Mexico and the Caribbean.)

Baker gives the names "verbatim style" and "independent intervention" as two extreme types of interpretation. He cites examples where following either of these extremes can cause misunderstandings by the social worker or the non-English speaking client. For example, several young people were placed in the custody of a resettlement agency and agreed to "follow the reasonable directions thereof." Later it was learned that they thought they had been placed into slavery because of the interpreter's close translation. In this case, the interpreter's "verbatim" rendering of the English was misunderstood by the client. In another case, a social worker offered to help a client be placed with his uncle or with a foster family. Although the boy at first said that he preferred to live with his uncle, the interpreter took the initiative to explain the advantages of foster care and apparently convinced the boy to tell the social worker that foster care was his preference. The social worker was successful in finding foster care, later learning that the boy had wanted to be with his uncle. This example shows the distortion following inappropriate intervention by the interpreter (Baker, 1981: 392-393). Interpreters who work with hearing and deaf people may be sufficiently aware to avoid the negative aspects of these styles. However, they do need to be aware, as well, that a social worker's previous experience with interpreters may have included performances like those cited above.

In order to achieve the best results in working as a social worker-interpreter team, Baker urges that interpreters be introduced to social work ethics and to practices such as the use of silence in an interview, client self-determination and the like. For interpreters from the foreign culture, he notes that empathy for one's own people cannot be assumed, and yet is an important attribute for the interpreter.

Consumer education

Clients in the rehabilitation process and counselors can both be considered clients of interpreting service. Clients may be unfamiliar with the appropriate role for the interpreter. The tendency for the client to address requests for assistance or information to the interpreter, rather than to the non-signing rehabilitation counselor is quite common. Similarly, the counselor who is unfamiliar with deafness and interpreting may turn to the interpreter as an expert in all areas related to hearing-impairment and the language and culture of deaf people. The interpreter's role includes educating the clients about the limits of an interpreter's functioning. The interpreter may find it difficult to remain neutral, to intervene neither in the counseling process nor as an advocate for the client. Adherence to the policy of simply interpreting will provide the best service in the long run, whatever the short-term frustration or annoyance. The benefits of educating the people who will continue to use interpreters will have long-lasting impact.

Dual roles

There are two circumstances in which the person serving as interpreter might be thought to have two roles. One is much like the dilemma that educational interpreters face when asked for information about the student. The interpreter may be expected to report facts about the assignment which seem to be revealing confidential information. If the interpreter reports the date and hours worked, this can be construed as providing information that permits the agency to pay the interpreter. The policy of many interpreters and agencies to have a fee for minimum number of hours (X dollars for N hours' work) may alleviate the need to reveal the interpreter's specific comings and goings. If the interpreter is expected to report client attendance, progress, or the outcome of an evaluation or meeting, the interpreter should be aware of this expectation, and needs to evaluate the request for such reports in light of the interpreter's understanding of the Code of Ethics. The interpreter would have to agree to the request before accepting the assignment. Likewise, the client should be informed ahead of time that the interpreter has this responsibility. Both the client and the interpreter need to be clear about what the conditions of their interaction are.

The second situation where two roles come into play is where the social service worker takes on the function of interpreting for the client with some third party. For example, some agencies do not hire separate interpreters for job interviews, trusting the ability of the job placement counselor to communicate between deaf applicant and personnel representative or prospective employer. Even making the assumption that the counselor has the communication skills in sign language and interpreting to accomplish the task, the client needs special briefing on the change in role of the counselor. No longer an advocate or explainer, the counselor will take on the neutral stance of the interpreter. At the same time, the employer may ask questions of the deaf person for which the client knows the counselor-cum-interpreter already has the answer. "Why are you asking me this? Why don't you just tell her about my training program?" the client asks the counselor. So the dual role of this second type requires extraordinary orientation for the deaf or hearing-impaired person to be able to know "which hat" the counselor-interpreter is wearing.

In Great Britain, social workers have functioned as the interpreters with deaf people for the past twenty years or more. Only recently have people begun to recognize the need for a separate profession of interpreter; even then, the financial support to make professional interpreting possible has not been forthcoming. Social workers often feel the dilemmas mentioned above, especially when they are called upon to interpret in contexts outside of social work. A deaf person whose spouse is abusive may want to seek a divorce. The social worker can assist with relocation, counseling, and other services. But who will interpret for the divorce hearing in the courts? The social worker is caught between the need for the service he or she can provide, and the obligations to the agency which is the employer and that agency's other clients. The client has no alternatives for interpreting but the social worker, and at the same time may be confused by the different stance this person takes in the office as compared with in the courtroom.

Summary

Vocational rehabilitation, social work and similar services have the goals of helping people seek and maintain employment, develop and maintain stable and meaningful relationships at home and in the community. When the service provider does not share the language or communication mode of the client, an interpreter may be called upon to assist. While interpreters need instruction in the expectations that social service personnel will have of them, the clients both need special orientation to the interpreter's role and function. In particular, the limits of the interpreter's responsibility need to be clarified.

Interpreting in Business, Industry and Government

Spoken language interpreters have been working in the fields of business and industry for many years, but this is a new area that many sign language interpreters have been entering recently (Figure 9-6). An American business person, for example, who is expecting to trade with organizations in other countries will often travel with a liaison interpreter along to interact with potential customers or vendors who are not comfortable in English.

Figure 9-6
One-to-one

The interpreter might be expected to advise the business person about protocol and procedures in the other countries; that is, the interpreter may be hired to interpret the culture of doing business, as well as translating the language meanings. Interpreters working on referral for the State Department of the United States accompany groups of foreign visitors. These visitors may be government officials, agricultural experts, manufacturers or any sort of business representative from another country. The interpreters may then have the responsibility of elaborating on American customs and culture for them.

Sign language interpreters are newer to the business world, although interpreters have been working with political groups and government agencies (Figure 9-7) for many years, as we have described in the early history of sign language interpreting. Studies show that deaf people as a group are underemployed and receive lower incomes than their educational achievement would predict. Nearly fifty per cent of all deaf employees work in the area of manufacturing (Schein and Delk, 1973). Prompted by recent federal legislation to remedy employer discrimination against disabled people, deaf people have been asserting their need for full communication in the work site and have begun to assume positions where immediate face-to-face or telephone communication is part of the job. Oral interpreters are also appearing in the business

Figure 9-7
National political convention

environment. In some cases, a deaf employee with strong speechreading and oral skills may not have realized that oral interpretation is a possible enhancement of the work place. Interpreters with deaf people have continued to maintain a non-involved stance, in business as in other contexts, relying instead on the participants to communicate and elaborate for each other.

Federal law

The Rehabilitation Act of 1973 includes several sections which have strong implications about access to employment for disabled people, including deaf people. As summarized in DuBow *et al.* (1982), Section 501 applies to the federal government and describes a qualified handicapped person as one who can, with or without reasonable accommodation, perform the job function without endangering the health or safety of self or others. Section 503 applies to employers that do business with the federal government (federal contractors), again using the phrase "reasonable accommodation." Section 504 applies to recipients of federal assistance, and again uses the pivotal phrase.

Business contexts and business concerns

In what sorts of business contexts do we find interpreters aiding the interaction between hearing and deaf people? Job interviews, the hiring process, training and orientation, re-training and staff meetings are the obvious contexts where deaf employees interact with hearing people for business purposes. The explanation of a new benefits package, the annual awards presentation and holiday party, and union negotiations may also need interpreters. Telephone calls present an immediate and continuing need for interpreting, and are dealt with in a separate section (see "Telephone Interpreting" in Chapter Ten.)

Levinson (1984) writes of his own experience in hiring an interpreter for telephone support, for meetings, and additional contexts. He justifies the cost of hiring an interpreter by noting that his own value to the organization increases when he can participate fully, and his visibility is heightened as he joins in discussions, returns phone calls promptly and is generally effective in his position. Before adding an interpreter to assist him, he would rely on secretarial staff to make phone calls. However, the impracticality of this make-shift solution was obvious: the secretaries have plenty of regularly scheduled work, and they were not available to accompany him to group meetings.

Bird and Smith devote a good deal of attention to the role of interpreters in industry. They remind us that using an interpreter can "clarify job responsibilities, avoid misunderstanding, prevent future problems, open all communication channels, and allow better opportunities for the advancement of deaf employees" (n.d.:6). They address the issue of cost effectiveness. During a period of training, Vocational Rehabilitation or a similar referral agency often picks up the fee until the eligible consumer becomes productive on the job. A number of large corporations absorb the whole fee, especially after an initial exposure to the use of interpreters. Jobs on the assembly line, or in some other production area of manufacturing may require less interpreting, since much of the communication needed can be done through demonstration and writing. Jobs in clerical, accounting, or management areas may require more frequent services from an interpreter. As deaf people become better educated and take positions in business, the need for qualified interpreters will grow.

Interpreting concerns

In some businesses, employees with basic signing skills may be asked to interpret, despite the fact that their skills are not adequate to

131

the task and their job descriptions say nothing about interpretation. They may find interpreting an interesting variation to their regular work, but for the deaf employee, interpreting by unqualified people is no avenue for understanding and may even prove detrimental. On the other hand, if employees can be found already on staff with appropriate sign language and interpreter instruction, it may be useful to add interpretation to their list of job responsibilities. The fact that the interpreter in this case is also an employee brings up potentially sticky issues of ethics, specifically relating to confidentiality. For example, an internal interpreter would be privy to communication regarding compensation, health and benefits, or job performance that might be reserved for an employee and manager. Therefore, co-workers, even those with adequate sign language skills, need special instruction in the role and ethics of interpreting. The solution to difficulties cited in using an internal interpreter is to employ someone specifically in the role of interpreter. Often a freelance interpreter from the community will have the skills needed to function as an occasional assist for communication. Should the interpreting needs of the organization become greater, an interpreter or staff of interpreters can be hired full-time.

Since few full-time interpreters in private industry have written about their experiences, we can look at in-house translators to anticipate the advantages and disadvantages for language specialists in these positions. Daly *et al.* (1981) discuss the variety of job titles, ranks and salaries that in-house translators in industry have. The salary scale cited ranged from a low of $12,000 to a high of $43,800, with anywhere from one to more than twenty-five years of experience. The lower figures were generally found among those with fewer years of experience, but among the drawbacks to the job is that there are limited opportunities for advancement and the translator may reach a peak of earnings after a relatively short career. The advantages of having a regular income with fringe benefits, opportunities for continued contact with professional colleagues, and timely information on developments in the technical area are all important. Among the disadvantages mentioned are the need for keeping regular hours, the high pressure and deadlines, the lack of understanding of the translator's work, and instruction within the organization requiring continuing efforts by the translators to educate management. Some of these positives and negatives would be easily extended to in-house interpreters. The pressure of deadlines for written work probably would translate into the pressure of competing schedule demands made on interpreters. We can also anticipate that the interpreter working in a business environment will require time to become technically fluent in the language of the industry. The American Translators Association Conference for 1984 had numerous talks given on topics such as "Translation of German Chemical Process Diagrams," and "An Introduction to Toxicology for Translators." We can anticipate future RID Conventions to include comparable technical addresses for sign language interpreters.

Interpreting in Religious Settings

Religion provided many early motivations for translation work, both for spoken languages and between spoken and signed languages. Bible translation and missionary work have been activities practiced by many clergy throughout history. Regular church services for deaf people have provided a socially acceptable meeting place, as well as supportive network for the delicate fabric of a few deaf families in a larger hearing community. One can find congregations of deaf people, ministered to by signing clergy, as well as deaf members in an otherwise ordinary congregation, where the religious leader may choose to use sign language or may use the services of an interpreter. Deaf people have also been ordained by several denominations and lead their own congregations. Deaf signing choirs have competitions in "precision hymn-sign-singing" in parts of the U.S.

Today, all sorts of religious occasions invite the presence of an interpreter: weddings, funerals, baptisms, christenings, naming ceremonies, confirmations, bar and bat mitzvahs, religious camp, retreats, and religious education. Because much of religion is ritualized, and the protocol, order of events and language are fixed (as opposed to spontaneous), an interpreter can familiarize herself or himself with the usual services and appropriate texts, and thus prepare more thoroughly than for many other settings. At the same time, the participants are likely to speak quickly (unless well trained); since they know the ritual so well, they forget that it may be new to the interpreter. Even when the interpreter is from the congregation, and therefore presumably familiar with the words, service and tradition, the process of interpretation will probably give the familiar a different cast.

Specialized language

Religious practice and belief have often been linked with special uses of language and with even special languages. Some religions use a language other than the language of daily conversation. Judaism, for example, uses primarily Ancient Hebrew, some Aramaic and a smattering of other languages in the Bible and other religious texts. Different religions or branches of a single religion may have slight variants in wording or choice of phrasing in prayers or other religious texts that seem trivial from the outside, but hold a great deal of meaning for the followers of that tradition. Interpreters working in a particular religious context need to become sensitive to the uses of language in that tradition. When a language is spoken that the interpreter does not understand (Hebrew, Latin, Greek, etc.), it is helpful to indicate why the interpretation has stopped, by saying a brief phrase, "they're using Hebrew now," or the like.

Texts that are part of the ritual may have a standard signed form, as the Lord's Prayer does. An interpreter who will be performing at a church would be well-advised to commit some or all of these ritualized parts of language to memory, both the spoken and the signed forms. In the example mentioned above of the signing deaf choirs, the choral portion of the service would also have a fixed form familiar to the congregation. Insofar as the deaf congregants are invited to participate in responsive reading, unison recitation or singing, having a consistent translation known to both the deaf members and the interpreter conveys a feeling equivalent to that of the spoken language: this text has a meaning and form determined from an authoritative source. "This is the same reading we had two weeks ago."

Sermons, Bible study, and other teaching activities related to religion often spend great amounts of time drawing fine distinctions between terms that appear to be synonyms in ordinary language. The challenge for the interpreter here is to find equally poetic and finely drawn distinctions in the signed translations of such passages.

Physical considerations.

Some religions have strict rules about who can stand in which parts of the house of worship. Others have spiritual significance to the architectural elements. For example, in an Orthodox synagogue, women and men sit in distinct areas of the sanctuary for worship; however, when the same space is used as a meeting room or lecture hall, seating is not restricted. A female interpreter can easily translate for the weekly lecture series (held on a weekday) from the main floor of the sanctuary, but cannot stand or sit in the same spot for the Sabbath worship ceremony.

The interpreter at a wedding will need to consider who is deaf and who is hearing. If the members of the wedding party, including the bride or groom or both are deaf, then that dictates one sort of arrangement of clergy and interpreter. If some guests are deaf and no members of the wedding party, then a different arrangement could be made. Figure 9-8 shows one possible arrangement for the interpreter near the minister, in the case when both bride and groom are deaf or hearing-impaired.

Figure 9-8
Wedding

Falberg, writing on interpreting in religious situations, gives the anecdote about the interpreter who arrives to translate for a funeral service where the parents of the deceased are deaf (Quigley and Youngs, 1965:79-80). The interpreter tried to introduce himself and explain his role to the minister, but everything was rushed and the interpreter felt he had not been understood. The interpreter chose to stand near the minister in the church, but from this position was cut off from his view of the deaf parents (and they from viewing him). Falberg indicates that in such a situation it is difficult to know what is the correct way to handle the dilemma. If the interpreter places himself near the immediate family, other people nearby may assume he is causing a distraction and not "officially" part of the proceedings. By taking a position near the minister, he indicates his formal status, but loses effectiveness by not being visible to the target audience.

Ethical concerns

Many people mention that it is preferable that the interpreter be of the same religious conviction as the congregation. Why is this? One reason is that religious beliefs are generally strongly held. The interpreter who is expected to interpret a message contrary to his or her own moral or religious belief may have a difficult time giving this contrary view with the genuine feeling expressed by the original speaker. Another reason is much simpler. The interpreter is likely to give a better translation in a context where more of the language is familiar and where the deeper meanings and connotations of both the words and the practice are part of the individual's religious education. An argument against the interpreter working in his or her own congregation would be that the individual has little or no opportunity to participate as a congregant.

The issue of payment in a religious context can be a sticky one. Religious institutions depend on contributions and volunteer activity, and some people may find it appropriate to donate their interpreting services. Others whose profession is interpreting, whose livelihood depends on fees for service, may choose to charge the going rate. A member of the congregation would be more likely to donate than someone from the outside; however, the congregant has no obligation to volunteer in this way. The awkward part can occur when a change in interpreting personnel happens: the previous interpreter was willing to undertake the work without being paid and the present interpreter looks mercenary by requesting payment. Where the interpreter works for the church or synagogue on a regular basis, the religious institution should be prepared to acknowledge the service as it does the work of the organist or the religious school teachers.

An interpreter who generally expects payment may choose to volunteer at times. It may happen that one is invited to interpret for a wedding. If the interpreter is well-acquainted with the couple or their families, the interpretation might be considered a wedding gift (or part of it). This is really a decision left to the interpreter and cannot be assumed by the wedding party.

A final note on ethics: the role of the interpreter in the religous setting needs to be clearly defined. An interpreter may also be a lay leader, and may with the religious leader's blessing teach Sunday School, organize spiritual or social activities with the deaf community. In other religious contexts, the interpreter functions only as the interpreter, conveying the services to the deaf congregation and helping them communicate with the religious leader and the rest of the congregation. Some religious workers may also be educated as interpreters. The deaf congregation needs to know how strictly the interpreter construes his or her role to be. The safest route, avoiding misunderstandings and conflicts, is for the interpreter to simply interpret.

Interpreting in Performing Arts

The following comments about the performing arts setting are more thorough and comprehensive than the treatments of the other seven sub-sections have been. Let us reiterate here what was mentioned at the beginning of the chapter. The fact that this section is longer is intended as a model of how each of the sub-sections could and should be developed. It does not imply any more importance of this sub-section in comparison to the other settings.

Several factors led to this expanded treatment. First, New York—where I have been living and working for the past six years—has a great deal of theater activity, including Broadway shows, off-Broadway music and drama, off-off Broadway theaters, Lincoln Center, traveling artists and shows. In the metropolitan area, at least a half-dozen organizations sponsor interpreted performances, including more than one theater with deaf performers. I have been active as an audience member, advisor, director and interpreter in many of these performance settings. Second, I had the pleasure of joining in an *ad hoc* peer support group in which many of these issues (and more) were thrashed around during a period of about a year. Third, I have been teaching courses in sign language and the performing arts, and directing student interpreters in theater for children for the past four years. In addition, performance interpreting is a wonderful field through which to gain exposure for both interpreting and accessibility for deaf and other disabled people. Therefore, it is my hope that people will approach this area responsibly. For all of these reasons, I offer more extensive guidance.

The objective of an interpreter in a performing arts setting is to communicate to the audience. Who is that audience, and who is performing? The answers to these questions will help define the task and setting more clearly for the interpreter.

Where the audience includes deaf people and the performers do not sign or communicate with that audience directly, then the interpreter will be performing an on-stage role. This need not be actually on the stage, as we will see, but let's call it that for the present time.

Where the audience includes hearing people and the performers do not speak or communicate with that part of the audience directly, then the interpreter may also take an on-stage role. The voicing reader for deaf theater is the most common example of this type. The audience will not necessarily see the interpreters, but will hear them.

Where at least some of the performers are deaf, and the other members of the cast or crew are hearing and do not communicate directly with the deaf performers, then the interpreters may take a back-stage role. In this case, it is possible the audience will not see the interpreter at all.

A performing interpreter will need to have a wide range of skills beyond the expected high level of interpreting and translation abilities. Concentration, an understanding of 'focus,' physical control, movement, and even acting are useful tools. Familiarity with the terminology of the theater is primary. More than that, interpreters working in performing arts will gain from understanding the division of responsibilities in and process of theater and performance: how to use the rehearsal time to best advantage, how to accept direction and suggestions from a director as the actors do, who has what responsibility and can help the interpreter accomplish his or her tasks effectively.

Where does performing arts interpreting happen? The first and most obvious answer is "at the theater"—Broadway and other professional theaters, touring companies, regional theater, dinner theater, community players' groups, college and university shows, and children's theater. Poetry readings, opera, folk festivals, popular music concerts, puppet shows, and even some dance productions (where taped or live spoken words are included) have included sign language interpretation. Large public events, such as community celebrations, holiday commemorative events, public rallies and demonstrations, are quite comparable to performances, in that they are generally scripted; they may have technical rehearsals if not full rehearsals, and the inclusion of interpreters will be most effective if planned early on. The pageantry around a birthday, anniversary, or civic commemoration of some other sort can become theatrical. Insofar as the people producing the event are organized and willing to meet at least some of the interpreters' needs, these assignments can be approached like performing arts events. Martin Luther King's birthday celebration, for example, has become an annual occasion for performance in many communities. Television is another medium, but many of the conventions of theater have been borrowed by television. The preparation and performance work an interpreter does for television may be compared to work set in a theater.

Sign language theater, deaf theater, and interpreters

Miles and Fant (1976) have made an interesting and important distinction between sign language theater and deaf theater. The first is essentially theater in translation: any play, poem, or selection of literature can be translated into sign language and performed. Sign language theater makes no attempt to deal with deafness, per se. The audience is expected to understand the convention, for example, that if one character complains to another about the noise in the next room, the second will respond as a hearing person might. In fact, the actors may be deaf or hearing, but hearing status is not important to the roles; "Hamlet," "Chorus Line," or any other show may be performed in sign language theater. Deaf theater adapts material from the conventional theater to "allow for realistic portrayal of deaf (people's) experience," or develops material directly about deaf people's experience. The actor's hearing status is a trait of the character played, and the presence of narrators (voicing for signing characters) or use of signing by hearing characters is given a logical explanation (1976:6).

137

Readers or narrators, sometimes called speaking actors, have long been employed with sign language theater where a sizeable non-signing audience is expected. In the simplest example, one, two or more people seated at the front facing the stage read the lines as the actors sign them. In other sign language theatrical experiences, the readers may be costumed and arranged on stage. The performance of the readers demands rehearsal, careful attention to timing and vocal modulation, and full fluency in the language to adjust if any unexpected changes happen during the performance. Readers may be assigned more than one character and then must work to differentiate characters by assigning distinctive vocal traits to differentiate among these characters. The National Theater of the Deaf, a company largely made up of deaf actors, has generally hired schooled hearing actors, and integrated them on stage, in order to assure high quality and consistent vocal performance.

In the play "Children of a Lesser God," the hearing character, James Leeds, speaks many of the lines signed by Sarah, a deaf woman. Sometimes he behaves as her interpreter, but more often he appears to be responding to her or translating her to himself: "You don't think you'd care for that." Sometimes it's only through his response that the non-signing audience understands what she has said. This play is written more in the style of deaf theater. (Deaf audiences may feel otherwise, since some of the characters have no signed accompaniment, and thus are not accessible.)

The following discussion expands on the notion of interpreters within performances initially planned for hearing audiences. Signing interpreters create a parallel sign language theater experience. We will also touch on the role of readers within sign language theater. Readers create a parallel spoken language theater experience. Neither should be confused with a deaf theater environment.

Elements to a successful interpreted performance

In order to have a successful interpreted performance, the following tasks need to be addressed, either by the interpreter or by someone else who is equally or better qualified:

—Script selection: What production will be interpreted? Some scripts lend themselves to sign language interpreting, while others do not. Is it possible to see a videotape of a touring group to see whether their material will accommodate an interpreter well? Can the interpreter be planned as part of a new production, rather than patched in at some later point? Having a well-informed director who prepares for the interpreter on the stage will make for a successful performance.

—Arrangement for contracts, payment of interpreters, advisors: Even something as simple as a letter of agreement from the production company to the interpreters and their advisors, should state who is taking responsibility for which parts of the interpreted performance. How many dates will interpreters work? For the full run of the show or only a limited number of performances? Will they have unlimited access to the rehearsal process or any performances before the target dates? Will the interpreters have a technical rehearsal prior to their performance, and will this rehearsal run at normal speed with all the regular lighting and sound cues? Will the interpreters be paid for rehearsal time separately from the performances? If the show closes before all of the interpreted performances are completed, what is the payment due to the interpreters? These are only a few of the questions that need to be answered early in the process.

In some communities, local arts councils or state arts commissions have been supportive of interpreted performances, granting funds to help defray costs. In other areas, the interpreters are paid from special corporate grants or the operating budget for the theater. Of course, the ideal arrangement is that the ticket sales to the signing audience will pay for the costs associated with interpreting, but it may take several seasons to build a sufficiently large deaf and hearing base of support for interpreted performances.

Is securing coaching, translation assistance, directing, and advising the responsibility of the interpreters or the theater company? Who selects the advisors and who pays them? These are two separate questions, and both need to be settled early to avoid misunderstandings later in the process. A fellow interpreter or deaf community member who is called upon for assistance in translation or to offer feedback during the rehearsal process is delivering a sophisticated service which deserves compensation.

—Selection of interpreters: There are any number of ways to decide who will interpret a particular show or series of shows. Often interpreters (like actors) are cast because they have the right 'look.' Sometimes the interpreter will be chosen because of a specific signing style, ability to convey several characters, or skill in setting the right moods. The selection process needs to have some attention to signing and interpreting skills.

How many interpreters will be involved with a particular production depends on several factors. How long is the performance? How large is the theater or hall? Will the whole audience be deaf or will it be a mixed audience? Is this a one-character show, or does it have a cast of thousands? Is there any obvious limit dictated from the budget? For example, one interpreter trying to portray six or eight characters over a two-and-a-half hour performance will probably not do the show justice; the interpreter's fatigue will be visible to the audience, and the separation of characters is unlikely to be maintained. Such a show calls for two or perhaps three interpreters.

Who selects the interpreters? An interpreter or group of interpreters can make an agreement with a theater or production company to handle all of the details for the interpreted performance. That person or group can then retain control over selection of the interpreters. Often, however, if a theater will be paying for the performance, it may want to have representation in the process. Following another model for selection, the theater company chooses an advisory panel who audition and recommend interpreters.

In many communities, the performing interpreters are chosen from the group of most proficient interpreters. However, some communities have found performance to be a good instructional practicum for novice interpreters. In these cases, the advisors (deaf and hearing) take more responsibility for translation, coaching, blocking, and directing than where the interpreters are accomplished professionals.

—Script and performance analysis: There are at least four aspects of a production which the interpreter needs to consider while preparing for the performance:
1. what is the artistic vision of this production?
   what is the director's interpretation of the script?
2. what is the direction of the performance? how are people arranged on stage, blocked, what does the show look like?
3. what is each actor's characterization? how have they chosen to present the roles?
4. what is the mood, style, tone, rhythm of the show?

Somehow, the performing interpreter has to find a way to integrate all of these elements into an understandable whole. These will color or even determine the nature of the interpretation. For example, the translation cannot be done without reference to a particular production, because the direction the signs move, the emphasis each receives, and the choice of signs depends in part on the way that the actors make their entrances and exits, how a particular character reacts to another, and so forth.

—Translation and rehearsal: The interpreter must have the full command of sign language resources available during the translation process. An interpreter who continually meets words or phrases that are beyond his or her language competence needs to call on an advisor for assistance.

A few general suggestions can be offered:
1. the size of the signing needs adjustment to the size of the performance space and the distance to the audience;
2. signs that make noise may need to be avoided or adapted to prevent interference with the production;
3. fingerspelling will generally be difficult to read at a distance and will not communicate most effectively;
4. creation of signs should follow the principles of coinage that are part of the target language.

Some good reading about the translation process for performance is available: Fant (1979); Klima and Bellugi (1980, especially Chapters 13 and 14); Eastman (1980); Malzkuhn (1980); Solow (1978); Golladay (1978); and Kirchner (1978).

—Blocking or positioning of interpreter(s): No single solution can be prescribed for all interpreted performances. In part, the positions of the interpreters depend on the seating of the signing audience. Generally, the director has the final say on where the interpreter(s) will stand or sit. The decision should be based on artistic criteria as well as visibility for the target audience. Where two or more interpreters divide several characters, the interpreters need to be positioned in relation to each other to permit the viewing audience to understand their alternating turns as alternating turns as conversation, responding to one another. Were the interpreters to be separated on either side of the stage, the deaf viewer would never catch both interpreters: the deaf viewer doesn't have the audio cue to know where to look next.

The interpreters who stand or sit in a single place throughout the performance are practicing position interpreting. The position may be stage right, stage left, on the apron, on a special platform so that trunk and head are above stage level and appropriately lit. Or the interpreters may be set on a platform or on piece of scenery above the action. Figure 9-9 shows the position of interpreters "house right." Presumably, they are standing on a raised platform or sitting on high stools to be seen by the whole audience in the section in front of them.

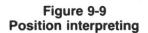

Figure 9-9
Position interpreting

Shadow interpreting occurs when the interpreters move with particular characters on the stage. This form is artistically the most demanding for the director, and the interpreter, and also the most rewarding when it succeeds. The audience is saved from the "ping-pong" effect of trying to catch the stage action and look back to the positioned interpreters' translations. Figure 9-10 shows the approach of having different interpreters shadow each of the three main characters on stage. The interpreter needs to find ways to indicate how the character is interacting with the other characters how the character moves, at the same time not overstepping the bounds from interpreting to acting.

Zone interpreting describes the interplay between two or more interpreters who each take responsibility for lines that are spoken within their "territory" on stage. Rehearsals will assist the interpreters in de-

141

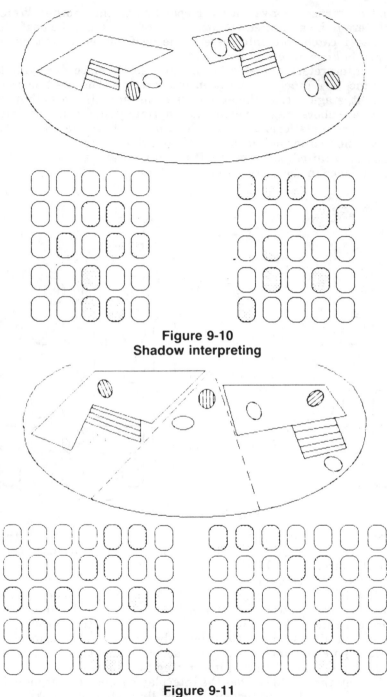

Figure 9-10
Shadow interpreting

Figure 9-11
Zone interpreting

termining where the boundaries for each zone are, so that two or more do not claim the same line. Figure 9-11 gives a rough idea of how zone interpreting might work. It is difficult from these static diagrams to have a sense of how the two, shadow and zone, might differ from each other. Factors such as the design of the set, the number of players on stage at once, and so on, will often be important in deciding which approach to take and how many interpreters to employ. In fact, some productions use shadow interpreters for the primary characters and zone interpreters for the secondary. In this way, there are not constantly four or five additional people running all over the stage, but there are sufficient interpreters to help differentiate the central cast from the support cast.

Closed-circuit interpreting happens when the theater or performance space is equipped with closed circuit television. The interpreters work from backstage and are video-projected onto television monitors in the house. The position of the target audience in relation to the monitors is important.

House interpreting puts the interpreter into position near the audience section reserved for deaf viewers, rather than on the stage. When the performance is a film, the audience will be able to see it as well from a distance, but may see the interpreter better close up. Lighting considerations are important here.

Will the interpreters stand or sit? If they will sit, then the seats must be checked for comfort and visibility. When the house is full, can the deaf audience still see a seated interpreter over the heads in front?

Similar considerations for voicing interpreters are necessary. The traditional spot at the front of the audience or in the front balcony is not the only place for readers to be placed. A thoughtful director may find a creative way to incorporate the readers into the production, given the appropriate text. "Our Town" has been performed in sign language with a chorus of readers designed into the production; "The Bald Soprano" incorporated the narrators as pieces of furniture, or other static set pieces; "The Gin Game," a dynamic interplay between two main characters with no supporting players, however, does not lend itself to such a treatment.

—Technical considerations (lighting, costuming and make-up): Lighting need not be elaborate, but does need to be considered. The faces, eyes, hands and forearms are most essential here. Whatever lighting is chosen for the interpreters should fit into the overall design for lighting. Lighting can do much to show off the interpreter as a subtle adjunct to the performance. Where the performance includes mime, or sections without speech or sound, the interpreters need not be lit; alternately they can move out of the light. Color of light will also need to be considered in relation to the interpreters' skin tones.

Shall the interpreter be costumed or wear street clothes? This decision rests in negotiation between the production staff and the interpreters or their director. When the production is highly elaborate and stylized, such as an opera, the interpreters will look out of place in contemporary street clothes. If the show is contemporary, perhaps street clothes are most appropriate. This again is an artistic decision to be determined early on. Where stage lighting is employed, stage make-up needs to be in use also. Both face and hands need make-up.

143

—Direction, professional advice: The involvement of specialists other than the interpreters themselves depends on budget, time and resources. Having an informed eye watch the rehearsal process can be extremely advantageous. Having an interpreter's producer, who will handle many of the details of liaison with the production staff, gives the interpreters clear focus on translation and rehearsal. Soliciting professional advice from educated deaf theater-goers, deaf performers, or colleagues in the interpreting world allows the interpreters the benefit of feedback and revision prior to the performance.

—Audience development: At the same time interpreters are engaged to rehearse and perform, the theater needs to think about audience development in the signing community. Gathering the appropriate audience for an interpreted performance is not an easy task. In fact, it entails on-going community education about theater, performance and the arts. Not every show will be an easy one to understand or a crowd-pleaser. The audience needs to be cultivated and encouraged to experience many kinds of performance art.

At the same time, producers and theater staffs need to develop realistic expectations about the size of a theater-going audience. Even though the deaf community in a particular area may be estimated at several thousand individuals, only a handful may show up at any performance; but isn't that true of the hearing audience as well? The number who attend any particular performance is only a sampling of all the members of a community.

Theaters should by all means attempt to attract a large deaf audience through advertising in deaf community newspapers, or mailings to target homes and agencies. The involvement of a community member as a resource to the theater will save the interpreters' attention for the task of interpreting. The budget for audience development needs to be determined as early as possible, with the realization that ordinary means of advertising will not necessarily be effective for letting the deaf audience know about an accessible performance.

—Audience accommodation: Will the box office be equipped to take phone reservations from TDD's? or is an alternate number available? Will an interpreter or signing staff member be available at the box office on the day of the performance? Will the ushers be briefed on what to expect, or will there be signing ushers? Will a special section be held for deaf audience members, their friends and families? Will a poster or insert to the program explain any special signs that are used in the performance (e.g., name signs of different characters)? Will the audience be able to read the script ahead, or have a synopsis prior to the performance? Will the director, performers, or interpreters meet with this audience before the show to orient them to the production? or after the show to discuss it? Someone should think about answers to these and similar questions; it need not be the interpreters; an informed member of the theater company, or the interpreter's producer may have these tasks as part of their assignment.

—Evaluation: There are many ways to judge the success of an interpreted performance. Personal interviews take time, but can dig for more detailed comments. Questionnaires, if well-designed, may give some indication of general areas, both in interpreting and accessibility, that have succeeded or need improvement. In any case, it will be helpful in planning for the next interpreted performance to have some perspective on the success of this event. The theater may only wish to know whether the audience would be willing to buy tickets for a similar performance in the future. The interpreters may prefer more detailed response about their performance in relation to the theater work.

One reviewer wrote of one interpreter in a few words while reviewing a performer:

> On the night that we saw Whoopi Goldberg, the audience was more racially mixed than any we had encountered in an Off-Broadway house in a long while. Goldberg's performance was also being simultaneously translated for the hearing-impaired by Hands On, a group whose goal it is to shepherd laughter across the sound barrier. The interpreter was inches away from Goldberg throughout the show, his hands and mouth working continuously. Yet to his great credit and hers, he was completely invisible to those who were not deaf and still communicated everything, even the foreign accents, to those who were.
>
> (Dworkin, 1984:10)

In summary, the performance interpreter working on-stage can only do exemplary work when all the business of the theater is taken into account in a timely manner: selection of script, translation and rehearsal time, positioning, costuming, lighting, and audience development are only some of the factors which will contribute to successful interpreted performance.

Backstage interpreting

A backstage interpreter's work is typically more like other sorts of interpreting work. The difference is that all that has been learned about the theater or performance becomes useful as background to the assignment. The backstage interpreter is the deaf performer's ears and possibly also voice. Rehearsals, auditions, cast meetings, even company parties and press conferences are within the venue of the backstage interpreter.

A backstage interpreter is often involved intensively with one or a few deaf people; all the strictures of confidentiality, faithfulness, and so forth that have been practiced for so long still apply. If the interpreter makes an error or is inattentive for an instant, the performers are aware of the interpretation. The interpreter might appear not to be working, because the deaf performer is doing a task which does not require continuous and instantaneous interpreting, and thus people assume the interpreter is approachable. They will come ask all the standard questions about one's involvement with this deaf actor, the interpreter's background in sign language and interpreting, and so on. But of course, the interpreter is working, and must excuse herself or himself.

A backstage interpreter need not only be part of theatrical events. The interpreter behind the scenes in a film, television program or any sort of public performance where the deaf person is featured can be considered a backstage interpreter. This role is not yet a very frequent one, but it is terribly demanding, since there are often no other signers around or people accustomed to communicating with deaf people. The deaf performer can feel left out of the sociability of the company and may depend on the interpreter as a companion. At the same time, the deaf performer wants to be independent and function naturally with colleagues in the world of theater, television or other performing arts. This relationship requires the utmost in diplomacy, the strictest discretion, and the greatest alertness and stamina.

Television interpreting

Interpreting on television happens in some communities with regularity, while it is only an incidental occasion in others. Certain programs (the daily news summary, a weekly religious program) are more often interpreted. Some stations, often the public network affiliate, agree to include interpreters. Occasionally a candidate for public office or a commercial sponsor will incorporate an interpreter in the short spot.

There are several methods of incorporating an interpreter on television. The *corner insert* is so familiar that it is emblematic of television interpreting; the popular show "Saturday Night Live" even parodied this use of interpreting. What is not so well known is which corner is most effective? What sort of background and costume will enable the viewer to read the interpreter's message? What camera angle is best? Shall the corner be squared off, or will an oval read better?

NTID's (1979) guidebook on television interpreting contains many good suggestions about how to produce effective interpreting for broadcast. Interpreters and producers will probably find that a hard-edged oval cameo reads better than soft-edged inserts. Solid, evenly lit background that separates background from interpreter helps the message stand out. Where there is more than one studio available, the interpreter may be placed out of the traffic, separate from the live production. The interpreter will need excellent audio feed in any case, in order to make the production accessible to the intended audience. The interpreter's choice of clothing should take into account not only the usual interpreting concerns, but also the technical considerations of television equipment. One particular shade of blue reads as invisible by the machinery that can take the signal from the camera on the interpreter and insert it to the signal from the pre-recorded or live material. Thus, the interpreter who wears this blue may appear to be a disembodied pair of hands below a floating head. Solid black and strong white are also difficult colors for the television camera to read. Interpreters who are familiar with these technical issues will be accepted as knowledgeable professionals by the technical television crew.

For interpreters, one of the biggest challenges is making the message understandable while working within a tightly constrained space. Where the interpreter might usually shift body angle to signal the change in

146

speakers or characters, this movement may need to be modified to fit the insert area available. It is helpful to read the script ahead, rehearse with any pre-recorded audio material, and have a video monitor available to check one's sign production. Again, checking the audio signal from the pre-recorded tape or live production area is imperative. Ear plugs with direct audio feed or a special audio monitor may be called for.

Interpreters will want to convey sound effects, insofar as they are important to the program. Doorbell rings, telephones, and footsteps off camera are the sort of auditory information that motivates characters' subsequent actions. In contrast, where graphics or captioned images convey the whole message, the interpreter's image can be faded, allowing for the slight lag from voice to hands. If a voice-over announcer explains the meaning of the graphics, then the interpreter will need to be seen by the audience. Because of these issues, planning for an interpreter insert needs to begin at the time the broadcast is planned. In this way, space in the picture can be left for the insert without diminishing the effect of the non-linguistic visual message.

Interpreters may also find themselves on screen mixed into the group in the camera's view, rather than inserted. For example, a local talk show may include both deaf and hearing guests. In order for the host and guests to talk together, an interpreter will be necessary. The interpreter, or the interpreter's advocate, will need to consult with the director well before the recording date in order to agree on the interpreter's position on the screen, the appropriate use of microphones for the interpreter, and so forth. In this case, the home viewing audience wants to see the interpreter as well as the deaf panelists. If the interpreter is on the set with the host and guests, then special care needs to be taken to consistently keep the interpreter on camera, whether the host or some hearing guest is speaking. This may involve the use of split-screen techniques or other multiple camera mixing. Of course, while the deaf guests sign, the interpreter will need to be voicing, but need not be visible. Perhaps the most successful way to handle this example involves the use of two interpreters, one for voicing and one for signing. The signing interpreter would need to be seen by the deaf panelists, but could also be inserted into the broadcast signal live using one dedicated camera.

In the above example, we have already anticipated questions about what to do with the interpreter for a deaf television performer or guest who does not speak. An off-camera interpreter equipped with appropriately checked microphone needs to be able to see the deaf person. It also helps if the interpreter can be seen by the deaf person.

In all of these cases, whether the interpreter is seen as a corner insert, incorporated on the set or functioning as an unseen voice, the interpreter is included in the AFTRA union regulations for professional broadcast performers. An interpreter who is unclear about how much to charge for televison work should consult with the AFTRA offices in New York or Los Angeles to help determine the appropriate fee. Interpreters who appear on television incidentally, e.g. as part of news coverage of some other event which included interpreting, will probably not be covered by these regulations.

147

speakers or characters, this movement may need to be modified to fit the insert area available. It is helpful to read the script ahead, rehearse with any pre-recorded audio material, and have a video monitor available to check one's sign production. Again, checking the audio signal from the pre-recorded tape or live production area is imperative. Ear plugs with direct audio feed or a special audio monitor may be called for.

Interpreters will want to convey sound effects, insofar as they are important to the program. Doorbell rings, telephones, and footsteps off camera are the sort of auditory information that motivates characters' subsequent actions. In contrast, where graphics or captioned images convey the whole message, the interpreter's image can be faded, allowing for the slight lag from voice to hands. If a voice-over announcer explains the meaning of the graphics, then the interpreter will need to be seen by the audience. Because of these issues, planning for an interpreter insert needs to begin at the time the broadcast is planned. In this way, space in the picture can be left for the insert without diminishing the effect of the non-linguistic visual message.

Interpreters may also find themselves on screen mixed into the group in the camera's view, rather than inserted. For example, a local talk show may include both deaf and hearing guests. In order for the host and guests to talk together, an interpreter will be necessary. The interpreter, or the interpreter's advocate, will need to consult with the director well before the recording date in order to agree on the interpreter's position on the screen, the appropriate use of microphones for the interpreter, and so forth. In this case, the home viewing audience wants to see the interpreter as well as the deaf panelists. If the interpreter is on the set with the host and guests, then special care needs to be taken to consistently keep the interpreter on camera, whether the host or some hearing guest is speaking. This may involve the use of split-screen techniques or other multiple camera mixing. Of course, while the deaf guests sign, the interpreter will need to be voicing, but need not be visible. Perhaps the most successful way to handle this example involves the use of two interpreters, one for voicing and one for signing. The signing interpreter would need to be seen by the deaf panelists, but could also be inserted into the broadcast signal live using one dedicated camera.

In the above example, we have already anticipated questions about what to do with the interpreter for a deaf television performer or guest who does not speak. An off-camera interpreter equipped with appropriately checked microphone needs to be able to see the deaf person. It also helps if the interpreter can be seen by the deaf person.

In all of these cases, whether the interpreter is seen as a corner insert, incorporated on the set or functioning as an unseen voice, the interpreter is included in the AFTRA union regulations for professional broadcast performers. An interpreter who is unclear about how much to charge for televison work should consult with the AFTRA offices in New York or Los Angeles to help determine the appropriate fee. Interpreters who appear on television incidentally, e.g. as part of news coverage of some other event which included interpreting, will probably not be covered by these regulations.

function, but did satisfy the goal of the rally organizers to make accommodations for everyone who might want to participate.

This example is only one of many possible similar ones which demonstrate the symbolic function of the interpreter. While deaf rally members might have actually seen an interpreter for all or most of some speeches, particularly in the afternoon, for large parts of the morning presentations the interpreting was an act of symbolic communication. No one in the immediate audience who could see the interpreting was deaf, and no deaf people in the mass audience could see the interpreting. The logistics of the rally and march prevented the communication from being completed. However, the shared understanding of the rally organizers and the deaf marchers was that the spoken remarks would be made accessible, and the presence of interpreters on the stage at the U.N. building fulfilled that understanding.

The symbolic nature of the interpreting was played out in another way, namely for the home viewing audience. The television coverage did not include closed or open captions, and did not use a corner insert for interpreting (or any other method we have discussed). However, insofar as the speakers from the podium were on the screen, there was a chance that the interpreters were also on the screen. The presence of the interpreters could communicate not only the meaning of the immediate remarks being spoken, but also the larger message that this rally was being made accessible for deaf people. The visibility of access for deaf people (through interpreting) communicates again a larger message that the rally was accessible to all disabled people.

Summary

Performing arts interpreting includes a variety of distinct contexts, from the obvious theatrical productions through civic or political events to television. Each of these draws on the interpreter's skills in translation as well as performance, where poise under difficult circumstances is vitally important. Performing arts contexts, such as those discussed above, generally are more effectively interpreted when the interpreters have both preparation time with a script and rehearsal time in the physical setting where the interpreting will take place. The technical considerations for theater differ from those for television, but the interpreter's overall concern in each of these settings is that the expected audience be able to understand and appreciate the intent of the production. There will even be cases, as we saw, when the interpretation remains largely symbolic, communicating to the immediate deaf audience a genuine effort at accessibility, or to a distant audience the notion that the event included or expected a deaf audience.

10 SPECIAL COMMUNICATION TECHNIQUES

This chapter will describe five types of situations calling for special communication techniques. Three of the situations are dictated because of the communication requirements of deaf or hearing-impaired people. People with limited language abilities (also called Minimal Language Skills), people who prefer an oral-visual representation of spoken language (the oral deaf), and people whose perceptual disabilities include severe visual impairment (also called deaf-blind) have additional communication needs beyond those which we have assumed up to this point. In addition, teams of interpreters may be required in other settings, where criteria of time, space, physical arrangement or language all contribute to complicating the interpreting context. Finally, telephones have become so much a part of our modern lives that people who do not have the ability to communicate directly by phone require sensitive and accurate assistance in completing communication in settings other than face-to-face.

Clients with Minimal Language Skills

Characterizing MLS

Minimal Language Skills is a term which characterizes the diminished or idiosyncratic communication system of some deaf individuals. The expression Minimal Language Skills (MLS) is considered more polite or precise than the older term "low verbal." There are not yet any tests or ways to determine exactly who is included in the MLS group. People who exhibit MLS may come from quite different backgrounds, and yet the interpreter's approach to communicating with them can be similar.

Most individuals who exhibit MLS also do not speak well, probably do not read or write, and in general are not familiar with English or any other spoken language. However, many deaf people who fit this description (do not speak well, not fluent in spoken or written language) are competent in a standard sign language such as ASL, and these people would not be considered MLS. Even someone who does not use fingerspelling and whose signing is full of localisms can still be considered a perfectly normal monolingual ASL user. It may require some adjustment on the part of the interpreter to accommodate the non-standard forms, but the grammar of the utterances may still be considered standard sign language.

Foreign deaf persons sometimes are labeled MLS until they acquire the sign language of the local community. Their signing appears highly idiosyncratic, and in fact many of the techniques suggested for communicating with an MLS signer will work well with a foreign signer. The difference is that the foreign signer is fluent, uses gesture and space efficiently, understands the role of eye gaze in sign language grammar, and is likely to be highly communicative and cognitively sophisticated.

MLS may describe a deaf person who uses a highly idiosyncratic signing system, for example, "home sign." Home sign in this context means a whole system of signing, not just a few homemade lexical items. A deaf person who has been isolated from other deaf people, but who has developed a gestural repertoire, probably can be characterized both as using home sign and having MLS.

MLS has never been the term to characterize the fluency or amount of communication that an individual exhibits. One person might be very gregarious, while another much more reserved, but both may exhibit minimal language skills. Similarly, intelligence is independent of language skills. Some people who show MLS have strong intellectual capabilities, while others have serious limitations. An equivalent term for minimal language skills is "minimal language competency."

Communication techniques

Since each person who exhibits MLS uses an individually determined symbol system, the hearing or deaf person who encounters a deaf person showing minimal language competency cannot be schooled reliably in advance in how to communicate. Interpreters, rehabilitation personnel, and others who need to communicate, however, should take several steps.

1) Become familiar with the usual context of the communication with family members or co-workers. Often the communicative, fluent MLS person is accustomed to introducing others to their own private gestural languages.

2) Use props and environmental objects to aid communication; maps, clocks, calendars, pictures, tactile stimuli and the like may be useful.

3) Highly recommended is the involvement of an intermediary RSC (deaf) interpreter, to assist in the communication, particularly when the consequences of the communication may affect the health or welfare of the deaf person classed as MLS.

An intermediary interpreter can be helpful for two reasons. First, deaf persons, especially those who have attended residential schools, have long experience in interacting with other deaf individuals. They will be familiar with gestural language skills in all stages of development and with people whose signing behavior ranges from totally nonstandard to totally conforming. Second, the presence of a deaf interpreter may relieve the anxiety of a deaf person who is having difficulty communicating to several hearing people. Deaf persons who have instruction as interpreters are likely to understand role-separation, and take on only the responsibility of relaying messages between the MLS person and the others who need to communicate with him or her. Not all RSC's will have equal ability for handling interpreting with MLS individuals.

Figure 10-1 illustrates one possible arrangement of hearing and deaf participants in a courtroom where an MLS witness is testifying. In this case, the hearing interpreter is standing near the witness, facing the attorneys and the deaf interpreter. The deaf interpreter stands near the attorneys facing the deaf witness. In this way, the judge and court reporter can hear everything the hearing interpreter voices, and the deaf witness will rely on the RSC interpreter for sending and receiving communication. As discussed below ("Teams of Interpreters"), this arrangement affords maximum separation of tasks for the two interpreters, ensuring that they will function in a mutually coordinated way.

4) Use pantomime, gestures, and adopt or adapt the MLS individual's own store of gestures. It may require the involvement of a family member or friend to help with the communication. While the involvement of relatives as aides in interpreting situations is not desirable in general, there are circumstances where communicating is more important than staying within the boundaries of the usual constraining rule.

Several sorts of ideas may be difficult to communicate with someone who does not have a standard sign language, or who does not share the interpreter's sign language. Expressing relationships in time (X happened before Y; three weeks ago . . .), pronouns, especially where several people or objects are discussed at once, comparatives (A is more _____ than B, C is as _____ as D), and negation are all potential stumbling blocks in interpreting and communicating with an MLS deaf person.

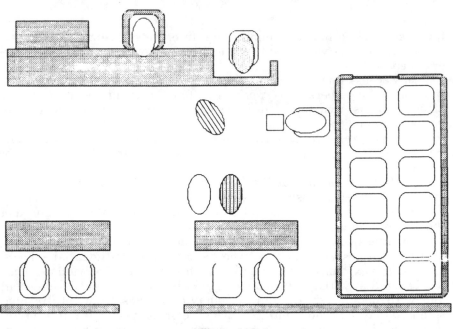

Figure 10-1
MLS witness

An unsuccessful interpreting assignment

Even when one follows all of the recommendations, it is not always possible to have a successful and satisfying interpreting encounter. The following story illustrates how communication might fail even when everyone is trying to cooperate.

In the past five years, I've been freelancing more or less full-time. Among the most difficult interpreting assignments I've had — emotionally — was a case where I was called to court to interpret with a rape victim before the grand jury. Both the young woman and her alleged attacker were deaf, and before the Assistant District Attorney (ADA) was willing to take the case before the Grand Jury, she wanted to be sure that the testimony would be sufficient to have them return an indictment. I happened to be assigned as the interpreter.

When the agency called me and told me which courthouse to go to, who to meet there and all the necessary information, I recall they also mentioned that this was expected to be a difficult interpreting assignment because of the witness's low language skills. Knowing that this sort of information often is filtered through the district attorney's office, on the basis of poor written or spoken communication skills, and then through the agency's staff, with an unknown number of intermediate steps of messages taken on one side or the other, I listen and take this information with a grain of salt. I decided to try it on my own the first time. I have sufficient experience in this area to know that

154

if my language and interpreting skills are not equal to the task, I will be able to bow out gracefully or call upon an intermediary interpreter.

When I arrived, I was introduced to the ADA, the witness, her sister (hearing), and the police officer who had driven them from their home, some distance away. The ADA gave me the barest outline of the case, some relevant dates and some background on the witness-victim. She had been attacked twice by the same man, with a period of one month intervening. The first attack had happened in another jurisdiction, and therefore could not come up in testimony before the Grand Jury. The second attack was the one which needed to be described; the questions that the ADA needed to ask were things like, what time did you leave home that day? where did you meet this man? is this the picture of the man you met on the bus? where did you get off the bus? when did he first threaten you? did he have a weapon? when did you find out? were you afraid of bodily harm? where was the building that he led you into?

I spent some time talking to the witness, introducing myself, explaining to her and her sister that I was the interpreter today, and what we were expecting to do. I said that the ADA wanted to ask some questions but she didn't know how to sign, so I would help her by signing, then I would tell her in voice what the answers were. We were not trying to hurry, and we understood that the re-telling might be emotionally difficult.

In the process of orienting the witness, and talking with her sister and the ADA, I learned that she was a client of Goodwill job training. This fact told me two things: 1) that her educational achievement was not the highest, and 2) I knew her job trainer who is also a certified interpreter. In fact that trainer's name sign came up and I asked about her. Apparently, when the witness had been taken to the hospital, it was her trainer who interpreted for her during the medical emergency. But this same person felt that her involvement with the client was too great for her to function properly as an interpreter in the court situation.

After more than two hours of working both in simultaneous and consecutive methods, with the aid of a calendar for the months in question, and a map of the area showing public transportation routes near the victim's home, the place where she had been picked up and her job training site, and with her sister aiding my identification of place names and family members' name signs, the ADA felt that the testimony was still too confused and inconsistent to go before the Grand Jury. We agreed to meet another day and I specifically requested that we include a deaf (RSC) interpreter who might be more familiar with the idiosyncratic sign usage of this witness.

Two weeks later, we met again. I encouraged the RSC interpreter to get acquainted with the witness, and helped him learn a few of her personal signs (names of relatives, job trainer, and so forth). Again the ADA gave us great latitude in formulating the questions in a way which would give her the testimony she needed to bring an indictment, and yet in a way which was intelligible to the witness.

We worked together and separately for several hours; the parts of the story which never quite became clear included the identification of the exact place where the victim and her attacker exited from the bus, and the relation to that place of the abandoned building the boy forced her into. The victim consistently picked the suspect's picture from a group of pictures. The police officer offered to drive us all (two interpreters and witness) to the end of the bus line in order to see if any particular place along the route sparked the witness's memory. We two interpreters were still hopeful that looking at the route in three dimensions would work some magic that we were unable to carry off using only language and maps.

The difficulty here was that the witness's sign language repertoire was so limited, both in terms of vocabulary and grammatical elaboration of that vocabulary, that we were unable to pose questions of much subtlety. It would be easy to label her as a person with Minimal Language Skills. The witness's memory or attention span, her ability to form syntactically complex responses, and her ability to respond appropriately were questionable.

The outcome of the interpreting assignment was that the case had to be dropped. The witness never went before the Grand Jury, because she could not consistently separate the two attacks, could not identify where it had taken place, how she had gotten home afterwards, or other details.

Prior to this interpreting job, both my RSC partner and I were confident that if only the right combination of people were put into a situation, and permitted sufficient freedom in posing the questions and voicing the answers, the communication would proceed — perhaps not smoothly or easily, but it would be possible. This assignment jolted both of us into a new and unpleasant reality. Even with our cumulative language skills and years of experience, this interpreting team was unable to communicate in the way that a court testimony would require.

This anecdote reminds us that an interpreter is not a panacea for all communication difficulties. Even two interpreters at the same time cannot guarantee the end of communication barriers. And clients who have limited language skills may present a challenge to an interpreting team, because of additional gaps in their cognitive development and social awareness. Fortunately, interpreting assignments which are unsuccessful like this one, i.e. where the communication does not happen, are relatively rare.

Summary

Interpreting with an MLS deaf person stretches the skills and creativity of the interpreter. The interpreter who accepts the client as an equal without looking down on the client's difference or limitations of language will have a better chance at successful communication. Working with MLS clients is a sensitive test of an interpreter's ability to judge his or her own skills. This context is one in which an interpreter may want to call in a replacement and may welcome the additional competence that an RSC brings to the communication.

Interpreting for deaf-blind people

Interpreting with and for deaf-blind people involves some special skills and special background knowledge. It often helps to understand how the person became deaf-blind.

Etiology of deaf-blindness

There are four possible profiles for people who are both visually-impaired and hearing-impaired:

1) born sighted and hearing, loses both senses one at a time or simultaneously through injury or illness.

When people lose hearing and sight after acquiring language and mobility, then it is difficult to predict what form of communication will be preferred. It is unlikely that they will have acquired much sign language, although they may understand one of the actile fingerspelling methods. They will probably be comfortable with some communication system that is based on English or their original spoken-written language;

2) born sighted and deaf, later loses vision through illness or injury.

About fifty per cent of the cases of deaf-blindness in the U.S. today are accounted for by Usher's Syndrome, that is, congenital deafness along with retinitis pigmentosa (RP). RP is a hereditary (not infectious or contagious) illness, which may not begin to express symptoms until the middle of childhood or even later. This degenerative condition is marked by diminished vision at night or in low-light areas, decreasing peripheral (side) vision, more often known as "tunnel vision," and possible eventual loss of central vision.

Other causes of blindness might be geriatric diseases of the eye, such as glaucoma, cataracts, and diabetic retinopathy.

If the person previously used sign language, this still may be the preferred form of communication, although reception may need to be modified to a tactile mode or adjusted to a smaller space within the tunnel range of the viewer. A deaf person who was raised orally may be able to learn how to receive information through the Tadoma method, a tactile technique for speechreading (lipreading). The deaf person places the thumb on the lips of the speaker and spreads the other fingers gently across the cheek, jaw and throat to sense movements involved in speaking, including vibrations of the vocal cords;

157

3) born hearing and blind, later loses hearing.

A small proportion of deaf-blind people originally could hear and thus probably acquired spoken language and Braille reading proficiency. They may prefer to use some form of tactile spelling including tactile Braille, and are likely to be able to speak intelligibly for themselves;

4) born deaf and blind, or becomes deaf-blind in early childhood.

Helen Keller is one of the best know examples of someone deafened and blinded in early childhood from illness. She preferred fingerspelling with the one-hand alphabet.

A large number of visually-impaired and hearing-impaired people were born during the rubella epidemic of 1963-65. Some of these people have additional handicapping conditions such as mental retardation or deformed limbs. The type of communication preferred by these deaf-blind people depends largely on their educational background. These people are now reaching adulthood and will pass from the supervision of the schools into the areas of vocational training, college, or jobs. Interpreters will be called upon more frequently to aid interaction between deaf-blind people and their communication environment.

Not all deaf-blind people are totally deaf or totally blind. They may retain some auditory perception, perhaps with a hearing aid. They may still have some light or movement perception. It depends on what sort of illness or injury occurred.

Communication techniques

Kates and Schein (1980) have catalogued a large number of techniques and devices for communicating with deaf-blind people. Interpreters who anticipate interacting with deaf-blind clients will want to familiarize themselves with some of these communication options.

Much interpreting with deaf-blind people requires one interpreter to one client, since each person's needs are different and so many of the clients require tactile reception. It is helpful if the interpreter and client can face each other for sending and receiving sign language or fingerspelling, as illustrated in Figure 10-2. An alternative is to sit side-by-side for one-handed transmission-reception (e.g., Braille manual, Lorm alphabet), as diagrammed in Figure 10-3. At the same time, the interpreter should be prepared for physical fatigue from the constant weight of the receiver's hands on the sending hands. The client also expends a high level of energy in receiving tactile information, keeping arms raised for long periods of time, and may therefore prefer to sit in a chair with arms or at a table in order to rest an elbow from time to time. Interpreters will find that it is not physically possible to interpret for thirty minutes or more, as it might be with a sighted deaf person. Interpreter teams, therefore, will need to be sensitive to each other's limits in tactile transmission. Where thirty minutes might be expected of each interpreter in a business meeting, classroom or convention presentation, fifteen minutes might be the limit in one-on-one tactile interpreting.

It is generally a good idea to agree on signals that will indicate that

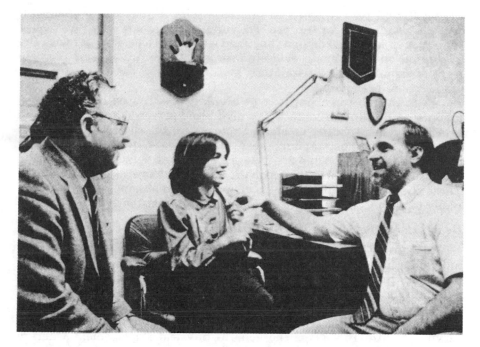

Figure 10-2
Deaf-blind

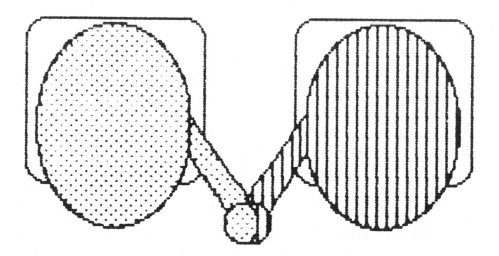

Figure 10-3
Side-by-side tactile

the deaf-blind person wants to interrupt with a question or comment, does not understand, or the like. The regulatory signals which we expect from spoken language or sign language will need to be adjusted with the deaf-blind client. Among deaf-blind people there are several possible ways of signaling these regulators, and interpreters need to learn individual client preferences.

Even though the client may be blind, it is still useful for the interpreter to maintain eye contact. The deaf-blind person's face may indicate a lack of understanding (a blank expression), the desire to interject a question, active understanding (head nod), and so on. Regular monitoring of the facial expression and eye gaze of a deaf-blind person will permit the interpreter to maximize the feedback and confidence in understanding. Those clients who could use their vision prior to blindness may be more likely to use facial cues more often and more consistently.

Deaf interpreters with deaf-blind consumers

In a group where both deaf and deaf-blind people are present, the individual interpreters for the deaf-blind people may themselves be deaf people. In this situation while someone is speaking, a hearing interpreter will interpret into an agreed variety of sign language. Each of the one-on-one RSC (deaf) interpreters will seat themselves so that they can see that interpreter and will relay the address to the deaf-blind person they are serving. Figure 10-4 gives the general physical arrangement where a deaf interpreter works with a deaf-blind client. When the person

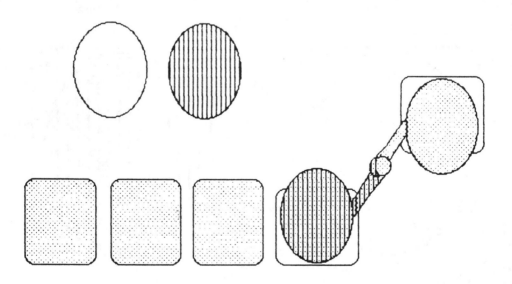

Figure 10-4
Relay tactile

160

addressing the group is signing, a speaking interpreter will voice, while each of the one-on-one interpreters can shadow or interpret from the original signer.

Deaf (RSC) interpreters can also assist deaf-blind clients with telephone calls (through the use of TTY's/TTD's).

Personal appearance

As in any other interpreting situation, clothing, make-up and other factors of personal hygiene are important to consider. When the client is relying on reduced vision, the interpreter will be wise to take special care to make the viewing task easy. Clothing that contrasts with skin color is, of course, appropriate. White or shiny fabric may cause a glare that makes viewing difficult, and thus should be avoided.

Jewelry, such as necklaces, bracelets and rings, can interfere with reduced visual reception by causing glare or distraction. In addition, it can scratch or lead to misunderstanding in tactile reception. For the same reasons, long, sharp, or ragged nails should be attended to before interpreting with deaf-blind people.

Because much interpreting with deaf-blind people happens in closer physical proximity than interpreting with other clients, the interpreter should take care to be aware of the olfactory impression he or she gives. Heavy fragrance (perfume, after-shave, and the like) is as undesirable as unpleasant body odor. Interpreters who smoke or have meals including onions or garlic just before working with a deaf-blind client can show sensitivity to the client by brushing the teeth or using a breath mint before beginning to interpret.

Additional roles

Interpreters with deaf-blind people also find themselves in the role of mobility aide. In an unfamiliar environment, a deaf-blind person is unlikely to be able to find the restrooms, negotiate the path from room to room or building to building, or even eat lunch independently. Preparation for interpreting with deaf-blind people will thus include some orientation to the alternatives available for guiding, orienting, and assisting deaf-blind people achieve maximum independence.

Petersen's (1984) interview with Linda Annala gives an interesting overview of the current attitudes and accommodations by and toward deaf-blind people. Kanda and Roy (1981) include a module by Rita De-Vries (329-370) on interpreting with deaf-blind clients, that gives student activities, group discussion topics, and further reading suggestions.

Oral transmission

For over two hundred years, there has been a controversy in philosophies of educating deaf children. In the common usage, this controversy is referred to as the "oral-manual" argument. Today it takes the form of exclusion of any form of manual communication under the oral option, or inclusion of some form of sign language or manual communication under the alternative. The consequence of the split of approaches in

161

education is that deaf adults do not share uniform communication skills. The goal of oral education is to integrate the hearing-impaired person into the mainstream of society, so as to avoid drawing attention to the hearing loss. Oral education promotes the view that the deaf person should be permitted and encouraged to interact with others on the basis of his or her own intelligence and interests. The goals of oral education should then make interpreters unnecessary, but as we will see there are more factors involved than simply speechreading spoken language under ideal conditions. Those deaf and hearing-impaired people who have exclusively relied on spoken language without signs for communication may still need assistance to participate fully in interaction with hearing people.

Barriers to lipreading

A skilled lipreader may be confident of his or her communication abilities in a one-to-one encounter. But the same person probably cannot follow a group discussion, where the turn-taking behavior is less than orderly, nor can such a lipreader participate in a large group lecture session where the lipreader must view the speaker's face obscured by a microphone, by distance from the podium, poor angle of view, or inappropriate lighting conditions. Similarly, lipreaders cannot function when the speaker turns to write on a blackboard, to face the slide screen or other visual aids. Personal characteristics of the speaker may also interfere with visual comprehension of spoken language: the speaker may have a beard or mustache covering his lips and parts of the cheeks and neck that precludes effective lipreading. Other speakers' movement of the lips may be insufficient to lipread, in which case an interpreter may be called upon even in a one-to-one situation. In fact, the term "lipreading" has gone out of fashion in technical circles, replaced by "speechreading" to indicate that not only the movements of lips, but also the action of cheeks, chin, jaw, neck are important indicators; facial expressions and body attitudes will be employed by the person receiving information in this way.

Techniques in oral transmission

Deaf individuals who prefer speechreading as their receptive mode may wish to request the services of an oral interpreter. This interpreter faces the deaf person and silently mouths the oral-aural message along with the speaker. Figure 10-5 shows one possible seating arrangement for the oral deaf adult and the interpreter. In some respects, oral interpreting is like shadowing, simply repeating the words after the speaker has uttered them. And for those few exceptionally skilled speechreaders, this is all the interpreter will need to do. In a large proportion of cases, however, the interpreter will need to re-phrase the utterance in order to maximize the comprehensibility of the spoken language. Facial expressions can be employed to indicate question, emphasis, or emotions such as anger, surprise, pleasure. In the case of low-visibility words, synonyms may be substituted, a clarifying word may be added, or the whole sentence may be rearranged. In addition, the interpreter should be aware of ways to clarify with paper and pencil when necessary.

Figure 10-5
Oral

As with sign language interpreting, the oral interpreter may be called upon to voice for the deaf individual. This part of the job requires great judgment and tact. Some deaf people realize that their voices will not be intelligible to a naive hearing audience, unfamiliar with deaf speech; they will understand that they cannot successfully use the microphone provided for speakers or modulate their volume to match the requirements of the space. In this case, the interpreter will need to lipread the deaf speaker and repeat the comments in an appropriate vocal manner. In other cases, the deaf person will want to try to speak for himself or herself. If the hearing participants do not understand the deaf speaker's voice, the interpreter faces a common, but sticky problem: letting the speaker know and then resolving the communication difficulty.

An interpreter who can function in the oral transmission mode will have training in understanding speechreading, knowledge of such communication techniques used by deaf people, will be able to anticipate which words or phrases in the spoken sentence will be difficult to uniquely identify through speechreading, and will know how to include commonly used gestures (or sign language) into the stream of silent mouthing. Like other interpreters, the oral interpreter will adhere to the Code of Ethics, will have an understanding of the social interaction between hearing-impaired and hearing people, and will have had an opportunity to practice, under supervision, these techniques and judgments. Northcott (1979b) outlines a curriculum for oral interpreter instruction. Kanda and Roy (1981:435-534) have fleshed this curriculum out further with student activities, readings, and classroom exercises.

163

Education and certification

Since the late 1970's, the Registry of Interpreters for the Deaf, in conjunction with the Alexander Graham Bell Association, has been offering training for oral interpreting. One purpose is to identify people who have some good practical experience but no formal instruction as interpreters and to introduce them to the whole range of ethical and protocol dilemmas that arise in professional interpreting. Another purpose has been to broaden the expectations and competencies of interpreters who have been educated for sign language work. Currently, RID offers separate certification for oral interpreting. These certificates parallel the certificates for spoken-to-sign language or sign-to-spoken language interpreting, and the testing procedure is much the same, with the additional element of a written test on the factual material included in the training.

Is oral transmission interpreting?

We should note that there have been some objections to give oral transmission the full recognition as "interpreting." The objections question whether the task of relaying a particular message within two forms of a single language really taps the same cognitive and behavioral processes that interpreting from a source language to a target language engages. The oral interpreter changes an auditory message to a visual one within the same language.

We might say that this is a controversy of semantics or theoretical consequence, but without practical implication. If, however, it can be shown that the processes involved in interpretation between two languages are not engaged in oral transmission, then several very practical issues become operative. Is it appropriate to offer equivalent professional recognition (e.g. certificates of proficiency, pay rates, etc.) to those who have practice oral transmission, but who do not have interpreting skills?

No one denies that the service being performed by oral interpreters is necessary; on the contrary, all hearing-impaired people are entitled to full access to information and interaction in legal, medical and educational settings, in professional life and cultural events. Nor do the objectors deny the complexity of the task, and that there are correct and incorrect ways to do it. Insofar as we understand it, the logistic and ethical issues are equivalent for simultaneous translation between two languages (interpreting), two codes (transliterating), and two modes (oral transmission). Therefore, those skilled in oral transmission enjoy recognition as interpreters.

Teams of interpreters

Several circumstances require the use of more than one interpreter to effectively provide communication to and from all participants. The factors which determine the number of interpreters include length of assignment (time), spatial arrangements or number of participants, and varieties of languages or communication systems used.

Length of assignment

Currently, the most frequent call for two interpreters is the assignment which will last longer than one interpreter can work with top performance. It is hard to give an absolute number of minutes beyond which one person cannot handle a job, since it depends on the particular dimensions of the communication setting. Are frequent breaks built into the meeting agenda? Perhaps the meeting can get by with fewer interpreters. Is it possible that it will go on all day with continuous talking and signing from any of several participants? Perhaps more than two interpreters will be required.

Consider the case of court reporters who work without relief for the length of the court business day (generally three hours in the morning session and three hours in the afternoon). Even in this relatively intensive work schedule there are generally frequent, albeit irregular, breaks in the day, for example when new cases are called, off the record remarks are exchanged, lawyers approach the bench, or retire to judge's chambers. In the event that a hearing is scheduled for a whole day and no regular opportunities for such rest intervals are anticipated, two court reporters may work in thirty-minute shifts, spelling one another.

Sign language interpreters have found that twenty- to thirty-minute shifts are comfortable. This length of interpreting turn compares well with the general practice of spoken language interpreters working in a booth above or beside the conference hall. The length of interval needs to be agreed upon at the beginning of the assignment, so that substitution of interpreters can happen with the least disruption to the proceedings. The context in which the interpreters are working must be considered as well, when planning for the substitutions. In a workshop or panel discussion, class lecture or group therapy setting, interpreters may feel comfortable switching at the point dictated by the clock. In a more formal presentation, for example, by the guest speaker at a convention, in a court of law, in a staged poetry reading, or at a political rally, interpreters may want to agree to relieve each other only at the end of one speaker's remarks, between direct questioning and the cross-examination, following the introduction of the guest speaker and then again between the formal address and the question and answer period. Figure 10-6 shows an interpreter working near the speaker at the podium. In the background are seated the chair of the meeting, and to the side, the interpreter's partner. The choice to be seated on the stage is only one of several alternatives available. The interpreting team or their supervisor will need to look at the physical arrangement of people and temporal arrangement of events to determine the best choice in each situation.

Physical and logistical considerations

When interpreting happens in a physically large space, several interpreters may be required. Even in the case where the speaker will sign for himself (that is, sign and speak simultaneously) guests may be seated at such a distance from the podium that they are effectively out of view of the remarks addressed to them. Alternatives here are determined

Figure 10-6
Teams/platform

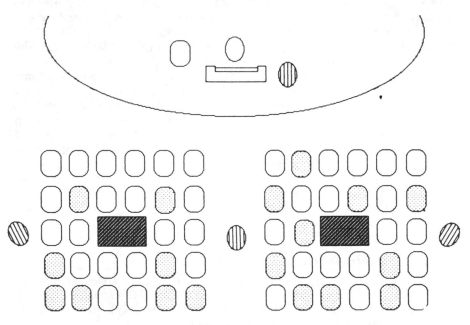

Figure 10-7
Visual obstructions

in part by budget and available equipment. Several interpreters might be hired and positioned around the room; planners will take into account the ability of these interpreters to hear the speaker from a distance, while presumably facing away from the podium. If a meal is being served and cleared at the same time as the guest is speaking, then each interpreter may need a monitoring loudspeaker or audio headset to hear the speaker well enough to interpret. In a large hall, where the interpreter is not positioned directly next to the speaker, audio levels again need to be checked so that the interpreter receives a good, direct audio signal rather than depending on possibly muffled, amplified sound which has bounced off of walls, windows or other surfaces of undetermined acoustic qualities. Figure 10-7 diagrams one situation where the architecture of the meeting room may prevent some deaf audience members from seeing the interpreter at the podium, so additional interpreters have been positioned farther back in the hall.

When both deaf and hearing participants are expected to address a group from podium or panel level, and both are expected in the audience as well, it is likely that two or more interpreters will be needed. A deaf person chairing the session or speaking as a panel member will not be able to see the interpreter who has been positioned inobtrusively behind the panelists or podium. This deaf presenter will need an interpreter positioned at the front of the audience section, facing the stage area. This interpreter will be able to sign the interpretation of the spoken remarks and will voice for the deaf panelist, should voicing be needed. In fact, the interpreter facing the panelists and the interpreter facing the audience will each need an alternate, relief interpreter if the discussion will continue for an extended period of time (e.g., more than one hour). Figure 10-8 illustrates this example: one interpreter faces the audience from the stage, while another faces the stage from the audience. The second interpreter may wish to change position from side (in front of the deaf presenter) to center as the hearing-impaired or deaf presenter moves from waiting to active presenting. Again, the specific arrangement of interpreting staff must be decided with a more complete understanding of the anticipated circumstances.

Another sort of space which might require several interpreters is the group discussion arranged around an open circle or square. At NTID in the early 1970's, the National Advisory Group included both deaf and hearing members. In addition, deaf and hearing staff members would be responsible for presenting information or answering questions during the discussions. Rather than restrict the deaf members of the group to particular seats in the room, at the same time restricting their freedom of visual contact around the table, the team of two interpreters were positioned back-to-back in the center of the room, surrounded by the group members. In this way, at least one of them could be seen easily from almost any position in the room. One opening was left in the circle of meeting tables so that the relief interpreters could enter the circle and make the substitution smoothly.

So far, physical factors, such as size of space, shape of seating arrangement, or extent of time, have led to recommendation of more than

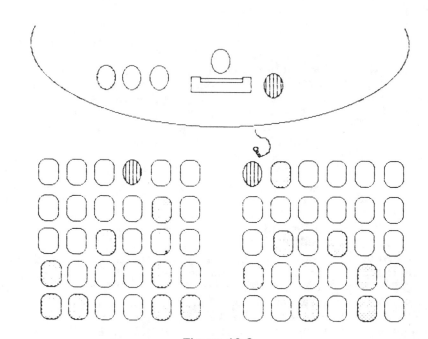

Figure 10-8
Deaf panelist, deaf audience

one interpreter. Another important reason for the use of more than one interpreter is the variety of communication skills of the participants.

Communication skills

Intermediary interpreters are those who have special communication skills for reaching deaf people who have idiosyncratic gestures or other signing varieties beyond the understanding of the originally scheduled interpreter. Often the intermediary interpreter is an RSC (deaf) interpreter. The interplay between the two interpreters makes it possible to communicate with this deaf person, whereas one alone would not have the appropriate skills.

For example, a deaf person may have been misdiagnosed as retarded or mentally ill, and placed in a mental institution for a long time. (Unfortunately, such cases are far too common; see Vernon and Hyatt (1981) for one such example.) Upon discovery that the source of the person's difficulty is deafness rather than mental illness, the responsible authorities may assign him or her to an agency responsible for rehabilitation. However, this agency will most likely be unable to communicate using traditional sign language forms. An experienced team of hearing and deaf interpreters may be able to assist the rehabilitation staff in appropriate psychological evaluation, adjustment to daily living skills outside of an institution, and additional aspects of rehabilitation.

Sometimes, a hearing interpreter will find a perfectly competent, but monolingual deaf signer whom the interpreter cannot understand. Rather than abandon the whole situation, the parties involved would be wise to call upon a certified RSC to work with the hearing interpreter and the consumers. Figure 10-9 gives two options for arranging deaf and hearing people and interpreters. In the view on the left, the deaf person must look to the side to communicate with the intermediary (RSC) interpreter. That interpreter then must turn to face the hearing interpreter, who will voice the message of the deaf person. In going the opposite direction, the intermediary interpreter and deaf person will again have to turn toward each other and away from the hearing people to communicate. The temptation for the hearing interpreter to voice for the deaf person, by-passing the intermediary interpreter, is heightened in this configuration. For these two reasons, comfort in communicating and full respect for the role of the RSC, we recommend the positions as shown on the right in Figure 10-9. In this view, since the hearing interpreter is standing next to the deaf person and the deaf interpreter opposite, the comfortable view of the deaf person will be look at the hearing speaker and the RSC interpreter. This positioning of interpreters encourages the hearing interpreter to fully utilize the skills of the RSC. (This arrangement was suggested to me by Jan Kanda and Bob Alcorn.)

Figure 10-10 shows the use of this arrangement in the situation where a deaf person is the plaintiff or defendant in a courtroom. The hearing interpreter here is positioned where he or she can be heard distinctly by the court reporter, and at the same time has a clear sightline to the deaf interpreter. The deaf person has a clear view of the deaf interpreter. The hearing attorneys need only remember not to block these

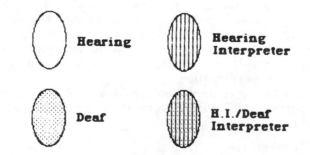

Incorrect   Correct

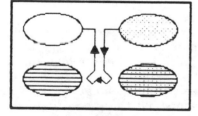 Hearing 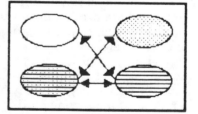 Hearing Interpreter

Deaf   H.I./Deaf Interpreter

Figure 10-9
Deaf-hearing teams

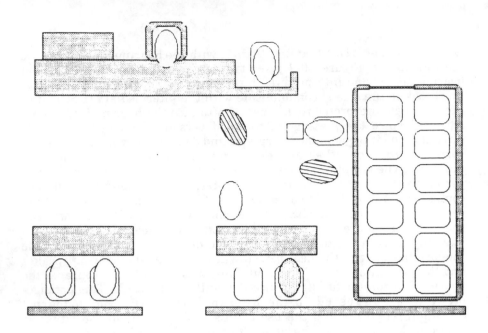

Figure 10-10
Deaf plaintiff/defendant

lines in addressing the witnesses. When the deaf plaintiff/defendant takes the witness stand, the interpreters will rearrange themselves, more in the positions suggested in Figure 10-1. The positions of the interpreters suggested here are not meant to be rigid.

Another type of communication setting may lead to the use of more than one interpreter. National conferences, technical meetings, and similar large group gatherings have included both interpreters and transliterators as part of the communication services available to deaf participants. In this case, people whose preferred language is ASL (or another deaf sign language) will understand the proceedings, as will those whose preferred form is signed English (or another manually coded spoken language). Providing both types of simultaneous translation will require planning before the meeting occurs, in order to schedule sufficient number of interpreters. Sometimes only the plenary sessions will have the choice of both types, while the break-out groups, discussion sessions, or special topics meetings will be limited to one interpreter. Often such limitations are a result of budgetary considerations rather than any intention to restrict participation.

As mentioned in previous sections, oral transmission and translation to deaf-blind participants would complete the interpreting picture at such large meetings.

International meetings

One last setting which involves the use of several interpreters is the international conference on a topic of interest to deaf participants. As

170

more deaf people receive broader education and achieve greater employment opportunities, such conferences will be found outside of the topics of sign language, deafness and deaf education. Consider the case of the Third International Symposium on Sign Language Research held in Rome, Italy, during the last week of June, 1983. Twenty-two countries were represented by participants. These participants saw ten simultaneous translations into different sign languages, from the audience's left to right: Belgian, Thai, French, British, American, Italian, Swedish, Danish, Norwegian, and Finnish sign language interpreters. The official spoken languages of the conference were Italian and English, so that every remark or address was either given in or translated into one of these two spoken languages. From the booths upstairs, Flemish and French were also available on the headphones.

Any deaf person who addressed the group would have to speak one of the two official spoken languages or have an interpreter voice into either of these spoken languages. All of the other interpreters then would follow that sign-to-voice translation or its translation into the other official spoken language. Deaf participants from some countries were not able to afford to bring their own interpreters; they had to rely on understanding an interpreter from one of the ten delegations with simultaneous sign language interpretation. For example, participants from Spain had to depend on their understanding of French Sign Langue, those from South Africa on American Sign Language. Other deaf people came from countries where two or more sign language systems are in use. Those from French-speaking parts of Switzerland watched the French interpreter, while those from French-speaking parts of Canada preferred to use the ASL interpreter.

Interpreters in this setting had real demands placed on their stamina. Meetings lasted from 9 am to 1 pm and again from 3 pm to 6 pm or later. For some languages, there was only one interpreter and several deaf audience members (e.g. Thai and Belgian). When simultaneous (competing) sessions were held some afternoons, the deaf people from these language groups had to decide which session would get to have the interpreter. Meanwhile, the interpreters had to meet each evening with the next day's speakers and also needed to prepare for the following day by reading as many of the presentations as possible.

One impressive feat was the ability of interpreters from countries where English is the second or third language to translate simultaneously from their familiar sign language into spoken English. For example, when two Danes presented their work, the first half was given by one who spoke directly in English. The second half of the presentation was given by the co-author in Danish Sign Language and voiced into spoken English (rather than Danish, which would be that interpreter's usual and expected task).

Not only were the interpreters at this meeting outstanding for their stamina and language abilities, but also for their teamwork. For example, when the speaker (positioned physically above and behind the interpreters at the podium) used slides or overhead projections, the relief interpreters might sit facing their interpreting colleagues holding a copy of the diagram for them to refer to. The off-duty teammate might also provide lip movements as cues for the interpreters who could not see the mouth of a heavily-accented speaker.

Summary

Several circumstances may lead to the necessity for more than one interpreter. Two or more interpreters are necessary when an assignment involves extensive time. Several interpreters may be required when an assignment will take place in a physically large space, or one which includes visual barriers for many participants.

Besides temporal, physical and logistic considerations, questions of language preference may make two or more interpreters a requirement. The deaf person who does not understand the hearing interpreter may function well when a deaf interpreter is included as part of the communication team. Individuals from different countries may also require different interpreters.

Telephone

How ironic that Alexander Graham Bell, who championed the cause of hearing-impaired people, who worked to help them overcome the handicaps of impaired speech, invented the device which effectively prevents people with severe hearing-impairment from participating fully and freely in the modern world. The ability to use the telephone is seen by many as an absolute necessity for living in highly technologized Western societies. There are several options open to the deaf and hearing-impaired who wish to make phone calls.

Telephone use without intermediaries

Some hearing-impaired people have sufficient residual hearing to be able to use the telephone in the ordinary way. With a well-fitted hearing aid, an amplifier in the handset and appropriate training, many people who were previously through to be unable to use a telephone independently can learn to make the machine work for them.

One accommodation to hearing loss can be to have the hearing-impaired person guide the conversation and the other party respond by agreed-upon codes. For example, many people find the distinction among "yes, yes," "no," and "I don't know" to function well as response codes. The deaf or hearing-impaired person with intelligible speech can ask questions which the other party answers using the response codes. The vowel sounds in the three expressions are quite distinct from one another, and the number of syllables can be recognized as well (two, one, three). Not all hearing-impaired people can use auditory signs, and so some visual signalling devices are also available to serve a similar purpose. Some of these devices show only the presence (or absence) of auditory signal, and so the difference among steady tone (dial tone), rapid burst (busy signal), slow on-off signal (ringing), and the voice codes are all accessible through vision.

Telecommunication devices for the deaf (TDD's) offer another alternative for long distance real-time communication. If both parties have a teletypewriter (TTY) or other compatible machine, they can take turns typing out messages, rather than depending on vocal-auditory means. TDD's send auditory signals over the telephone lines that are decoded into letters by the device at the other end of the line. Some of these devices use paper print-out, while others have light diode displays for the message. As long as the machinery is compatible, both sides will be able to function independent of intermediaries. (There are even some machines which translate the electronic tones into Braille printed codes, rather than lights or ordinary print, for deaf-blind people.) More recently, TDD's are being equipped with both the older Western Union-type (Baudot) signals and the newer computer-compatible (ASCII) signals.

All of these alternatives permit independent telephone interaction by a deaf or hearing-impaired person. However, each of these alternatives requires auditory discrimination ability and training, speech intelligibility, or available equipment on the part of the deaf person, and equipment or a willingness to let someone else define the direction of the conversation on the part of the hearing person. When the necessary factors are not in place, introducing an interpreter into the picture may define the optimal solution. Figure 10-11 shows a typical interpreted telephone call.

Figure 10-11
Telephone

Telephone use with interpreters

As with other settings for interpreting, the interpreter is responsible for facilitating the communication, but the deaf person is responsible for the telephone call. All of the guidelines below have the goal of providing the deaf person with the maximum control of both the procedure during the call and the outcome of the call.

Most of the discussion below assumes that a professional interpreter will assist during a phone call between a deaf and a hearing person. It also happens that deaf people whose work requires phone contact regularly depend on a hearing member of the staff to assist. The hearing person may be a secretary, administrative assistant or co-worker. The role, while on the telephone, is still simply voice and ears for the deaf person. Any greater flexibility, such as direct discussion between the hearing person assisting with the call and the party on the other end of the line, will need to have the full understanding and cooperation of the deaf person making the call.

Preliminaries

The deaf person will provide the telephone number (with area code) or the name and address of the party to be called, if the phone number needs to be requested from the appropriate directory assistance operator. The deaf person also needs to provide the interpreter with additional calling and billing information (collect call, person-to-person call, etc.). It often helps to explain briefly the nature of the phone call before actually dialing, so that the interpreter is ready for what might happen. The interpreter who agrees to interpret a phone call without an introduction of what sort of call it will be does so at his or her own peril. The deaf person may be calling a family member to discuss personal matters of some intimacy, may be calling a business to complain about poor service, or may be trying to deal with the bureaucratic organization to get some information. Each of these calls would demand a different emotional or personal style from the interpreter. A briefing before the call will assist the interpreter in being maximally effective.

After the deaf person dials the number, the interpreter will indicate the meaning of any auditory signal, such as "ringing," "busy," "recorded announcement," or similar information. When the party on the other end answers, "Good afternoon, V.N. and R," the interpreter repeats the greeting for the deaf person. The deaf person will respond, "Extension 322, please," and the interpreter will repeat that message for the hearing party on the other end.

Introducing the Interpreter

The deaf person making the phone call can also ease the way by letting the interpreter know ahead how she or he wants to inform the other party that they are using an interpreter. Notice that there are several choices of how the interpreter can be introduced, and that each of these may lead to a different outcome. For example, the interpreter can take the lead and say: "Hi, this is Sally McDermott, interpreting with Marianne Smith who is deaf. . . ." However, this sets up Sally as the person to talk to rather than Marianne. On the other hand, the interpreter can wait for the deaf person to begin with, "Hello, this is Marianne Smith calling. I'm deaf and I'm speaking to you through an interpreter right now." While it's not guaranteed, and every interpreter with even a bit of phone experience will have stories of telephone misunderstandings, this second method of introduction is more likely to achieve the desired results. One might wonder why even think of using the interpreter's name; there appears to be no reason for it. If the deaf person is of one sex and the interpreter the opposite, it may be helpful to clarify this by using both names: "Hello, this is Marianne Smith calling. I'm deaf, and so I've asked Tom McDermott to interpret this call for us."

There may be times when no announcement is required or expected. A deaf business person calling a familiar associate to confirm a lunch date has no fear that the party at the other end of the line will hang up when a woman's voice says, "Hi, Sam? It's George Martin calling to confirm lunch at 12:30." The same would hold true for a deaf person calling a family member. There may be cases when the deaf person prefers to avoid mentioning the interpreter's presence. In general, however, it is helpful to mention that an interpreter is being used, since this statement then can account for unexpected silences, slight delays in responding, and the like.

Even when the deaf person makes the introduction of the interpreter at the beginning of the conversation, the hearing person who has not experienced this type of phone call before may be confused. Receptionists, operators, and others whose job is handling a large volume of phone calls expect rapid responses; the nature of telephone calls with interpreters leads to some lag while the voice message is translated and then while the non-vocal message is voiced. In these lags, operators often jump in ("Are you still there?") which, of course, must be interpreted (interrupting the deaf person's response in the meantime). A supplementary or expanded explanation of the fact that there is an interpreter involved may help to alleviate the difficulties.

Interpreting on the telephone can occur simultaneously or consecutively. The usual way is for the hearing-impaired person to interact immediately (as in simultaneous interpretation) with the other party. The alternative (more like consecutive interpretation) is for the hearing-impaired person to write or explain the message to the interpreter and let the interpreter make the call. Some calls include both written information and simultaneous messages. In either case, the hearing-impaired person does not leave the interpreter's view while the call is in progress, without telling the other party to "please hold on." The interpreter cannot respond to unexpected questions or comments without direction from the maker of the call, the hearing-impaired person. In either of these methods, it is the hearing-impaired person who determines the close of the call. A classic error of the "nice neighbor" who is doing the deaf person a favor by making a phone call is to hang up without checking that the caller has finished, and before making sure the caller understands what has transpired. In contrast, the "consecutive" method of phone calling demands a great deal of judgment on the part of the interpreter. The interpreter must be certain that the information which has been transmitted includes all that the deaf person wanted to know or tell.

When a decision is required, the interpreter may want to ask the other party to hold while getting the appropriate response from the maker of the call.

The maker of the phone call, the hearing-impaired person, may choose to write down specifics of appointment times, meeting places, and the like, as the interpreter gives it. As a practical matter, it may be simpler to have the interpreter write down complicated information, such as travel arrangements, as it is received over the telephone. The hearing-impaired person can then confirm the message while reading it off, and keep the paper as a permanent record. The decision about who writes should be left to the people in the telephone situation, but having pencil and paper handy is helpful.

Hearing-impaired people who prefer to speak for themselves may use one telephone receiver to speak into, while the interpreter listens and translates using another receiver connected to the same line. Neisser (1983:34) includes an example of this sort of "ancillary transmission" in which the hearing-impaired person reads the lips of the intermediary and responds vocally. In a pinch, the interpreter and hearing-impaired person can pass the phone receiver back and forth between themselves. Another option, which requires only one receiver, is for the hearing-impaired person to speak (rather than sign) to the interpreter who then repeats the message to the party on the end of the line. The interpreter can give the message from the distant party to the hearing-impaired person through silent mouth movements to speechread.

Interpreters as instructors

Since many hearing-impaired and deaf people have little experience in telephone etiquette or telephone procedures, interpreters sometimes find themselves in the role of instructor, orienting the person to the use of the phone. How to dial, how to wait for an outside line when dialing from an office phone, how to ask a receptionist or switchboard operator for the appropriate party, how to introduce the interpreter, and how to open and close a conversation by phone may all be new to the deaf person. Even some deaf people who are experienced phone users may still have gaps in their understanding of the conventions that have grown up around the telephone. For example, when someone asks for your phone number, the area code and exchange are read as single digits, and the last four numbers may be given as single digits or as two pairs. For example (212) 555-3478 might be read as "Two one two, five five five, three four seven eight," or as "Two one two, five five five, thirty-four seventy-eight." (But these numbers are not read, "Two hundred twelve, five hundred and fifty five, three thousand four hundred seventy-eight.") And, even though we write a hyphen between the exchange and the last four digits, we do not read the hyphen or say it out loud. A deaf person might assume that the precise way to give the phone number is with the punctuation.

The interpreter who is working with a novice phone user will find the extra time spent in rehearsing the procedure has long term payoff. The deaf person may initially be timid or uneasy about dialing or talking directly with someone unseen, and all too willing to relinquish control of the phone call to the interpreter. With a bit of practice, the novice will gain feelings of self-confidence and comfort in the newly found power of communication. The deaf person can then rely on any equally skilled interpreter to facilitate a phone call, and is not dependent on the person who handled the matter previously to know how to follow up.

Summary

Deaf and hearing-impaired people have several options for using the telephone. With appropriate training, some can use existing phones or phones supplemented by additonal equipment. Others will rely on interpreters. The use of an interpreter for telephone communication is different from having someone else make a call and relay a message. With the interpreter, the hearing-impaired person can maintain full control of the conversation. Since using interpreters for phone calls is not a widespread experience for all deaf people, many still require orientation to telephone apparatus, procedures and etiquette. Interpreters often serve to orient deaf clients to the telephone.

11   Practical Considerations in Employing Interpreters

The experience of sign language interpreters in working with new groups who have not accommodated signing, deaf people, and mixed hearing and deaf audiences is that several types of problems recur regularly, and yet most can be avoided with proper planning.

Logistics, Planning, Physical Factors

Sight lines

The interpreter must be seen to successfully accomplish the task of facilitating communication. Hearing people may be half the consumers, but deaf or hearing-impaired people are the other half of this communication event.

Unobstructed sight lines—the open path of communication between signers—are crucial to successful transmission of message. It's really that simple. Let's make "common sense" explicit and highlight the best procedures:

a) standing next to, not in front of the interpreter

Often the hearing person who is inexperienced at using an interpreter will stand in front of the sign language interpreter. It's natural enough to understand why: if you, the speaker, see your audience looking at some other spot, and some or all of your audience continues to look NOT at you, you may be inclined to put yourself in the place where everyone is looking.

I remember an occasion when I observed an interpreter working in a museum. About five deaf people were along for a tour of a special exhibit. A sort of dance occurrred, with the group looking at the interpreter, the speaker moving into the visual gaze, the group shifting counterclockwise, both interpreter and deaf audience. The most surprising part is that the speaker never realized what was happening.

A colleague of mine is a professor who only recently learned to sign. She intellectually knows that the majority of the class is looking at the interpreter because they can understand her that way, but at the same time she has had feelings of jealousy that her words don't matter, that everyone is looking at something much more interesting. This feeling persisted for as long as five or six weeks of the first semester—until she had sufficient receptive skills to monitor the deaf students interaction with her on her own, but not sufficient skill to send the messages she wanted to send.

b) seating the deaf person and interpreter opposite one another

The ideal arrangement of deaf participants and interpreters depends on the size of the room or space in which the event will be held, and the kinds of activities that will go on. But in the simplest case, where one interpreter will be working with one deaf person, the optimal distance between the two is approximately six to eight feet apart and facing one another. When possible, the interpreter seated slightly to the side and behind the primary hearing participant is the best arrangement. The possibility of mutual gaze between the deaf and hearing persons is greater if the deaf person doesn't have to look away from the interpreter too far or with too great an adjustment for distance.

Figure 11-1 shows a mixed group seated for comfortable discussion. The (hearing) interpreter is positioned nearly across from the deaf participant, so that she can see him in order to voice for any comments or questions he may have. He can see the interpreter as well, and can take in the view of much of the group.

Inappropriate seating for deaf participants and interpreters includes hearing interpreter next to deaf viewer, or equal distance between hearing participant, deaf participant, and interpreter. The side-by-side arrangement is the preferred one for liaison spoken language interpreting, since a whispered or low voice simultaneous interpretation is possible; the latter is sometimes unavoidable given particular room sizes. Figure 11-2 shows one of these unavoidable situations. The counter comes between the clerk and

Figure 11-1
Small group (voicing)

the clients. In this case, the interpreter is not part of the regular staff, but has come to assist the deaf person, and thus stands outside the counter. At the bank, in the precinct house, at the information booth in a department store, in the library, and many other settings, the architecture may present some obstructions.

c) group (mixed hearing and deaf), especially without fixed seating
For the deaf participant, it is as important to take in the rest of the action in the room as it is to view the interpreters. The film or slide presentation, mounted displays that will be discussed, and the expressions of the speakers on the platform are all a part of the visual context and content. Seating of deaf participants must be considered carefully.

At the same time, deaf people generally can be accommodated in the general seating area. Unless there are special reasons to do so, meeting organizers would do well to plan the interpreter's position so that the deaf participants need not feel segregated.

Will there be reserved seating and the interpreters visible from only parts of the audience? In this case, the organizers need to make sure those audience seats are as good for viewing the action in the room as others. This is a challenge for performance spaces and theaters which are beginning to include deaf audiences and interpreters.

Will there be open seating and the interpreters visible to all? Then, any seats that are blocked from the view of the interpreters because of architectural features of the space must not be occupied by deaf people.

Figure 11-2
Counter obstruction

Will the group be moving or standing without fixed locations? Both the museum example above, where a tour takes the group through several galleries, and the prepared childbirth class having a tour of the hospital are good examples of events that might happen in a space without fixed seating. Such moving groups require special sensitivity from the group leader.

Lighting

Under ordinary circumstances, room light is sufficient for viewing the sign language interpreter and for the interpreter to view the signing person. When planning seating arrangements or room configuration, considerations of lighting need attention.

[A whole separate issue concerns lighting for theatrical events. This is covered in a surface manner under the heading "Performing Arts."]

a) avoid backlight

A window or bright source of light behind the interpreter makes viewing difficult. Even if the interpreters are well-illuminated from the front, strong backlight may cause them to appear dark or indistinct, facial expressions and lip movements difficult to read. If the communication setting is expected to have two-way turn-taking, then the deaf people also need to be able to sit where they will not be backlit. In the small office shown in Figure 11-3, the hearing person has not blocked the interpreter, but they may not be totally comfortable either. At least they avoided having the interpreter sit with her back to the window, although

182

if the deaf fellow moves too far to his right, he may have some undesirable backlight effect.

b) avoid direct frontlight

Direct light from in front of the interpreter may cause two undesirable effects. First, the interpreter will appear washed out or indistinct

Figure 11-3
Cramped office

in contrast with the rest of the visual environment. Second, the light may prevent the interpreter from seeing the audience clearly, and thus may limit effective two-way communication.

c) low light or no light (e.g. slides, films)

An interesting challenge for the interpreter comes from low light settings, such as those where visual aids are used, or theater productions. College classes and business events often have films, slide presentations, and the like. Anticipating the interpreting needs is the first step toward making sure that such events are accessible. The light "spill" from the slide or film screen may be sufficient to permit the deaf audience to view the interpreter. Alternatively, some auditoriums have spotlights that can be focused to the side of the screen and adjusted to a low level matching that of visual media.

Some schools, colleges, and other educational institutions make a high-intensity lamp available for the interpreting staff. This lightweight piece of equipment can be easily taken to the particular job site for the hour or two needed, then returned to a central location. Interpreters who regularly find themselves in need of such a light might purchase one to carry along with them.

Figures 11-4 and 11-5 show two approaches to the problem of a darkened room with visual aids, in these cases a slide projector. Figure 11-4 shows one possible position, where the interpreter relies on the light spill from the projector. Figure 11-5 gives an alternative in which the interpreter has a separate source of light directly focused on him or her. A combination of lighting effects might occur when the interpreter is positioned near the screen and an audience member focuses a hand-held flashlight toward the interpreter. Such an improvised solution can be effective in providing adequate light in a relatively small space. In contrast, some very elaborate arrangements of lights within a frame have been devised where an interpreter regularly translates films for a large deaf audience.

Background, audio and visual

The ideal background will be a solid color, not too bright or too strong a hue. If textured, it will be relatively unobtrusive. Problems occur in rooms, halls and other enclosures where the bold decor conflicts with the quiet viewing needs of the deaf audience and the interpreters.

a) wallpaper, wall design, decorative curtains, etc.

Many times a large dining room, reception hall or other formal space will be decorated in an overall pattern. Somehow, the rooms that are

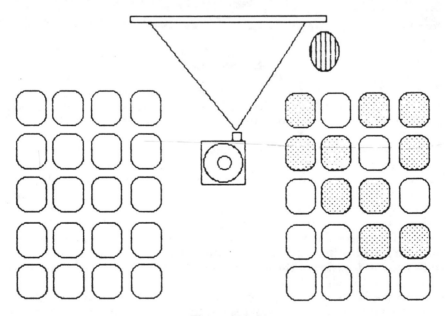

Figure 11-4
Using the light spill

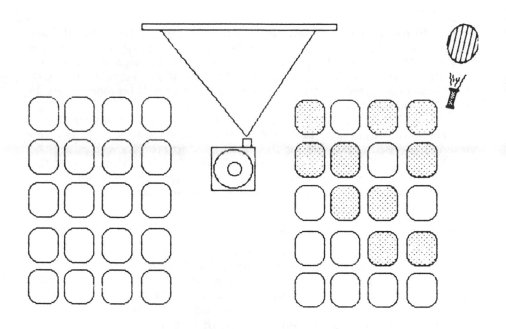

Figure 11-5
Interpreter's light

chosen for interpreting always seem to have the largest brightly colored flowers, or decorative optical illusions, or strongly colored draperies on the walls. Even a plain auditorium with a stage may be too busy visually.

A variety of solutions are available, limited only by the creativity of the meeting organizers and interpreter coordinator. Some facilities where interpreters work regularly have portable plain-colored panels in blues and greens available to use as background. On other occasions, meeting organizers have hung improvised curtains of plain dark cloth across a stage when pulling the curtain limits the amount of stage space available.

b) doorways, traffic pattern through the space

Even though the problem of light through the windows has been discussed, the issue of doorways and entry/exit through the space is important to consider separately. A busy traffic pattern will distract the attention of the deaf audience much as the noise from a radio playing loudly in the next room would disturb a hearing audience. Planning the layout of the group before they arrive can permit least interference from doorways and visible outside activity.

c) placement of loudspeakers, microphone, audio equipment

If speakers will use microphones, the interpreter needs to be standing in a position where the loudspeakers are behind him or her. If the amplified sound is in front of the interpreter, he or she will only hear the

185

distorted reflections of the amplification, and will not be able to deliver the message clearly. In cases where a musical or dramatic group will perform on a stage, the interpreter may want to request a personal monitor. A separate loudspeaker placed facing the interpreter and with the volume adjusted for the interpreter's comfort will be more likely to ensure good audition.

When both hearing and deaf presenters face a large audience, the hearing presenters will probably be using a microphone. A separate microphone will be needed for the voicing interpreter as well, since the interpreter will be seated or standing facing the deaf presenter at the podium. The interpreter may be positioned some distance from the podium and will also need to voice for deaf audience members' remarks.

Anticipating audience needs

a) estimating length of assignment

Two issues for interpreters in estimating the length of an assignment are: how many interpreters will be needed and how often breaks should be scheduled. Fatigue is a difficult condition to quantify, but jobs longer than one and one-half to two hours will likely require more than one interpreter. Some people recommend that interpreters take a break every 20 to 30 minutes, and will not tolerate a single interpreter working longer than this at one stretch. More commonly, interpreters are accustomed to handling a session like a two-hour class with a break in the middle. It is important to remember that the interpreter is "talking" whenever any other person is talking; the interpreter never gets a break unless there is silence, and even then, must remain "at the ready" to continue. The interpreters remain on duty during formal luncheons or dinner meetings where deaf participants get to know hearing colleagues, so mealtimes cannot be assumed to be break periods for the interpreters.

A related issue is the number of hours that one interpreter can realistically be expected to work in a single day. Conference interpreters for spoken languages expect to work no more than five to eight hours per day with partners; that is, the two interpreters would work a five-hour day, each taking half of the working time, following a relief schedule that they or their coordinator devised. We know of cases where a single sign language interpreter worked as many as eleven hours in one day with only a half-hour for lunch and short breaks to travel between locations within one institution. This schedule can not be justified even for a young, healthy person. The individual in question reported impaired functioning in physical energy, mental alertness, and emotional steadiness on the days after these eleven-hour workdays. A more reasonable schedule will yield more consistent performance from the interpreter.

b) estimating number of languages/modalities

When the deaf audience includes members whose language preferences are diverse, more than one interpreter will be working at any given moment. The Conference of Interpreter Trainers and the Registry of Interpreters for the Deaf have tried to model appropriate interpreter

186

services at their conventions. What has been found to work best in these large mixed audiences is the simultaneous presentation of at least two signing varieties, and the availability of tactile interpreting and oral transmission on request.

At international meetings, we have seen as many as ten simultaneous translations occurring in the signed languages, with three or more spoken languages as well. Budgeting for such extensive interpreting services must begin early in the planning process.

Whenever deaf-blind individuals will be a part of the group, additional interpreters will be necessary for one-on-one service.

c) planning for simultaneous sessions

A large meeting or convention may begin with a keynote address or similar plenary session, but later may break up into simultaneous smaller workshops or special sessions. Meeting planners cannot assume that all deaf participants will want to attend the same session at the same time. Where hearing participants are assigned to particular groups, deaf participants can be assigned also. However, planners may want to weigh the costs of hiring an extra interpreter or two against the too frequent assumption that all the deaf people can be put together in one group. Where hearing participants are left to their own choice in selecting a time to join a group, deaf participants must also be afforded similar opportunity of choice. A coordinator of interpreters will help to negotiate the most economical and practical solution for each specific event.

d) budgeting

Appropriate planning is the only way to make sure that the budget for interpreters is going to be adequate. Both the interpreters and the meeting planners need to bring up this issue directly and well ahead of the event, so that no one is surprised at the time of the actual event or when the bill is submitted.

When the report on this year's conference is sent in complete with suggestions for next year's annual meeting, the time is right to recommend any budget revisions for the interpreting needs for the following year's meeting. Were there interpreters at all of the sessions where they were needed? Were there sufficient relief interpreters? Were the interpreters needed during luncheon meetings, and had this been pre-scheduled?

Protocol and Language Use

Interaction with the interpreter

Most hearing presenters become comfortable with the interpreter after a few minutes. Getting used to part of the audience being visually attentive to another person while you're talking is not simple, but it is straightforward. There are a few habits to adopt that will put the interpreter at ease as well.

a) avoid touching the interpreter

Touching the interpreter while she or he is working is a "no-no." A hearing speaker who is unfamiliar with interpreters and the interpreting situation may try to relieve his or her own anxiety about communicating through the interpreter by putting an arm around the working interpreter; the gesture may be intended as friendly and casual: it is neither. On the contrary, touching the interpreter is distracting to both the hearing and deaf audience, disrespectful to the working interpreter, and inappropriate. Since the interpreter is bound by a behavior protocol that precludes participation as himself or herself, the interpreter may choose to say nothing rather than step out of role. While he or she may prefer to avoid a confrontation in the midst of the communication event, any member of the audience, hearing or deaf, can remind the offending speaker not to touch the interpreter.

Equally inappropriate is using the interpreter as a prop. The speaker who needs to demonstrate a particular life-saving maneuver, how to drape fabric, or any other similar display for which a still human figure is needed would do better to choose a member of the audience to act as model. The interpreter is working while interpreting and needs an unobstructed view of the audience as they do of the interpreter.

b) talking to the interpreter

Among the more awkward moments in interpreting comes when the hearing people address the interpreter directly. Even such innocent questions as "How did you get involved in this work?" or "Will you be available for another meeting with us next week?" can cause difficulties. The interpreter would prefer to wait until the end of the interaction to step out of role and participate. When the group is large or even moderate in size, with several members in each primary language/mode, the interpreter's task is difficult enough without having to distinguish between "interpreter is talking" and "someone else is talking."

The hearing or deaf person who is experienced at using interpreters will wait for a break to talk about personal matters to the interpreter. The interpreter caught on the spot may choose not to respond to a speaker's question ("Am I talking too fast for you?") or may find a quick answer more satisfying for both ("Just speak as you would ordinarily; I'll let you know if there's a problem."). The speaker who asks such a question is acknowledging the interpreter as a person, and deserves to be recognized. The interpreter, however, wants to avoid drawing attention to himself or herself during the interaction. The choice of appropriate response may depend on the deaf participants' familiarity with interpreted interactions.

c) walking while talking

When a group of hearing people walk, nothing about the channels of transmission prevent their talking at the same time. Deaf people left to themselves will similarly gather in small conversational twos and threes while strolling from place to place. The interpreter, however, who must be sure that all of the deaf participants in a group can see the message will be unlikely to join a single such group; he or she would be leaving out the others. Thus, in a guided tour or any similar speech events that may involve steps between utterances, it is important that the leader of the tour talk only when not walking and walk only when not talking. If you think it through, this reminder is really for the health and safety of the interpreter, who should not be required to add walking backwards through crowded halls, galleries, or unfamiliar terrain to the repertoire of competencies.

Interaction with the deaf person

A hearing person who has not experienced using an interpreter before can be expected to indulge in some of the classical *faux pas*, which may be avoided by following the hints below:

a) speak directly to the deaf person

There is a fiction that we *all* engage in when we use interpreters. That is that the interpreter is not there—by magic or some other means the people who do not speak the same language or share the same modality are able to speak to each other. Addressing the deaf person as "you" (and similarly for deaf people, addressing the hearing person as "you") shows acceptance of this fiction.

The speaker who always begins, "Tell him . . ." as in "Tell him to check with the 'lost and found' on the third floor" is not participating in this fiction. The interpreter will give the translation into signing exactly as the hearing person says it, "Tell him. . . ." The deaf signer may be clever enough to remind the hearing person that he can be addressed directly. Alernatively the deaf person who does not have experience with an interpreter may adopt the same locution, "Ask her if they have a TTY in this building," thus making the interpreter's job that much more complicated.

b) avoid speaking about the deaf person present

A slight variation on the above problem comes up when the hearing person asks the interpreter about the deaf person, rather than addressing such inquiries to the deaf person directly. "Can your client lipread?" "Was she in the left hand lane when she signaled the turn?" The assumption that the interpreter has special information about the deaf person involved is natural enough, since it is likely that the hearing person has never met the deaf person before and both the interpreter and the deaf person show up at the same time. The interpreter will simply relay such questions directly to the consumer, who may understand them to be directed to him or her, or who may be confused by the third person locution. Similarly, when the hearing person makes an aside to the interpreter, that comment will be interpreted.

In fact, the reverse situation occurs as well, where the deaf person asks the interpreter about the hearing person: "What's this doctor's name?" And the interpreter will voice such questions and comments in the manner that they are said.

c) "Don't interpret this . . ." will be interpreted

By the time a hearing person has uttered the whole sentence that begins, "Don't interpret this, but . . ." the interpreter has already gotten most of it out onto the hands and face. If hearing people want to say something to one another without the deaf person knowing what it is, then they need to get out of range of the interpreter's hearing. In a court of law for example, the interpreter may want to step out of role long enough to say something like, "If you don't want me to interpret this, then please have me leave the room." The judge or administrator would then be free to dismiss the interpreter and the deaf participant to make whatever off the record remarks desired.

Deaf people similarly may need to be reminded that comments signed among themselves within the view of the interpreter will be voiced. Signed comments addressed to the interpreter will probably be taken as addressed to the hearing speaker. Private conversations between interpreter and deaf person would better wait until outside of the communication event involving the interpreter as an interpreter.

d) eye gaze directed toward the deaf people

A hearing person who is not experienced at interacting with deaf people may use the same eye contact behavior that he or she uses with hearing people or colleagues, namely no attention to eye contact. The doctor who is messing in the files, the clerk who is gazing off in space will be seen by the deaf person as inattentive or impolite.

Equally inappropriate is the habit of hearing people of looking at the interpreter rather than the deaf audience. The deaf audience may need to direct their gaze primarily at the interpreter, but they will check back with the speaker at pauses or occasional moments. The hearing speaker should arrange for appropriate seating to maximize the possibility of direct eye gaze with the deaf participants.

Persistent difficulties

The following several points illustrate difficulties that may persist, even among speakers who are experienced at working with sign language interpreters. Still, the list is offered in the hope that awareness of the difficulties will lead to more sensitive treatment by the hearing speaker who is preparing to address a group that includes deaf members.

a) lists of names, technical terms that need spelling

An awards ceremony, graduation, sales meeting, or any other gathering may involve the naming of a large number of individuals. The interpreter would be well advised to look at the list of names sufficiently ahead, and ask for pronunciation of any unfamiliar spellings. When the names are called out, the interpreter will need to keep pace with the most rapid speech rates. If the speaker reads at a slightly more relaxed pace, the interpreter will look equally relaxed.

b) turn-taking behavior in group discussions

Spoken language users know how to judge another speaker's comments, and can interrupt or take up the next turn at speaking without much difficulty. The cues for turn exchange are primarily vocal-auditory, and only to a lesser degree visual or gestural. Indeed, the deaf participants in a group discussion may not be physically able to follow the visual-gestural cues of all the members of the group while at the same time understanding the message through viewing the interpreter. Occasionally two people will speak at one time in a heated discussion, in making asides, or when both want to speak next.

Signers use overlap (signing at the same time as one another) in conversation more extensively than non-signers. The question of why this might be so need not concern us at the moment. The fact that different cues permit people to interrupt or take up the next turn in the two different modalities means that group moderators must be especially careful to recognize both deaf and hearing participants in discussions.

It is easy to let speakers carry on with their familiar habits, but the consequence is that signers in the group may be excluded from participation. Alternatively, in a primarily signing group where the deaf individuals recognize one another rather than waiting for the moderator, the interpreter may not be able to keep up with the turn-exchanges. A strong moderator can prevent exclusion of any part of the group by requiring participants to indicate their interest in talking, and formally recognizing each person in turn. Such a procedure may seen overly formal for some groups, but it permits all segments of the group the opportunity to communicate.

c) visual aids, demonstrations (permitting viewing time)

Of course, any speaker will be more effective if he or she accompanies the spoken message by visual aids, slides, charts, graphs, photographs or demonstrations of objects. The secret to making the most of the visual aids when part of the audience is depending on an interpreter is to pause following the mention of the place to look on the visual aid. Hearing people who are accustomed to a uniformly hearing audience expect that speaking while demonstrating or pointing to the focused object, segment of a graph or the like, will be easy for all. This expectation is not borne out for a deaf audience who use the same channel (visual) for verbal communication (interpretation of the spoken message) as for taking in the visual aid. In order for the deaf audience to keep pace with the full meaning of the presentation, speakers must point or demonstrate *without speaking,* having first alerted the audience that they ought to direct their vision at the screen or demonstration area. In this way, the impact of the visual aids will be maximized for the whole audience. Using a light arrow or pointer to show where to look on slides or overhead transparencies can be helpful, but only in conjunction with pausing time for viewing.

An additional hint: avoid words like "here," "there," "this," and "that" when referring to the visual aids. "In the shaded portion of the third column of this graph . . . " may be initially more taxing for the speaker, but such locutions will make the interpretation come out more clearly, and will prepare the audience to know where to view when the speaker does pause.

Even the most practiced speaker will probably need reminding in order to develop this new habit of pausing. Hearing speakers who know how to sign may even need coaching in this procedure and will occasionally fail to remember. Deaf participants may need to demonstrate their assertiveness in asking for viewing time.

d) parenthetical remarks (volume, pitch, speed)

Many speakers depart from a prepared script or from the main body of their presentation to add a parenthetical remark, some extra comment or elaboration which is peripheral to the general point of the presentation. In English at least, the vocal cues for parenthetical remarks include lowering the volume, lowering the pitch (tone of voice), and speeding up the rate. These three cues together make the parenthetical comment less audible and less intelligible to the interpreter. Even though the comments may be off the main point, the interpreter nonetheless has the responsibility to convey them to the deaf audience. Speakers would do well to make their offhand comments audible to the interpreter as well as to the rest of the audience and not be surprised if asked to repeat seemingly unimportant details. The deaf audience expects the full flavor of the presentation complete with departures from the prepared text.

e) reading from prepared text (speed, language usage)

Two problems occur when the speaker reads from a prepared text, namely language choice and rate of production.

The speaker who has written his or her comments out ahead generally has written in a style which is intended to be read by the audience, rather than heard. The prepared written text is likely to be more formal (include more passive voice, and the like), with word choice heavily dependent on technical jargon. Moreover, the speaker has done most of the thinking before the actual time of presentation. Thus, he or she will read along at a rapid clip, since no time is needed to put the ideas into sentences. Speakers who talk "off the cuff" or even from notes or an outline have to compose their utterances on the spot. Their spontaneous discourse gives meaning through the use of phrasing, pausing, emphasis and loudness (as well as the words themselves)—factors that may be lost or severely diminished when reading from a written text. Such factors of spontaneous speech are likely to help the interpreter understand the meaning and intention of the speaker better, and thus to create an equally effective interpreted form.

Secondly, as alluded to above, the speaker who reads from a fully written-out version of his or her remarks is likely to read more quickly than the same person would speak spontaneously. Therefore, the interpreter is dealing with two factors which compound the dilemma of interpretation: speed and complexity of spoken delivery. The speaker who cannot depart from the prepared text to give the same message in a spontaneous style can still aid the interpreter (and probably the whole of the audience) by slowing down slightly. Rather than adjust one's speech rate, simply pause at punctuation marks. The interpreter will appreciate receiving a copy of the speech to be read well ahead of time; in the case of a professional or technical conference, lead time of a week would be appropriate.

Summary

The list given here mentions only the most common dilemmas that are faced in effectively incorporating interpreters. Problems under the first three headings, relating to physical aspects of the setting, are generally possible to anticipate and prepare for. Anticipating personnel and budget issues involving interpreters can be difficult the first time deaf people and interpreters are included, but thereafter becomes part of the ordinary planning for a meeting. Those issues relating to interactions with the interpreter and with the deaf people disappear as hearing people and deaf people become familiar with appropriate interaction involving an interpreter. The last group of problems may only be reduced by all participants developing sensitivity to this sort of mixed group. For example, the turn-taking problem is among the most persistent and least satisfying parts of interaction in mixed groups where an interpreter facilitates communication. Still, even this can be successfully negotiated with the awareness of responsible parties.

Appendix A

Registry of Interpreters for the Deaf, Inc.
Code of Ethics

The Registry of Interpreters for the Deaf, Inc. refers to individuals who may perform one or more of the following services:

Interpret

Spoken English to American Sign Language
American Sign Language to Spoken English

Transliterate

Spoken English to Manually Coded English/Pidgin Sign English
Manually Coded English/Pidgin Sign English to Spoken English
Spoken English to paraphrased non-audible spoken English.

Gesticulate/Mime, etc.

Spoken English to Gesture, Mime, etc.
Gesture, Mime, etc., to Spoken English

The Registry of Interpreters for the Deaf, Inc. has set forth the following principles of ethical behavior to protect and guide the interpreter/transliterator, the consumers (hearing and hearing-impaired) and the profession, as well as to ensure for all, the right to communicate.

This Code of Ethics applies to all members of the Registry of Interpreters for the Deaf, Inc. and all certified non-members.

While these are general guidelines to govern the performance of the interpreter/transliterator generally, it is recognized that there are ever increasing numbers of highly specialized situations that demand specific explanation. It is envisioned that the R.I.D., Inc. will issue appropriate guidelines.

CODE OF ETHICS

INTERPRETER/TRANSLITERATOR SHALL KEEP ALL ASSIGNMENT-RELATED INFORMATION STRICTLY CONFIDENTIAL.

Guidelines:

Interpreter/transliterators shall not reveal information about any assignment, including the fact that the service is being performed.

Even seemingly unimportant information could be damaging in the wrong hands. Therefore, to avoid this possibility, interpreter/transliterators must not say anything about any assignment. In cases where meetings or information becomes a matter of public record, the interpreter/transliterator shall use discretion in discussing such meetings or information.

If a problem arises between the interpreter/transliterator and either person involved in an assignment, the interpreter/transliterator should first discuss it with the person involved. If no solution can be reached, then both should agree on a third person who could advise them.

When training new trainees by the method of sharing actual experiences, the trainers shall not reveal any of the following information:

name, sex, age, etc., of the consumer

day of the week, time of the day, time of the year the situation took place

location, including city, state or agency

other people involved

unnecessary specifics about the situation

It only takes a minimum amount of information to identify the parties involved.

INTERPRETER/TRANSLITERATORS SHALL RENDER THE MESSAGE FAITHFULLY, ALWAYS CONVEYING THE CONTENT AND SPIRIT OF THE SPEAKER, USING LANGUAGE MOST READILY UNDERSTOOD BY THE PERSON(S) WHOM THEY SERVE.

Guidelines:

Interpreter/transliterators are not editors and must transmit everything that is said in exactly the same way it was intended. This is especially difficult when the interpreter disagrees with what is being said or feels uncomfortable when profanity is being used. Interpreter/transliterators must remember that they are not at all responsible for what is said, only for conveying it accurately. If the interpreter/transliterator's own feelings interfere with rendering the message accurately, he/she shall withdraw from the situation.

While working from Spoken English to Sign or non-audible spoken English, the interpreter/transliterator should communicate in the manner most easily understood or preferred by the deaf and hard-of-hearing person(s), be it American Sign Language, Manually Coded English, fingerspelling, paraphrasing in non-audible spoken English, gesturing, drawing, or writing, etc. It is important for the interpreter/transliterator and deaf or hard-of-hearing person(s) to spend some time adjusting to each other's way of communicating prior to the actual assignment. When working from Sign or non-audible spoken English, the interpreter/transliterator shall speak the language used by the hearing person in spoken form, be it English, Spanish, French, etc.

INTERPRETER/TRANSLITERATORS SHALL NOT COUNSEL, ADVISE, OR INTERJECT PERSONAL OPINIONS.

Guidelines:

Just as interpreter/transliterators may not omit anything which is said, they may not add anything to the situation, even when they are asked to do so by other parties involved.

An interpreter/transliterator is only present in a given situation because two or more people have difficulty communicating, and thus the interpreter/transliterator's only function is to facilitate communication. He/she shall not become personally involved because in so doing he/she accepts some responsibility for the outcome, which does not rightly belong to the interpreter/transliterator.

INTERPRETER/TRANSLITERATORS SHALL ACCEPT ASSIGNMENTS USING DISCRETION WITH REGARD TO SKILL, SETTING, AND THE CONSUMERS INVOLVED.

Guidelines:

Interpreter/transliterators shall only accept assignments for which they are qualified. However, when an interpreter/transliterator shortage exists and the only available interpreter/transliterator does not possess the necessary skill for a particular assignment, this situation should be explained to the consumer. If the consumers agree that services are needed regardless of skill level, then the available interpreter/transliterator will have to use his/her judgment about accepting or rejecting the assignment.

Certain situations may prove uncomfortable for some interpreter/transliterators and clients. Religious, political, racial or sexual differences, etc., can adversely affect the facilitating task. Therefore, an interpreter/transliterator shall not accept assignments which he/she knows will involve such situations.

Interpreter/transliterators shall generally refrain from providing services in situations where family members, or close personal or professional relationships may affect impartiality, since it is difficult to mask inner feelings. Under these circumstances, especially in legal settings, the ability to prove oneself unbiased when challenged is lessened. In emergency situations, it is realized that the interpreter/transliterator may have to provide services for family members, friends, or close business associates. However, all parties should be informed that the interpreter/transliterator may not become personally involved in the proceedings.

INTERPRETER/TRANSLITERATORS SHALL REQUEST COMPENSATION FOR SERVICES IN A PROFESSIONAL AND JUDICIOUS MANNER.

Guidelines:

Interpreter/transliterators shall be knowledgeable about fees which are appropriate to the profession, and be informed about the current suggested fee schedule of the national organization. A sliding scale of hourly and daily rates has been established for interpreter/transliterators in many areas. To determine the appropriate fee, interpreter/transliterators should know their own level of skill, level of certification, length of experience, nature of the assignment, and the local cost of living index.

There are circumstances when it is appropriate for interpreter/transliterators to provide services without charge. This should be done with discretion, taking care to preserve the self-respect of the consumers. Consumers should not feel that they are recipients of charity. When providing *gratis* services, care should be taken so that the livelihood of other interpreter/transliterators will be protected. A free-lance interpreter/transliterator may depend on this work for a living and therefore must charge for services rendered, while persons with other full-time work may perform the service as a favor without feeling a loss of income.

INTERPRETER/TRANSLITERATORS SHALL FUNCTION IN A MANNER APPROPRIATE TO THE SITUATION.

Guidelines:

Interpreter/transliterators shall conduct themselves in such a manner that brings respect to themselves, the consumers and the national organization. The term "appropriate manner" refers to:

(a) dressing in a manner that is appropriate for skin tone and is not distracting.

(b) conducting oneself in all phases of an assignment in a manner befitting a professional.

INTERPRETER/TRANSLITERATORS SHALL STRIVE TO FURTHER KNOWLEDGE AND SKILLS THROUGH PARTICIPATION IN WORKSHOPS, PROFESSIONAL MEETINGS, INTERACTION WITH PROFESSIONAL COLLEAGUES AND READING OF CURRENT LITERATURE IN THE FIELD.

INTERPRETER/TRANSLITERATORS, BY VIRTUE OF MEMBERSHIP IN OR CERTIFICATION BY THE R.I.D., INC. SHALL STRIVE TO MAINTAIN HIGH PROFESSIONAL STANDARDS IN COMPLIANCE WITH THE CODE OF ETHICS.

October 1979

Appendix B

AIIC

CODE OF PROFESSIONAL CONDUCT

1983 VERSION
Code of Professional Conduct
(English translation of original French version)

ASSOCIATION INTERNATIONALE DES INTERPRÈTES
DE CONFÉRENCE
INTERNATIONAL ASSOCIATION OF
CONFERENCE INTERPRETERS

I. PURPOSE AND SCOPE

Article 1

a) This Code of Professional Conduct and Practice (hereinafter called "the Code") lays down the conditions governing the practice of the profession by members of the Association.

b) Members are bound by the provisions of the Code. The Council, with the assistance of the Association's members, shall ensure compliance with the provisions of the Code.

c) Candidates for admission shall undertake to adhere strictly to the provisions of the Code and all other AIIC rules.

d) Penalties, as provided in the Statutes, may be imposed on any member who infringes the rules of the profession as laid down in the Code.

II. CODE OF ETHICS

Article 2

a) Members of the Association shall be bound by the strictest secrecy, which must be observed towards all persons with regard to information gathered in the course of professional practice at non-public meetings.

b) Members shall not derive any personal gain from confidential information acquired by them in the exercise of their duties as interpreters.

Article 3

Members of the Association shall not accept engagements for which they are not qualified. Their acceptance shall imply a moral undertaking on their part that they will perform their services in a professional manner.*

Article 4

a) Members of the Association shall not accept any employment or situation which might detract from the dignity of the profession or jeopardize the observance of secrecy.

b) They shall refrain from any conduct which might bring the profession into disrepute, and particularly from any form of personal publicity. They may, however, for professional reasons advertise the fact that they are conference interpreters and members of the Association.

---

*The moral undertaking given by AIIC members under article 3 of the Code of Professional Conduct shall apply equally to the performance of services by interpreters who are not members of AIIC but are engaged through a member.

Article 5

a) It shall be the duty of members of the Association to afford their colleagues moral assistance and solidarity.

b) Members shall refrain from statements or actions prejudicial to the interests of the Association or its members. Any disagreement with the decisions of the Association or any complaint about the conduct of another member shall be raised and settled within the Association itself.

c) Any professional problem which arises between two or more members of the Association may be referred to the Council for arbitration.

d) As regards candidates, however, infringements of the Code or other rules of the Association shall be adjudicated by the Admissions and Language Classification Committee.

Article 6

Members of the Association shall not accept, and still less offer, conditions of work which do not meet the standards laid down in the Code, either for themselves or for interpreters engaged through them.

[Editor's Note: This portion of the AIIC Code is reproduced by permission.]

Appendix C

Compilation of State Interpreter Laws
Revised May, 1985

PUBLIC SERVICE OF GALLAUDET COLLEGE
reprinted here with permission of:

National Center for Law & the Deaf
800 Florida Avenue, N.E.
Washington, D.C. 20002

[Editor's Note: Reference is made throughout to "LSC" and "NRID." These should be understood to represent SC:L and RID. This compilation is updated regularly; current changes can be obtained directly from NCLD.]

STATE	STATUTES	SCOPE	PAYMENT	QUALIFICATIONS
Alabama	Ala. Code §12-21-131 (criminal & probate) Rules of Civil Proceedings 43(f) (1978)	Court may appoint interpreter for deaf party or witness in any state court proceeding—civil, criminal or probate	In civil: by state or by parties; may be taxed as costs. In criminal/probate: by state.	In civil is court's choice. In criminal/probate the interpreter must be adept and fluent in sign language, meet deaf party's approval, and be approved by the Alabama Association of the Deaf.
Alaska	Alaska Administrative Rules 6 (fees) (1981)	Silent on appointing interpreter	By the court in criminal cases and coroner's inquests; civil can be, by parties as taxed by the court or paid by the court.	Silent on qualifications
Arizona	Ariz. Rev. Stat. Ann. §11-601 (compensation) §12-241 (penal sanction) §12-242 (criminal) (pretrial) (administrative) §36-1946 (Interpreters for the deaf and their duties) Arizona Rules for Criminal Proceedings: Rule 12.5 (grand jury) (1982)	Interpreter must be appointed for deaf party or witness in: 1. grand jury proceedings 2. any court proceedings which may result in confinement or penal sanction of deaf person 3. civil cases 4. administrative agency proceedings 5. at time of arrest	Appointing authority	Appointing authority must first determine that interpreter can readily communicate with and translate statements of deaf persons. Intermediary interpreters may be appointed. Interpreter must be "qualified."

		6. pre-trial interrogation of deaf criminal defendant 7. criminal procedures 8. juvenile cases		
Arkansas	Ark. Stat. Ann. §5-715 (administrative) §5-715.1 *et seq.* (qualifications) §27-835 §43-2101.1 (criminal) §22-148 to 153 (court interpreter program) (1981)	Interpreter must be appointed for deaf parties in any state court proceedings: 1. criminal proceedings from time of arrest and custody, if deaf defendant 2. civil proceeding 3. administrative agency proceedings	Based on standards established by Arkansas RID. If court appointed, payment from general county funds; otherwise, by appointing authority or by private retainer. No acquitted defendant is required to pay for an appointed interpreter.	Certified by National RID, Arkansas RID or if such not available one otherwise qualified. Preliminary determination that interpreter can readily communicate with and interpret statements of deaf person and interpret proceedings involved.
California	Cal. Evid. Code §750-54 (criminal, juvenile, mental, administrative) (West) Cal. Govt. Code §68560-68564 Cal. Govt. Code §11002 (employment services) Cal. Evid. Code §750-754 (criminal, civil, juvenile, administrative, mental competency, traffic violation) (1984) (West)	Interpreter must be appointed for deaf party or witness in any: 1. criminal proceeding, including juvenile cases 2. mental competency hearing 3. administrative proceeding 4. civil proceeding 5. pre-trial interrogation of deaf defendant 6. worker compensation proceeding 7. state employment services 8. traffic violation proceedings	In criminal, juvenile, mental competency proceedings by county; in administrative hearing by appointing authority; in civil, as determined by court.	Certificate by NRID or state affiliate or court-approved agency and on list of recommended court interpreters established by each county's superior court. If only available interpreter inadequate, deaf party may nominate another to act as intermediary between self and appointed interpreter. Interpreters subject to testing of competency by State Personnel Board.

STATE	STATUTES	SCOPE	PAYMENT	QUALIFICATIONS
Colorado	Colo. Rev. Stat. §13-90-113 §13-90-114 §13-90-201 to 205 (1978)	Interpreters must be appointed for deaf party or witness in: 1. grand jury proceedings 2. any court proceeding which may result in confinement or penal sanction for deaf party 3. any administrative proceeding 4. at time of arrest and pre-trial interrogation of a deaf criminal defendant Court may appoint interpreter in all other cases.	By the state.	Appointing authority must first determine that interpreter is readily able to communicate with and translate statements of the deaf person.
Connecticut	Conn. Gen. Stat. Ann. §17-137(k) thru (p) §K(a) qualifications of interpreters §K(b)(1) criminal & civil actions §K(b)(2) criminal investigations §K(b)(3) deaf parents of a minor child §K(c) administrative §K(d) employee grievance procedure §K(e) any school or college,	Interpreter must be appointed for deaf party or witness or for a deaf parent of a minor child who is a victim, witness or suspect in any: 1. criminal proceeding 2. civil proceeding 3. administrative proceeding 4. employment grievance procedure 5. education or human	By State Commission on Deaf; reimbursement to commission by appointing authority.	Approval by State Commission of Deaf and Hearing-Impaired which makes appointments to requesting court or agency.

	Citation	Appointment	Payment	Interpreter Qualification
	human services agency §P(a)&(b) compensation §1-25 oath (West) (1984)	services agency; agency may request interpreter 6. law enforcement agencies must provide qualified interpreters for any deaf involved in a criminal investigation, whether as a victim, witness, or suspect		
Delaware	Del. Code Ann. 10 §8907 (1976)	Interpreter must be appointed in any criminal or civil court proceeding where deaf person is party or witness.	State pays in criminal proceedings or court assigns between litigants in civil court.	Interpreter must be "qualified."
District of Columbia	D.C. Code Ann. §1-1509, §1-1511 (1982)	Interpreters must be appointed for deaf parties or witnesses in contested agency proceeding.	Not clear, seems to be paid by agency.	Interpreter must be "qualified."
Florida	Fla. Stat. Ann. §90.606, §905.15 (grand jury), §90.606.3 §901.245 (arrest) (West) (1981)	Interpreter must be appointed for deaf witness in: 1. grand jury proceeding 2. criminal action, interpreter must be appointed for deaf defendant in custody prior to interrogation (unless impossible, then interrogation must be in writing) 3. all judicial proceedings	Criminal: general county funds Civil: court has discretion to issue as costs	Interpreter must be certified by NRID or Florida RID or certified by the appointing agency as able to communicate readily with the deaf person and able to repeat and translate accurately.

STATE	STATUTES	SCOPE	PAYMENT	QUALIFICATIONS
Georgia	Ga. Code Ann. §24-9-100 thru 108 §24-9-107 (oath) proceedings may be videotaped §24-9-108 (compensation) §24-1-5 (arrest) Art. 5 (evidence) (1983)	Interpreter must be appointed for deaf party or witness in any: 1. grand jury proceeding, licensing commission 2. criminal proceeding 3. civil proceeding 4. administrative proceeding 5. at time of custodial arrest and during pretrial interrogation of deaf criminal defendant	By county in which proceeding occurs if court appointed; otherwise by appointing authority.	Interpreter must be either certified by NRID or Georgia RID. When certified interpreter is unavailable, appointing authority must determine qualifications. Must be able to communicate accurately with and translate information to and from the hearing-impaired person.
Hawaii	Hawaii Rev. Stat. §606-9 (1979)	Courts and administrative judges may appoint interpreter when "necessary."	Not stated.	Not stated.
Idaho	Idaho Code §9-205 (criminal & civil) §19-1111 (grand jury) §9-1603 (fees) (1975)	Interpreter must be appointed for deaf party or witness in: 1. civil action 2. criminal action 3. grand jury proceeding	By county in which proceeding occurs.	Interpreter must be "qualified."
Illinois	Ill. Ann. Stat. ch. 38 §165-11 thru 13 (criminal) 51 §47 51 §48.01 (criminal & civil)	Court must appoint interpreter for deaf party or witness in "any legal proceeding of any nature."	By county in which proceeding is held.	Interpreter must be "qualified."

State	Citation	Appointment / Proceedings	Payment	Qualifications
Indiana	(Smith-Hurd 1971); Ill. Code Civ. Proc. Ch. 110 §8-1402 (1982) Ind. Code Ann. §4-22-1-22 5 (administrative) §34-1-14-3 (civil); Ind.R.Tr.P.43(f) (West 1984)	Court must appoint interpreter for deaf party in any court proceeding.	By the discretion of the court, may be taxed as costs or funds provided by law. Administrative boards or agencies pay.	Appointing authority may inquire into the qualifications of the interpreter.
Iowa	Iowa Code Ann. §622A.1 et seq §622B.1 et seq §622B appendix (West 1980)	Interpreter must be appointed for deaf party or witness in: 1. grand jury proceeding 2. criminal proceeding 3. civil proceeding 4. administrative proceeding 5. proceedings preparatory to appearing before any court	By appointing agency, if hearing-impaired person is not a party, payment must be charged to costs.	Interpreter must be listed in state directory as certified under the NRID system; must hold CSC or MCSC or SCL or specialized certificate.
Kansas	Kan. Stat. Ann. §60-243 (appointment & fee) §60-243(e) §75-4351 thru 4355 (all cases) (deaf mute) §60-417 Rules of Evidence (qualifications of interpreter) (1972)	Interpreter must be appointed for deaf party or witness in: 1. grand jury proceeding 2. any court proceeding which may result in confinement or penal sanction against the deaf person 3. any civil proceeding	Appointing authority determines who pays.	Appointing authority must first determine whether interpreter can readily communicate with and translate statements of deaf person. Limitation on use of spouse, relative, other interested party.

STATE	STATUTES	SCOPE	PAYMENT	QUALIFICATIONS
		4. any administrative proceeding 5. time of arrest for alleged violation of a criminal law 6. pre-trial interrogations of deaf criminal defendant		
Kentucky	Ky. Rev. Stat. §30A.400 to .435 (1978)	Interpreter must be appointed for deaf parties or witnesses: 1. at all stages of criminal, juvenile, or mental inquest cases including custody arrest, probation, & parole hearings. 2. administrative agency proceedings. 3. at pre-trial interrogation of deaf criminal defendant. Interpreter may be appointed in civil cases.	State pays for interpreter in criminal, juvenile and mental inquest cases and administrative hearings. In civil cases, court determines whether losing party or state pays.	Qualified by training or experience. State Supreme Court may prescribe further standards after consulting with Kentucky RID or the Kentucky School for the Deaf.
Louisiana	La. Rev. Stat. Ann. 15§270 (criminal) 49§181 (administrative) La. Code Crim. Proc. Ann. art. 433, 441 (grand jury) La. Code Civ. Pro. Ann. art.	Court must appoint interpreter for deaf party or witness in: 1. all civil cases and depositions 2. criminal trials	Fees are to be established by Louisiana Commission of the Deaf. State or agency pays. In court cases, court	Interpreter must be qualified. Appointing auth. must make preliminary determination based on the hearing-impaired person's needs and rec-

State	Citation	Proceedings	Fees/Certification	Qualifications
	192.1 La. R.S. 46:2361 to R.S. 46:2372 La. Rev. Stat. Ann. (West 1982)	3. mental commitment proceedings 4. grand jury proceedings 5. any state examination which is a prerequisite for state employment or licensing 6. legislative bodies 7. administrative agencies 8. licensing commissions 9. juvenile proceeding 10. time of arrest	determines and pays the interpreter fees.	ommendation of La. Commission for the Deaf which is to maintain a list of qualified interpreter transliterators from LRID or NRID; must be able to communicate with the hearing-impaired person.
Maine	Me. Rev. State Ann. tit. 5§48 (all proceedings) Rules of Civ. Proc. §43(L) Rules of Crim Proc. §6(D) (grand jury), §28 criminal (1979)	Court or agency must appoint interpreter whenever any personal or property interest of a deaf or hearing-impaired person is the subject of a proceeding before any agency or court and rehabilitation services.	By State Bureau of Rehabilitation on certification by appointing authority (unless employed by appointing authority as full-time interpreter).	Interpreter must have knowledge and understanding of NRID's Code of Ethics, be able to recognize deaf person's comprehension level, be able to communicate effectively with deaf person and interpret accurately, first consideration given by interpreter certified by National RID or Maine RID.
Maryland	Md. Cts. and Jud. Proc. §9-114 Md. Ann. Code art. 27	Interpreter must be appointed for deaf party or witness in:	In civil, court determines if losing party or county	Interpreter must be "qualified."

STATE	STATUTES	SCOPE	PAYMENT	QUALIFICATIONS
	§623A (criminal) art. 30 §1 (administrative) art. 30 §2A (employee grievance) (1979)	1. any civil proceeding, on application of deaf person 2. any criminal action 3. any "contested" case before an administrative agency. Interpreter may be appointed: at any public hearing if conducted by a state agency, if "feasible," following written request of deaf person. Feasibility determined by nature of hearing and the number of deaf persons making request. 4. employee grievance proceedings	pays in criminal, by court in administrative, tax as costs if agency so empowered; otherwise by agency. In employee grievance, payment is divided equally between employer and union or employee and organization.	
Massachusetts	Mass. Gen. Laws Ann. Ch. 221§§92 to 92A Mass. Gen. Laws Ann. Ch. 234A§69 (interpreter for deaf juror) (West 1983)	Court must appoint interpreter at time of arrest, in "any proceeding in any court in which deaf person is party or witness," or proceedings before an executive or legislative board, commission, agency, bureau, or other body of state.	By state.	Interpreter must be qualified. As determined by Office of Deafness, and other appropriate agencies.

State	Statute	Conditions	Appointed by	Qualifications
Michigan	Mich. Comp. Laws Ann. §393.501-509 (West 1982) (Deaf persons' interpreter act)	Appointing authority other than a court and court must appoint interpreter for deaf witness, plaintiff, or defendant in criminal or civil proceeding, grand jury, at time of arrest, during administrative and political subdivision proceedings. Clerk of political subdivision may hire interpreter to aid in voter registration & voting.	By court or appointing authority.	Interpreter must be able to readily communicate with the deaf person. The Michigan Division of the Deaf and Deafened is responsible for compiling and maintaining list of interpreters.
Minnesota	Minn. Stat. Ann. §546.42-546.44 (civil) §611.30-611.34 (criminal, grand jury, time of arrest, preliminary proceedings) §15.44 (state meetings) §204 C.15 (voters) (West 1984)	Interpreter must be appointed for deaf party or witness in: 1. mental commitment proceedings and mental health examination connected with the proceedings 2. civil action 3. criminal action 4. administrative agency proceedings 5. proceedings preliminary to any action in which deaf person may be confined or penalty sanctioned, including coroner's	By appointing authority; by county for court appointed.	Interpreter must be readily able to communicate with and translate statements of and translate proceedings to the deaf person.

STATE	STATUTES	SCOPE	PAYMENT	QUALIFICATIONS
		inquest and grand jury proceedings 6. at time of arrest and during pre-trial interrogation of deaf criminal defendant 7. state agencies sponsoring meetings or conferences for the public or for state employees must provide effective means of making orally delivered materials available to hearing-impaired participants		
Mississippi	Miss. Code Ann. §13-1-16 §99-17-7 (criminal cases) §11-7-153 (oath) (1972)	Interpreter must be appointed for deaf party or witness in "any legal proceeding of any nature" including administrative proceeding.	If deaf person is plaintiff, he pays. If deaf person is defendant, fee is treated as other court costs. If deaf person is non-party witness, fee is paid by the party calling the witness.	Interpreter must be qualified.
Missouri	Mo. Ann. Stat. §476.060 (civil) §490.630 (evidence) §491.300 (fees)	Court must appoint interpreter in all criminal and mental commitment proceedings.		

	§540.150 (grand jury)			
Montana	Mont. Code Ann. §§49-4-501 to 49-4-511 §§25-404, 25-413, 93-514, M.R. Civ.Pr. Rule 43(f) Montana Code Ann. Ch.245 §§1-14 (1979)	Interpreter must be appointed for deaf party or witness in: 1. any case before any court or grand jury 2. all stages of any administrative proceeding of judicial or quasi-judicial nature 3. any proceeding whereby deaf person may be subject to confinement or criminal sanction, or any proceeding preliminary thereto including: coroner's inquest, grand jury, and mental commitment proceedings 4. pre-trial interrogation of deaf defendant	In criminal action by county; otherwise, by appointing authority.	Approval by Montana Association of the Deaf and Montana RID. Preliminary determination that interpreter is able to accurately communicate with and translate information to and for the deaf person.
Nebraska	Neb. Rev. Stat. §25-2401 to 25-2406 (1973)	Interpreter must be appointed for deaf party or witness in "any legal proceeding or hearing preliminary thereto including administrative agency proceedings."	By county.	Interpreter must be readily able to communicate with, translate statements of, and translate proceedings to the deaf person.

STATE	STATUTES	SCOPE	PAYMENT	QUALIFICATIONS
Nevada	Nev. Rev. Stat. §50.045 (qualifications) §50.050 (criminal & civil) §171.1535 (definition) §171.1536 (time of arrest) §171.1537-171.1538 (waiver of rights) Rules of Civ. Pro. 43(f) (1975)	Interpreter must be appointed in: 1. all proceedings in which deaf person is witness 2. at time of arrest, pretrial interrogation of deaf criminal defendant, and in criminal proceedings 3. may be appointed in civil proceedings	By county in which proceeding is held, or by the parties as the court decides	Interpreter must be readily able to communicate with, translate proceedings for, and translate statements of deaf persons.
New Hampshire	N.H. Rev. Stat. Ann.§§ 521-A: 1 et seq 521-A: 2 521-A: 3 (criminal) 521-A: 4 (competency) 521-A: 5 (administrative hearings) 521-A: 8 (compensation) 521-A:11 (privileged communication) (1977)	Interpreter must be appointed: 1. at all stages of any court of administrative proceedings in which deaf person is "principal party in interest," when deaf person makes request 2. before any pre-trial interrogation where deaf defendant may be subject to imprisonment or fine in excess of $100 or both 3. when deaf person is party to or receiving services from any	By appointing authority	Certification by NRID or New Hampshire RID or, if unavailable, one whose actual qualifications have been "appropriately determined."

		state health, welfare, or educational agency; to assist in providing such services Interpreter may be permitted: in any administrative judicial "interested" and interpreter would be required for deaf principal party in interest; to aid deaf person in presenting testimony or comments.		
New Jersey	N.J. Stat. Ann. §2A: 11-28.1 (West 1971) repealed and replaced by Chapter 564 (approved Jan. 1984)	Court must appoint interpreter for deaf witness or party in any civil or criminal proceeding; grand jury; juvenile proceeding; administrative or quasi-judicial proceeding; mental health commitments; coroner's inquest; and at the time of arrest.	The court pays; agency or municipal body pays.	Certified by NRID or list of interpreters developed by the N.J. Dept. of Labor.
New Mexico	N.M. Stat. Ann. §38-9-1-1 to 38-9-10 (1979)	Interpreter must be appointed in any judicial or administrative proceeding in which deaf person is "principal party in interest" and deaf person has provided notice (2 weeks) (and proof of disability if court or agency so requires). In-	By appointing authority	Certification by NRID or by joint action of Vocational Rehabilitation Division of New Mexico RID and New Mexico Association of the Deaf; or by nomination by deaf person or appointing authority of one acceptable to both

217

STATE	STATUTES	SCOPE	PAYMENT	QUALIFICATIONS
		terpreter may be appointed: 1. whenever deaf person is requesting or receiving services from any state health, welfare, or educational agency 2. in any judicial or administrative proceeding where deaf person is "interested" and interpreter would be required for deaf principal party in interest of the purpose of translation and also in presenting testimony or comment.		
New York	N.Y. Jud. Law §390 N.Y. A.P.A. §301 N.Y. Exec. §259(i) (Parole) N.Y. Lab. §620 (4) N.Y. Work. Comp. §150(b), §927 (McKinney 1981)	Court must appoint interpreter for deaf party or witness to any civil or criminal legal proceeding of any nature; administrative agency proceeding; parole hearings (preliminary, revocation, or release); workman's compensation proceeding.	By county in which proceeding is held; in administrative proceedings, by the appointing agency; in parole hearings, by the division of parole	Must be "qualified."
North Carolina	N.C. Gen. Stat. §§8B-1 thru 8B-8 (1981)	An interpreter must be appointed for any deaf party or witness in: ● any criminal proceeding or upon arrest;	Court funds in civil, criminal, and juvenile proceedings; General Assembly funds in	Interpreter must be certified as qualified under standards of the Department of Human Resources or, if none so cer-

218

State	Citation	Proceedings for Which Interpreter Provided	How Appointed/Paid	Qualifications
(continued)		civil proceedings in superior or district court, including juveniles and proceedings before a magistrate; legislative committee proceeding; administrative proceeding; for deaf parents of juveniles in juvenile proceedings.	Legislative Committee proceedings; by appointing agency in administrative agency proceedings	tified are available, interpreter must be able to communicate and interpret effectively, simultaneously, and accurately for the deaf person.
North Dakota	N.D. Cent. Code §28-33-01 to 28-33-08 (deaf parties) §31-01-11 (deaf Witnesses)—oath of interpreter §31-01-12 fees Rule of evidence 604 (oath) (1979)	Court must provide interpreter: • at all stages of any judicial or administrative proceeding where deaf person is "principal party in interest" • before any pre-trial interrogation of deaf defendant where penalty may include imprisonment or fine over $100 or both • for deaf witness in any courts	By appointing authority	Certified by NRID or approved by State School for the Deaf. If unavailable, then one whose actual qualifications have been "appropriately determined."
Ohio	Ohio Rev. Code Ann. §2311.14, §2335.09 (courts) §3501.22 (elections) (Baldwin 1976)	Court must appoint interpreter for deaf party or witness in civil or criminal proceeding, including grand juries and coroner's hearings. May also appoint interpreters to assist in elections.	In civil, may be taxed as costs; in criminal and grand jury by county	Must be "qualified."

STATE	STATUTES	SCOPE	PAYMENT	QUALIFICATIONS
Oklahoma	Okla. Stat. Ann. tit. 12§2604 (oath) tit. 63 §2407 to 2412 tit. 22 §340 (grand jury) tit. 22 §344 (grand jury) tit. 22 §1278 (criminal & mental) (West 1982)	Oral or sign language interpreter must be appointed for deaf criminal defendant from time of arrest; for deaf defendant in mental commitment case; or deaf party in civil case; before any court where deaf person is a complainant, defendant, or witness; administrative proceedings; grand jury.	Taxed as costs in civil case, by county in criminal.	If court proceeding, must make efforts to obtain LSC interpreter. Qualified interpreter must be able to readily communicate with the deaf person and interpret accurately the deaf person's statements.
Oregon	Or. Rev. Stat. §44.095 (criminal & civil)—repealed C.892§98 §132.090 (grand jury) §133.515 (time of arrest) §183.310 (administrative definition) §183.418 (administrative) §151.050 (public defender's staff) §151.240 (Administrative powers of public defender's staff) (1973)	Interpreter must be appointed for deaf party or witness in: 1. civil proceedings 2. criminal proceedings 3. pre-trial interrogation of deaf criminal defendant 4. "contested" administrative agency proceedings 5. grand jury	By party needing interpreter in civil case. In criminal and administrative proceedings payment by county if party is financially unable to do so.	Interpreter must be readily able to communicate with, translate proceedings for, and translate statements of deaf persons.
Pennsylvania	Pa. Stat. Ann. tit. 16§1608, §3101 Rules of Crim. Proc. 209 (grand jury)	Interpreter must be appointed for deaf criminal defendant from time of arrest and throughout all	By state in criminal cases; may be taxed as costs in civil.	Interpreter must be either certified by NRID or local RID or otherwise qualified and trained to

State	Citation	Provisions	Appointment	Qualifications
	tit. 42§§1726, §§2301, 3722 (fees) tit. 42 §8701 (criminal, arrest) tit. 43 §476 (employee-note of hazards) tit. 72 §3191 tit. 72 §5020-309 (assessors) (Purdon 1978)	criminal proceedings. May be appointed in civil cases.		translate for and communicate with deaf persons.
Rhode Island	R.I. Gen. Laws §§8-5-8; (civil & criminal) §9-29-7 (fees) Superior Court Rule of Crim. Proc. 28. District Court Rule of Crim. Proc. 28. (1969)	Interpreter must be appointed for deaf party or witness in all civil and criminal trials. Interpreter may be appointed in other situations.	By state in criminal proceedings. Unstated for civil.	Interpreter must be "qualified."
South Carolina	S.C. Code Ann. §15-27-10 (Law. Co-op. 1972)	Court may appoint interpreter for deaf party or witness to any criminal or civil legal proceedings, or commitment proceeding.	By state or county as designated by the court.	Interpreter must be appointed by either S.C. RID or NRID.
South Dakota	S.D. Comp. Laws Ann. §15-6-43 f (civil) §19-3-7 thru 19-3-14 §19-3-10 (grand jury, penal sanction & criminal) (1974)	Interpreters must be appointed: 1. in grand jury proceedings for deaf witnesses; 2. in any court proceedings which could result in confinement or penal sanction against deaf persons;	By state through court of appointing agency.	Appointing authority must make preliminary determination that interpreter can readily communicate with and translate statements of deaf person. Deaf person must approve interpreter.

STATE	STATUTES	SCOPE	PAYMENT	QUALIFICATIONS
		3. in administrative proceedings where deaf person is principal party; 4. for deaf person in all court proceedings; 5. for pre-trial interrogation of deaf criminal defendant.		
Tennessee	Tenn. Code Ann. §24-1-103 Rules of criminal procedure: Rule 28. (1977)	Interpreter must be appointed for deaf party or witness in: 1. criminal trials; 2. civil trials; 3. grand jury proceedings; 4. administrative agency proceedings; 5. pre-trial interrogation of deaf criminal defendant.	By appointing authority.	Appointing authority and deaf person must first determine that interpreter can readily communicate with and interpret statements of and proceedings to the deaf person.
Texas	Tex. Stat. Ann. art. 6252-18 to 18a; Tex. Rev. Civ. Stat. Ann. art. 3712(a) (Vernon, 1979); Tex. Code Crim. Proc. Ann. art. 38.31; art. 15.17; art. 38.22; Rules of Civ. Proc. 183	Interpreters must be appointed: 1. in all criminal prosecutions of deaf defendants including pre-trial interrogation and hearing, arraignment, examining trial, and trial. Inter-	By county	Approved by State Commission for the Deaf

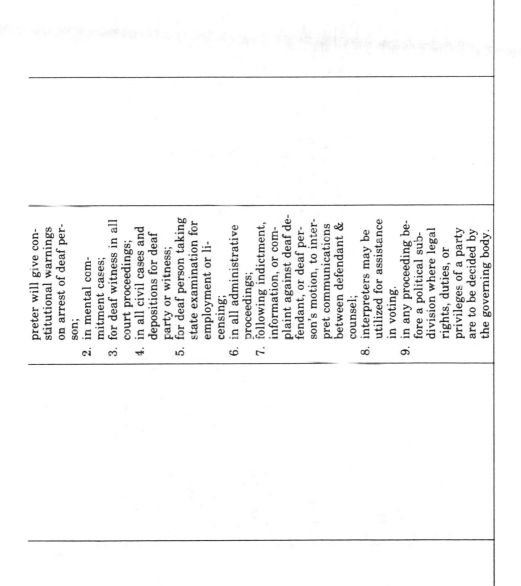

preter will give constitutional warnings on arrest of deaf person;

2. in mental commitment cases;

3. for deaf witness in all court proceedings;

4. in all civil cases and depositions for deaf party or witness;

5. for deaf person taking state examination for employment or licensing;

6. in all administrative proceedings;

7. following indictment, information, or complaint against deaf defendant, or deaf person's motion, to interpret communications between defendant & counsel;

8. interpreters may be utilized for assistance in voting.

9. in any proceeding before a political subdivision where legal rights, duties, or privileges of a party are to be decided by the governing body.

STATE	STATUTES	SCOPE	PAYMENT	QUALIFICATIONS
Utah	Utah Code Ann. §21-5-17 (fees) §77-35-15 §77-35-14 (subpoena) §78-24a-1 thru 11 (interpreters for hearing-impaired—any action) (1983)	Court may appoint interpreter for deaf party or witness at any court or quasi-judicial, grand jury, juvenile proceedings, adoption proceedings; mental health commitment proceedings; administrative, legislative, time of arrest.	Assessed the same as other court costs. Appointing authority pays if interpreter is not otherwise compensated.	Interpreter must be qualified and readily able to communicate with and translate information to and from the hearing impaired person involved. Utah D.V.R. shall establish update, and distribute list of qualified interpreters.
Vermont	VRCP 43(f) VRCrP 28	Court may appoint interpreter for civil and criminal proceedings.	By state in criminal case; civil, paid by one or more of the parties.	Unstated.
Virginia	Va. Code 2.1-570-§§573 (agency proceeding) 19.2-164.1 (1982 Amendd. Crim.) 63.1-85.4 (V.C.D. Law) 8.01-400.1 (priv. comm.) 37.1-67.5 (commitment) 8.01-384.1 (civil 1982) (1982)	Interpreter must be appointed for deaf party or witness for: 1. grand jury proceedings; 2. civil actions; 3. criminal proceedings; 4. from time of arrest of deaf criminal suspect; 5. administrative agency proceeding.	By appointing authority.	Interpreter must be certified by NRID or VRID and/or approved by Virginia Council for the Deaf.
Virgin Islands	T.4§323 Interpreters Ch. 19	In court of justice.	By appointing authority.	Interpreter must be "qualified."

Washington	Wash. Rev. Code Ann. §2.42.010 thru 2.42.050 (1973)	Interpreters must be appointed for deaf party or witness in: 1. grand jury proceedings; 2. hearings before an inquiry judge; 3. civil proceedings; 4. criminal proceedings; 5. administrative agency proceedings.	By state in criminal, grand jury, coroner's inquest, mental commitment proceedings and all other proceedings initiated by government agencies. In all other legal proceedings, deaf person must pay, unless he/she is indigent, but may be taxable cost in any proceeding in which costs ordinarily taxed.	Interpreter must be readily able to translate statement to and from deaf person.
West Virginia	W.Va. Code §57-5-7 (1982)	Interpreter must be appointed for deaf party or witness at every stage of: 1. criminal proceeding; 2. civil proceeding; juvenile proceeding; 3. grand jury proceeding; 4. coroner's inquest; 5. administrative agency proceeding.	By appointing agency if the deaf person is unable to pay for the service rendered.	Must be readily able to communicate with and translate proceedings for deaf person and accurately translate statement of that person; certified by RID, if available and need for such skill indicated or "otherwise qualified."
Wisconsin	Wis. Stat. Ann. §§ §59.77 (fee) §879.41 (probate) §885.05 (fee), §814.67	Interpreter must be appointed in any trial or examination in which deaf person is:	By appointing authority if deaf person is unable to pay.	Must be competent to converse in language used by deaf person.

STATE	STATUTES	SCOPE	PAYMENT	QUALIFICATIONS
	§885.37 (criminal, commitment, administrative) (West 1978)	1. accused of crime or misdemeanor 2. subject to a judgment as to "fitness for a place in society;" 3. party in administrative proceeding.		
Wyoming	Wyo. Stat. §5-1-109 (civil, criminal, arrest) Rules of Civ. Proc. §43(f) Rules of Crim. Proc. 29 (1979)	Court must appoint interpreter on petition of deaf person in: 1. all civil or criminal cases in which deaf person is a party; 2. a grand jury proceeding where deaf person is a witness; 3. before pre-trial interrogation of deaf defendant unless waived by deaf person or interrogation conducted entirely in writing and deaf person able to read and write.	Court determines; may be taxed as costs.	Must be "qualified."

226

Bibliography

Acevedo, Janet. 1981. Guidelines for Field Experience. Valhalla, NY: Westchester Community College (memoranda from November, 1981).

Ahlgren, Inger; Bergman, Brita. (eds.) 1980. Papers from the First International Symposium on Sign Language Research. Leksand, Sweden: The Swedish National Association of the Deaf [Sveriges dovas riksforbund].

Andereck, Paul. 1981. The Barney Miller Episode: Fantastic!. The Deaf American. 33.7:17–18.

Anderson, Crystal M. 1982. The Interpreter Trainer: Guidelines for Professional Development. The Reflector. 4:21–25.

Anderson, Crystal M. 1984. The Interpreter Trainer: Guidelines for Professional Development. In McIntire (ed.). pp 151–168.

Anderson, R. Bruce. 1976. Perspectives on the Role of Interpreter. In Brislin (ed.). pp. 208–228.

Anderson, R. Bruce. 1978. Interpreter Roles and Interpretation Situations: Cross-Cutting Typologies. In Gerver and Sinaiko (eds.). pp. 217–230.

Arjona, Etilvia. 1978. Intercultural Communication and the Training of Interpreters at the Monterey Institute of Foreign Studies. In Gerver and Sinaiko (eds.). pp. 35–44.

Arjona, Etilvia. 1984a. Education of Translators and Interpreters. In McIntire (ed.). pp. 1–35.

Arjona, Etilvia. 1984b. Testing and Evaluation. In McIntire (ed.). pp. 111–138.

Art, Carole. 1981. Refugees and Emigres and Their Language Problems. ATA Chronicle. 10.10:18–20.

ATA Chronicle. 1980. Registry of Certified Interpreters. 9.4–5:15.

Austin, Bruce A. 1980. The Deaf Audience for Television. Journal of Communication. 30.2:25–30.

Austin, Gary F. 1982. Secondary Education Sign Language Interpreters: A State of the Art Survey. RID Interpreting Journal. 1.2:38–46.

Baker, Charlotte. 1976. What's Not on the Other Hand. Papers from the Twelfth Regional Meeting of the Chicago Linguistic Society. Chicago, IL: CLS.

Baker, Charlotte. 1977. Regulators and Turn-Taking in American Sign Language. In Friedman (ed.). pp. 215–236.

Baker, Charlotte. 1980. How Does "Sim-Com" Fit into a Bilingual Approach to Education? In Caccamise and Hicks (eds.). pp. 13–26.

Baker, Charlotte; Battison, Robbin. (eds.) 1980. Sign Language and the Deaf Community: Essays in Honor of William C. Stokoe. Silver Spring, MD: National Association of the Deaf.

Baker, Charlotte; Cokely, Dennis. 1980. American Sign Language: A Teacher's Resource Text on Grammar and Culture. Silver Spring, MD: T. J. Publishers.

Baker, Nicholas G. 1981. Social Work Through an Interpreter. Social Work. 26.5:391–397.

Ballard, Betsy Ann. 1982. Theatrical Interpreting: State of the Art. RID Interpreting Journal. 1.2:47–54.

Barik, Henri C. 1973. Simultaneous Interpretation: Temporal and Quantitative Data. Language and Speech. 16:237–270.

Barik, Henri C. 1975. Simultaneous Interpretation: Qualitative and Linguistic Data. Language and Speech. 18:272–297.

Baron, Naomi. 1981. Speech, Writing, and Sign. Bloomington, IN: Indiana University.

Barrett, Wayne. 1984. The Deaf Deserve to Serve. Village Voice. May 29, p. 5.

Battison, Robbin M.; Jordan, I. King. 1976. Cross-Cultural Communication with Foreign Signers: Fact and Fancy. Sign Language Studies. 10:53–68.

Bearden, Carter E. 1975. Handbook for Religious Interpreters for the Deaf. Atlanta, GA: Home Mission Board of the Southern Baptist Convention.

Beekman, John; Callow, John. 1974. Translating the Word of God. Grand Rapids, MI: Zondervan Press.

Benderly, Beryl. 1980. Dancing Without Music. Garden City, NY: Anchor Press.

Bird, Barbara J.; Smith, T. Michael. n.d. Communication Needs of Deaf People in Industry. Rochester, NY: NTID. (Technical Report #2, Interpreter Education Program).

Brasel, Barbara B.; Brasel, Kenneth. 1974. The RID Scoring System and How It Works. Journal of Rehabilitation of the Deaf. 7.3:76–79.

Brasel, Barbara B.; Montanelli, Dale S.; Quigley, Stephen. 1974. The Component Skills of Interpreting as Viewed by Interpreters. Journal of Rehabilitation of the Deaf. 7.4:20–28.

Brislin, Richard. (ed.). 1976. Translation: Applications and Research. New York, NY: Gardner Press.

Brook, Rollins. 1983. Sound Systems for the Hearing-Impaired. Theater Design and Technology. 19.2:22–25.

Bruce, Robert V. 1973. Bell: Alexander Graham Bell and the Conquest of Silence. Boston, MA: Little, Brown and Company.

Bruck, Lilly. 1978. Access: The Guide to a Better Life for Disabled Americans. New York, NY: Random House.

Caccamise, Frank. 1978. New Myths to Replace Old Myths? (Comment). American Annals of the Deaf. 123.5:513–515.

Caccamise, Frank; Blasdell, Richard. 1977. Reception of Sentences under Oral-Manual Interpreted and Simultaneous Test Conditions. American Annals of the Deaf. 122.4:414–421. (Appears in shortened form in the Deaf American of November, 1977):

Caccamise, Frank; Hicks, Doin. (eds.) 1980. American Sign Language in a Bilingual, Bicultural Context (Proceedings of the Second National Symposium on Sign Language Research and Teaching). Silver Spring, MD: National Association of the Deaf.

Caccamise, Frank; Stangarone, James; Caccamise, Marilyn; Banner, Elizabeth. (eds.) 1978. Interpreting Potpourri (Proceedings of the 1978 RID Convention). Silver Spring, MD: RID, Inc.

Caccamise, Frank; Stangarone, James; Mitchell-Caccamise, Marilyn. (eds.) 1980. A Century of Deaf Awareness (Proceedings of the 1980 RID Convention). Silver Spring, MD: RID, Inc.

Carlson, Becky. 1984. The Code of Ethics: Some Interpretations. In Northcott (ed.). pp. 221–228.

Carter, S. Melvin, Jr. 1982. In Communication. The Deaf American. 34.5:21–22.

Carter, S. Melvin; Lauritsen, Robert R. 1974. Interpreter Recruitment, Selection and Training. Journal of Rehabilitation of the Deaf. 7.3:52–62.

Casagrande, J. 1954. The Ends of Translation. International Journal of American Linguistics. 20:335–340.

Chatoff, Michael. 1976. Legal Interpreting. Journal of Rehabilitation of the Deaf. 9.3:22–24.

Chough, Steven K. 1964. Casework with the Deaf: A Problem in Communication. Social Work. 9.4:76–82.

Cogen, Cathy. 1982. Northeastern University: A Program Description. The Reflector. 2:8–10.

Cokely, Dennis. 1980. Sign Language: Teaching, Interpreting and Educational Policy. In Baker and Battison (eds.). pp. 137–158.

Cokely, Dennis. 1981a. Sign Language Interpreters: A Demographic Survey. Sign Language Studies. 32:261–286.

Cokely, Dennis. 1981b. Demographic Characteristics of Interpreters. The Reflector. 1:21–28.

Cokely, Dennis. 1982. The Interpreted Medical Interview: It Loses Something in the Translation. The Reflector. 3:5–10.

Cokely, Dennis. 1983. Metanotative Qualities: How Accurately Are They Conveyed by Interpreters? The Reflector. 5:16–22.

Cokely, Dennis. 1984a. Editor's Comments. The Reflector. 8:3–4.

Cokely, Dennis. 1984b. Editor's Comments. The Reflector. 9:3–4.

Collins, Kevin J. 1972. The Deaf and the Police. Training Bulletin. New York, NY: Police Department of the City of New York. 1.2

Colonomos, Betty M. 1982. Reflections of an Interpreter Trainer. The Reflector. 2:5–14.

Condon, John C.; Yousef, Fathi. 1975. An Introduction to Intercultural Communication. Indianapolis, IN: Bobbs-Merrill.

Congrat-Butlar, Stefan. 1979. Translation and Translators: An International Directory and Guide. New York, NY: R. R. Bowker Co.

Crittenden, Jerry. 1975. Psychology of Deafness: Some Implications for the Interpreter. Journal of Rehabilitation of the Deaf. 8.4:19–23.

Crump, Ted. 1984a. Translators in the Federal Government—1984. In Newman (ed.). pp. 45–49.

Crump, Ted. 1984b. Quantity versus Quality in the Federal Government. In Newman (ed.). pp. 61–66.

Culton, Paul M. 1975. Deaf Students in Community Colleges. Community College Social Sciences Quarterly. 5:42–44.

Culton, Paul. 1981. A Study of the Validity and Reliability of the Comprehensive Skills Certificate Evaluation for Sign Language Interpreters. Salt Lake City, UT: Brigham Young University. (Unpublished doctoral dissertation).

Culton, Paul. 1982. A Study of the Validity and Reliability of the CSC Evaluation for Sign Language Interpreters—A Report to the Profession. RID Interpreting Journal. 1.2:16–37.

Daly, Marilyn. 1980. Registry of Certified Court Interpreters. ATA Chronicle. IX.4/5:15.

Daly, Marilyn; Gingold, Kurt; Newman, Patricia; et al. 1981. In-House Translators in Industry. ATA Chronicle. 10.10:28–30.

Deaf American. 1980. Careers for Deaf People in the Sign Language Field (Part Two). The Deaf American. 32.6:20–23.

DeJong, Gerben; Lifchez, Raymond. 1983. Physical Disability and Public Policy. Scientific American. 248.6:40–49.

Deuchar, Margaret. 1983. British Sign Language. London: Routledge & Kegan Paul.

Dicker, Leo. 1982. Facilitating Manual Communication for Interpreters, Students, and Teachers (revised). Washington, D.C.: RID, Inc.

DiPietro, Loraine J. 1970. Registry of Interpreters for the Deaf. Hearing Speech News. 38.5:8–9.

Domingue, Rita L.; Ingram, Betty L. 1978. Sign Language Interpretation: The State of the Art. In Gerver and Sinaiko (eds.). pp. 81–86.

DuBow, Sy. 1979. Federal Actions on Interpreters and Telecommunications. American Annals of the Deaf. 124.2:93–96.

DuBow, Sy; Goldman, Larry. 1981. Legal Strategies to Improve Mental Health Care for Deaf People. In Stein, Mindel, and Jabaley (eds.). pp. 195–209.

DuBow, Sy; Penn, Andrew; Goldberg, Larry, *et al*. 1982. Legal Rights of Hearing-Impaired People. Washington, D.C.: Gallaudet College Press. (Compiled by the staff of the National Center for Law and the Deaf).

Dworkin, Susan. 1984. Whoopi Goldberg—In Performance. Ms. Magazine. 12.11:20.

Earwood, Carl. 1983. Will You Please Sign? The Deaf American. 36.1:15–16.

Earwood, Carl. 1984. Providing for Comprehensive Practicum Supervision. In McIntire (ed.). pp. 251–290.

Eastman, Gilbert C. 1980. Nonverbal Communication as a Sign Language Base & Sign Language Translation for the Theatre. In Ahlgren and Bergman (eds.). pp. 121–128.

Evans, J. William, M.D.; Elliot, Holly. 1981. Screening Criteria for the Diagnosis of Schizophrenia in Deaf Patients. Archives of General Psychiatry. 38.7:787–790.

Fant, Louie J. 1972. The CSUN Approach to the Training of Sign Language Interpreters. The Deaf American. 25.3:56–57.

Fant, Louie. 1980. Drama and Poetry in Sign Language: A Personal Reminiscence. In Baker and Battison (eds.). pp. 193–200.

Fant, Louie. 1974. The California State University, Northridge Approach to Training Interpreters. Journal of Rehabilitation of the Deaf. 7.3:44–47.

Fant, Louie. 1980. Drama and Poetry in Sign Language: A Personal Reminiscence. In Baker and Battison (eds.). pp. 193–200.

Federlin, Tom. 1978a. Interpreter Evaluation—A Trainer's Perspective. The Deaf American. 30.11:17.

Federlin, Tom. 1978b. Sign Language Interpreters: The Changing Role. The Deaf American. 31.3:17–18.

Federlin, Tom; Muller, Keith; Waldman, Lester J. 1978. Training Interpreters for Criminal Court Work. The Deaf American. 30.8:7.

Fink, Barbara. 1982. Being Ignored Can Be Bliss: How to Use a Sign Language Interpreter. The Deaf American. 34.6:5–9. (Reprinted from Disabled USA, Fall 1981.)

Fitz-Gerald, Della; Fitz-Gerald, Max. 1978. Deafness: Implications for Sexuality. ERIC Document #153411.

Fitzhugh, Kristene. 1983. Free lance Interpreting: A Professional Method for Billing. The Reflector. 7:19–23.

Fleischer, Lawrence R. 1975. Sign Language Interpreting Under Four Interpreting Conditions. Salt Lake City, UT: Brigham Young University. (Unpublished doctoral dissertation).

Fleischer, Lawrence R. 1976. Is Our Professional Interpreting at the Ceiling? The Deaf American. 23.2:15.

Frid, Arthur. 1974. Interpreter in Criminal Cases: Allrounders First. Translation News. 4.4:1–6.

Friedman, Lynn A. (ed.). 1977. On the Other Hand: New Perspectives on American Sign Language. New York, NY: Academic Press.

Frishberg, Nancy; Enders, Marilyn. 1974. Prediction of Interpreting Skills. ISP #T4. Unpublished. NTID.

Fritsch Rudser, Steven. 1980. The Revised Code of Ethics: Some Issues and Implications. In Caccamise, *et al.* (eds.). pp. 58–63.

Gallaudet College. 1979. Interpreting and Interpreters: The Deaf Student in College. Washington, D.C.: Gallaudet College. (With the support of the W. K. Kellogg Foundation). pp. 59–61.

Gallaudet College. 1981. Interpreting at Gallaudet College. Washington, D.C.: Gallaudet College. (A Deafness-Related Concerns Committee report.)

Gardner, E. Elaine. 1983. Legal Implications of Professional Sign Language Interpreting. NCLD Newsletter. March. pp. 2–5.

Gerver, David. 1976. Empirical Studies of Simultaneous Interpretation: A Review and a Model. In Brislin (ed.). pp. 165–207.

Gerver, David; Sinaiko, H. Wallace. (eds.) 1978. Language Interpretation and Communication. New York, NY: Plenum Press. NATO Conference Series, Series III: Human Factors.

Gesue, Rita. 1981. Interpreter Referral Service and Registry of Interpreters for the Deaf: A Cooperative Venture. RID Interpreting Journal. 1.1:32–38.

Getzin, Margaret. 1981. Opportunities for Interpretation and Translation in State and County Government. ATA Chronicle. 10.10:28.

Gingold, Kurt. 1984. Quality and Quantity in Translation: An Industrial Translator's Viewpoint. In Newman (ed.) pp 73–77.

Godin, Lev. 1967. Interpreters for the Deaf in Russia. American Annals of the Deaf. 112.2:95–97. (Translated by Grozny.)

Goffman, Erving. 1963. Stigma. Englewood Cliffs, NJ: Prentice Hall.

Goldin-Meadow, Susan J.; Feldman, Heidi. 1975. The Creation of a Communication System. Sign Language Studies. 8:225–234. (Also in Stokoe (ed.), 1980.)

Goldin-Meadow, Susan; Feldman, Heidi. 1977. The Development of Language-Like Communication Without a Language Model. Science. 197:401–403.

Goldman-Eisler, Frieda. 1968. Psycholinguistics: Experiments in Spontaneous Speech. London, England: Academic Press.

Goldman-Eisler, Frieda. 1972. Segmentation of Input in Simultaneous Translation. Journal of Psycholinguistic Research. 1.2:127–140.

Goldman-Eisler, Frieda; Cohen, M. 1974. An Experimental Study of Interference Between Receptive and Productive Processes Relating to Simultaneous Translation. Language and Speech. 17:1:10.

Golladay, Loy. 1978. Interpreting Poetry into Sign Language. In Caccamise, *et al.* (eds.). pp. 187–191.

Goodman, Michael J. 1978. The Deaf Student in Your Class. Golden West College, Huntington Beach, CA: ERIC Document #160163.

Greenberg, Joanne. 1970. In This Sign. New York, NY: Holt, Rinehart and Winston.

Greenberg, Joanne. 1972. And Sarah Laughed. In Rites of Passage. New York: Avon Books. pp. 158–175.

Greenberg, Joanne; Doolittle, Glenn. 1977. Can Schools Speak the Language of the Deaf? The New York Times Magazine. December 11. pp. 50ff.

Grosjean, François. 1982. Life with Two Languages: An Introduction to Bilingualism. Cambridge, MA: Harvard University Press.

Hairston, Ernest; Smith, Linwood. 1983. Black and Deaf in America. Silver Spring, MD: T. J. Publishers.

Halliday, M. A. K. 1970. Language Structure and Language Function. In Lyons (ed.). pp. 140–165.

Harkins, Judy; Vernon, McCay. 1977. Community Colleges and Handicapped Students. Community and Junior College Review. 48:35–37.

Harris, Robert I. 1981. Mental Health Needs and Priorities in Deaf Children and Adults: A Deaf Professional's Perspective for the 1980's. In Stein, Mindel, and Jabaley (eds.). pp. 219–250.

Hartman, Mike. 1977. How to Convince 15 Interpreters to Interpret in Sub-Freezing Weather. The Deaf American. 29.8:12.

Heath, Kareena; Lee, Dorothy. 1982. Interpreters as Boring Monotones: A Solution. The Reflector. 4:27–30.

Heinlein, Robert A. 1972. Stranger in a Strange Land. New York, NY: Berkley Medallion Edition.

Herbert, Jean. 1968. The Interpreter's Handbook: How to Become a Conference Interpreter. 2nd edition. Geneva: Georg & Cie, S.A.

Heymont, George. 1983. Singing Opera . . . Signing Opera. The Deaf American. 35.5:2–6.

Higgins, P. C. 1980. Outsiders in a Hearing World. Beverly Hills, CA: Sage Publications.

Hoemann, Harry; Mullin, Darlene. 1983. Interpreters' Perspectives on Deafness and Deaf People. The Reflector. 6:25–28.

Holcomb, Roy L.; Corbett, Edward E. 1975. Mainstreaming—The Delaware Approach. Newark, Delaware: Newark School District (Sterck School).

Holm, Carol S. 1978. Deafness: Common Misunderstandings. American Journal of Nursing. 78.11:1910–12.

Hughes, Virginia; Wilkie, Faye; Murphy, Harry J. 1974. The Use of Interpreters in an Integrated Liberal Arts Setting. Journal of Rehabilitation of the Deaf. 7.3:17–19.

Hurwitz, T. Alan. 1980a. Interpreters' Effectiveness in Reverse Interpreting: PSE and ASL. Rochester, NY: University of Rochester. (Unpublished doctoral dissertation).

Hurwitz, T. Alan. 1980b. Interpreters' Effectiveness in Reverse Interpreting: PSE and ASL. In Caccamise, et al. (eds.). pp. 157-187.

Hurwitz, T. Alan. 1983. Growing up in a Mainstreamed Education: Reflections of a Deaf Person. The Deaf American. 35.8:15–18.

Hurwitz, T. Alan. 1984. Use of an Interpreter: A Deaf Person's Perspective. The Deaf American. 36.4:22–25.

Ingram, Robert M. 1977. Teaching Deaf Students How to Purchase and Use Interpretation Services. The Deaf American. 29.9:3–6.

Ingram, Robert M. 1978. Sign Language Interpretation and General Theories of Language, Interpretation and Communication. In Gerver and Sinaiko (eds.). pp. 109–118.

Ingram, Robert M. 1978b. Letter to the Editor. The Deaf American. 30.5:25–26.

Ingram, Robert; Ingram, Betty. (eds.) 1975. Hands Across the Sea: Proceedings of the First International Conference on Interpreting. Silver Spring, MD: RID, Inc.

Isham, Bill. 1983. Beyond the Classroom: Self-Directed Growth for Interpreters. The Reflector. 6:15–17.

Jacobs, L. Ronald. 1978. The Efficiency of Interpreting Input for Processing Lecture Information by Deaf College Students. Journal of Rehabilitation of the Deaf. 11.2:10–15.

Jacobs, Leo. 1980. A Deaf Adult Speaks Out. Second edition. Washington, D.C.: Gallaudet College Press.

Jakobson, Roman. 1960. Linguistics and Poetics. In Sebeok (ed.). pp. 350–377.

Jamison, Steven. 1984. Signs for Computing Terminology. Silver Spring, MD: National Association of the Deaf.

Jones, Ray L.; Murphy, Harry J. 1974. Integrated Education for Deaf College Students. Phi Delta Kappan. 55:542.

Joos, Martin. 1967. The Five Clocks. New York, NY: Harbinger Books.

Kanda, Jan. 1984. Response to Sylvie Lambert on Consecutive Interpretation. In McIntire (ed.). pp. 99–110.

Kanda, Jan; Alcorn, Bob. 1984. New Directions in Interpreter Training. The Reflector. 8:18–22.

Kanda, Jan; Roy, Cindy. 1981. Continued Development of Curriculum for Interpreter Training Programs in Vocational Education. Waco, Texas: Texas State Technical Institute. Final Report (July 1, 1980—June 30, 1981).

Kane, Joseph; Shafer, Carl. 1970. Personal and Family Counseling Services for the Adult Deaf. Final Report. Los Angeles, California: Family Services of Los Angeles. ERIC Document #052303.

Kannapell, Barbara; Hamilton, L.; Bornstein, H. (eds.) 1969. Signs for Instructional Purposes. Washington, D.C.: Gallaudet College Press.

Karmiloff-Smith, Annette. 1978. Adult Simultaneous Interpretation: A Functional Analysis of Linguistic Category and a Comparison with Child Development. In Gerver and Sinaiko (eds.). pp. 369–384.

Kates, Linda; Schein, Jerome D. 1980. A Complete Guide to Communication with Deaf-Blind Persons. Silver Spring, MD: National Association of the Deaf.

Kay, Carol R. 1980. Post-Secondary Programming for Hearing-Impaired Students. LINC Paper No. 802. Columbia, MO: Missouri LINC, Department of Special Education, University of Missouri.

Keiser, Walter. 1978. Selection and Training of Conference Interpreters. In Gerver and Sinaiko (eds.). pp. 11–24.

Keller, Helen. 1964. The Story of My Life. Clinton, MA: Airmont Publications.

Kirchner, Suzie. 1978. Sign a Song. In Caccamise, et al. (eds.). pp. 192–203.

Klima, E. S.; Bellugi, U. 1979. Signs of Language. Cambridge, MD: Harvard University Press.

Kolod, Susan Yabroff. December 18, 1979. The Role of Sign Language Interpreters. New York Law Journal.

Krakenberg, Susan J. 1981. Application of American Sign Language to the Psychiatric Setting. American Journal of Orthopsychiatry. 51:715–718.

Kummer, Karl. 1984. Quality and Quantity of Translations in a Nonprofit Organization. In Newman (ed.). pp. 67–71.

Lambert, Sylvie-Michèle. 1984. An Introduction to Consecutive Interpretation. In McIntire (ed.). pp. 76–98.

Lamendola, Linda. 1979. Working to Bridge Communication Gap with the Deaf. The Sunday Star-Ledger. May 27. (Bergen County, NJ). (Quoted in Benderly, 1980.)

Lane, Harlan. 1984. When the Mind Hears: A History of the Deaf. New York, NY: Random House.

Lane, Harlan; Battison, Robbin. 1978. The Role of Oral Language in the Evolution of Manual Language. In Gerver and Sinaiko (eds.). pp. 57–80.

Lane, Harlan; Grosjean, François. 1980. Recent Perspectives on American Sign Language. Hillsdale, NJ: Lawrence Erlbaum Associates.

Lang, Ranier. 1978. Behavioral Aspects of Liaison Interpreters in Papua New Guinea: Some Preliminary Observations. In Gerver and Sinaiko (eds.). pp. 231–244.

Latimer, Glenn; Vollmar, Guy; Vollmar, Sheryl. 1982. "Macho-Sign" or Merely a Gesture? The Deaf American. 35.2:25–27.

Lauritsen, Robert R. 1973. Reflections ... Hearing Children of Deaf Parents. In Lloyd (ed.). pp. 22–26.

Leonard, Isabel A. 1984. Productivity and the Freelance Translator. In Newman (ed.). pp. 79–81.

Levinson, Ken. 1984. Satisfied Yankee Fan. In Northcott (ed.). pp. 229–232.

Llewellyn-Jones, Peter. 1981. Simultaneous Interpreting. In Woll, Kyle, and Deuchar (eds.). pp. 89–104.

Lloyd, Glenn. 1971. Problems Associated with Interpreting for the Deaf Person in Large Groups. In Lloyd (ed.). p. 4.

Lloyd, Glenn. (ed.) 1971. Guidelines for Effective Participation of Deaf Persons in Professional Meetings. Washington, D.C.: U.S. Department of Health, Education and Welfare.

Lloyd, Glenn T. (ed.) 1973. The Deaf Child and His Family. Washington, D.C.: U.S. Department of Health, Education and Welfare (ODH/RSA 73–25075). Proceedings of the National Forum VI, Council of Organizations Serving the Deaf.

Long Island Registry of Interpreters for the Deaf. 1984. Directory of Members.

Longley, Patricia. 1968. Conference Interpreting. London, England: Pitman & Sons, Ltd.

Longley, Patricia. 1978. An Integrated Programme for Training Interpreters. In Gerver and Sinaiko (eds.). pp. 45–56.

Loomis, Lynne. 1982. Signed—With Love: Mildred Lewis. The Deaf American. 35.1:19–23.

Lowe, Ed. 1984. Learning the Language of Bureaucracy. Newsday. November 11.

Lyons, John. (ed.) 1970. New Horizons in Linguistics. London: Harmondsworth.

MacEachin, Aralyn D. 1982. Experiences of a Psychiatric Interpreter. The Reflector. 3:17–20.

Malzkuhn, Eric. 1980. Nonverbal Utterances. In Alhgren and Bergman (eds.). pp. 235–246.

Marmor, Gloria; Petitto, Laura. 1979. Simultaneous Communication in the Classroom: How Well is English Grammar Represented? Sign Language Studies 23:99–136.

Martin, David S. 1982. Mainstreaming the Hearing-Impaired Teacher. Paper presented at the American Association of Colleges for Teacher Education.: ERIC Document #214918.

Maxwell, Madeline M.; Boster, Shirley. 1982. Interpreting Hymns for Deaf Worshippers. Sign Language Studies. 36:217–226.

McElroy, Linda Jeanne Rupp. 1979. Community College Services for Hearing-Impaired Students in Arizona. ERIC Document #16818.

McIntire, Elliot G. 1981. The Deaf Student from Across the Lectern. The Deaf American. 33.11:9–10.

McIntire, Marina L. (ed.) 1984. New Dialogues in Interpreter Education (Proceedings of the Fourth National Conference of Interpreter Trainers Convention). Silver Spring, MD: RID Publications.

Mehta, Ved. 1971. A Second Voice. In John is Easy to Please. New York, NY: Farrar, Straus, & Giroux. pp. 3–25.

Merrill, E. C. 1976. The Responsibilities of Professionals to the Deaf Consumer. The Deaf American. 29.4:14–16.

Mikkelson, Holly. 1983. Consecutive Interpretation. The Reflector. 6:5–9.

Miles, Dorothy S.; Fant, Louie J. 1976. Sign Language Theatre and Deaf Theatre: New Definitions and Directions. Northridge, CA: Center on Deafness, California State University. Center on Deafness Publication Series No. 2.

Mitchell, Marilyn; Jones, James; Allen, June, et al. (eds.) n.d. Signs for Technical Vocational Education. St. Paul, MN: St. Paul Technical Vocational Institute. (Companion document to film cassette series.)

Moody, Bill. 1983. La langue des signes. Paris: Ellipses.

Moores, Donald F. 1982. Educating the Deaf: Psychology, Principles and Practices (Second edition) Boston: Houghton Mifflin Co.

Morgan, Susan. 1974. Interpreting as an Interpreter Sees It. Journal of Rehabilitation of the Deaf. 7.3:28–32.

Moulton, Janice. 1981. The Myth of the Neutral "Man". In Vetterling-Braggin, et al. (eds.). pp. 124–137.

Murphy, Harry J. 1978. Research in Sign Language Interpreting at California State University, Northridge. In Gerver and Sinaiko (eds.). pp. 87–98.

Murphy, Harry J.; Fleischer, Lawrence R. 1977. The Effects of Ameslan versus Siglish upon Test Scores. Journal of Rehabilitation of the Deaf. 11.2:15–18.

Myers, Lowell. 1964. The Law and the Deaf. Washington, D.C.: Rehabilitation Services Administration, HEW.

National Evaluation System Study Committee. 1980. Report to R.I.D. Members.

N.T.I.D. 1979. Interpreting Television for Hearing-Impaired Viewers: A Guidebook for Producers. Rochester, NY: Instructional Television Department, NTID.

Neesam, Ralph. 1966. Rating Forms and Check Lists for Interpreters. Journal of Rehabilitation of the Deaf. 2.1:19–28.

Neesam, Ralph. 1972. The Registry of Interpreters for the Deaf. In O'Rourke (ed.). pp. 62–67.

Neisser, Arden. 1983. The Other Side of Silence. New York: Alfred A. Knopf.

Newman, Patricia. 1983. ATA Certification Program. ATA Chronicle. 12.9:6.

Newman, Patricia E. (ed.) 1984. Silver Tongues: Proceedings of the 25th Annual Conference of the American Translators Association. Medford, NJ: Learned Information, Inc.

New Yorker. 1984. Babel (in Talk of the Town). The New Yorker. 59.49:29–32. January 23.

Nida, Eugene A. 1964. Toward a Science of Translating. Leiden: E. J. Brill.

Nida, Eugene A.; Taber, Charles. 1974. The Theory and Practice of Translation. Leiden: E. J. Brill.

Northcott, Winifred H. 1977. The Oral Interpreter: A Necessary Support Specialist for the Hearing-Impaired. The Volta Review. 79.3:136–144.

Northcott, Winifred H. 1979a. Letters to the Editor. American Annals of the Deaf. 124.1:4.

Northcott, Winifred H. 1979b. Guidelines for the Preparation of Oral Interpreters: Support Specialists for Hearing-Impaired. Volta Review. 81.3:135–145.

Northcott, Winifred H. (ed.) 1984. Oral Interpreting Principles and Practices. University Park, MD: University Park Press.

Nowell, Richard C.; Stuckless, E. Ross. 1974. An Interpreter Training Program. Journal of Rehabilitation of the Deaf. 7.3:69–75.

O'Rourke, Terrence J. (ed.) 1972. Psycholinguistics and Total Communication: The State of the Art. Washington, D.C.: American Annals of the Deaf.

Padden, Carol. 1980. The Deaf Community and the Culture of Deaf People. In Baker and Battison (eds.). pp. 89–103.

Palmer, Jim (ed.) 1972. Proceedings of the Second National Workshop/ Convention of the RID. Washington, D.C.: Registry of Interpreters for the Deaf.

Per-Lee, Myra. (ed.) 1980. Interpreter Research: Targets for the Eighties. Washington, D.C.: National Academy, Gallaudet College.

Petersen, Gene. 1984. An Interview With . . . Linda Annala. The Deaf American. 36.5:17–23.

Peterson, Paul C. 1976. The Influence of Horizontal Camera Angle on Deaf Viewers' Understanding of and Preference for a Televised Presentation Using Simultaneous Sign and Speech. Syracuse, NY: Syracuse University. (Unpublished doctoral dissertation.)

Pimentel, Albert. 1970. Interpreting Services for Deaf People. Journal of Rehabilitation of the Deaf. 3.1:112–120.

Pinchuck, Isadore. 1977. Scientific and Technical Translation. Boulder, CO: Westview Press.

Pricket, Bill; Rash, Norman. 1975. Use of Interpreters in the Vocational

Rehabilitation Process. Journal of Rehabilitation of the Deaf. 9.4:11–15.

Public Employee. 1980. Breaking the Sound Barrier. Public Employee. 44.11:16. (Newspaper of the American Federation of State County and Municipal Employees.)

Quigley, Stephen; Brasel, Barbara B.; Wilbur, Ronnie. 1973. A Survey of Interpreters for Deaf People in the State of Illinois. Journal of Rehabilitation of the Deaf. 6.1:7–11.

Quigley, Stephen; Youngs, Joseph. (eds.) 1965. Interpreting for Deaf People. Washington, D.C.: U.S. Department of Health, Education, and Welfare.

Rainer, J. D.; Altshuler, K. A.; Kallmann, F. J. 1963. Family and Mental Health Problems in a Deaf Population. New York, NY: Columbia University.

Redden, Martha R. 1976. Barrier-Free Meetings: A Guide for Professional Associations. Washington, D.C.: American Association for the Advancement of Science.

RID National Office. 1983. Consumer Column. Views. 8.3:2–3.

Reisman, Gloria; Scanlan, John; Kemp, Kay. 1977. Medical Interpreting for Hearing-Impaired Patients. Journal of the American Medical Association. 237.22:2397–2398.

Renzulli, Don. 1982. Ohlone College: A Program Description. The Reflector. 2:23–27.

Repa, Jindra. 1981. A Training Program for Court Interpreters. Meta. 26.4:394–396.

Riekehof, Lottie, L. 1974. Interpreter Training at Gallaudet College. Journal of Rehabilitation of the Deaf. 7.3:47–51.

Riekehof, Lottie. 1976. Factors Related to Interpreter Proficiency. Language and Communication Research Problems. Washington, D.C.: Gallaudet College Press. (also ERIC Document #138020.)

Robinson, Luther. (ed.) 1978. Sound Minds in a Soundless World.: U.S. Department of Health, Education, and Welfare (No. ADM 77–560).

Roy, Cynthia Bilderback. 1979. ASL: Training Program at IRS for Deaf Data Transcribers. The Deaf American. 31.7:15.

Roy, Cindy. 1980. Developing Curriculum For Interpreter Training Programs in Vocational Education. Austin, TX: Texas Education Agency. (Final Report: July 1, 1979—June 30, 1980).

Roy, Cindy. 1983. A Reader Responds. The Reflector. 5:23–24.

Roy W. F. 1982. The Southwest Collegiate Institute for the Deaf: Interpreter Training Certificate Program. The Reflector. 3:23–25.

Royster, Mary Anne. 1981. Deaf Parents: A Personal Perspective. The Deaf American. 34.3:19–22.

Rozek, Michael. October 1983. When Seeing is Hearing. American Way pp. 149–151.

Rudner, Lawrence M.; Getson, Pamela; Dirst, Richard D. 1981. Interpreter Competence. RID Interpreting Journal. 1.1:10–17.

Rust, Kenneth, 1981. Sign Language Studies at Madonna College. The Reflector. 1:15–20.

Sabatino, Lois. 1976. Dos and Don'ts of Deaf Patient Care. RN. 39.6:64–68.

Schein, Jerome D.; Delk, Marcus, R., Jr. 1974. The Deaf Population of the United States. Silver Spring, MD: National Association of the Deaf.

Schlesinger, Hilde; Meadow, Kathryn. 1968. Interpreting for Deaf Persons: A Contribution to Mental Health. The Deaf American. 20.11:5–8.

Schlesinger, Hilde S.; Meadow, Kathryn P. 1974. Sound and Sign: Childhood Deafness and Mental Health. Berkeley: University of California Press.

Sebeok, Thomas A. (ed.) 1960. Style in Language. Cambridge, MA: MIT Press.

Seleskovitch, Danica. 1976. Interpretation, A Psychological Approach to Translating. In Brislin (ed.). pp. 92–116.

Seleskovitch, Danica. 1978. Interpreting for International Conferences. Washington, D.C.: Pen and Booth.

Siegel, Mark Alan. 1979. When to Grant Licensure: New York's Solution. State Government News. November 10.

Silvern, Cathy. n. d. Visual Music: Interpreting Opera into Sign Language. (Insert to New York City Opera program, 1983.)

Siple, Linda A. (ed.) 1982. A Resource Guide of Training Programs (Interpreting for the Hearing-Impaired). Silver Spring, MD: Registry of Interpreters for the Deaf.

Siple, Patricia (ed.) 1978. Understanding Language Through Sign Language Research. New York, NY: Academic Press.

Smith, Sharon Winfield. 1982. A Very Special Gift. Modern Secretary. pp. 4–5.

Smith, Theresa B. 1983. What Goes Around, Comes Around: Reciprocity and Interpreters. The Reflector. 5:5–6.

Solow, Sharon Neumann. 1978. American Sign Language (ASL) Technique in Interpreting/Translating. In Caccamise, et al.(eds.). pp. 144–148.

Solow, Sharon Neumann. 1981. Sign Language Interpreting: A Basic Resource Book. Silver Spring, MD: National Association of the Deaf.

Solow, Sharon Neumann. 1983. An Interpreter's Guide to Life in the Fast Lane. The Reflector. 5:10–11.

Stagehands, Inc. 1980. Shadowing: Interpreting Performances in Sign Language. P.O. Box 1111, Decatur, GA 30031: Stagehands Inc. (A videotape and printed discussion.)

Stansfield, Millie. 1981. Psychological Issues in Mental Health Interpreting. RID Interpreting Journal. 1.1:18–31.

Stawasz, Pat. 1983. Interpersonal and Group Dynamic Skills for the Educational Interpreter. CIT Newsletter. 3:5–6.

Stein, Laszlo K.; Mindel, Eugene D.; Jabaley, Theresa. (eds.) 1981. Deafness and Mental Health. New York, NY: Grune & Stratton.

Sternberg, Martin L. A. 1974. Brief, Intensive Training to Develop Interpreters. Journal of Rehabilitation of the Deaf. 7.3:63–68.

Sternberg, Martin; Tipton, Carol; Schein, Jerome. 1973. Interpreter

Training: A Curriculum Guide. New York, NY: Deafness Research & Training Center, New York University.

Stinson, Michael; Macleod, Janet. 1980. Recall of Thematically Relevant Material by Deaf Students as a Function of Interpreted Versus Printed Presentation. (Paper presented at the American Educational Research Association). ERIC Document #188363.

Stokoe, William C., Jr. 1972. Semiotics and Human Sign Languages. The Hague: Mouton.

Stokoe, William C., Jr. (ed.) 1980. Sign and Culture. A Reader for Students of American Sign Language. Silver Spring, MD: Linstok Press.

Stokoe, William C., Jr.; Battison, Robbin M. 1981. Sign Language, Mental Health, and Satisfactory Interaction. In Stein, Mindel and Jabaley (eds.). pp. 179–193.

Stokoe, William C., Jr.; Bernard, H. Russell; Padden, Carol. 1980. An Elite Group in Deaf Society. In William C. Stokoe (ed.). pp. 295–317.

Stokoe, William C., Jr.; Casterline, Dorothy, C.; Croneberg, Carl G. (eds.) 1965. A Dictionary of American Sign Language on Linguistic Principles. Washington, D.C.: Gallaudet College Press. (Reprinted by Linstok Press, Silver Spring, MD, 1976.)

Stout, Nancy L.; Krulwich, Maxine T. 1982. Hearing-Impaired Students in Post-Secondary Education. Washington, D.C.: Higher Education and the Handicapped/Closer Look Resource Center.

Straub, Edward. 1977. Interpreting for the Deaf in a Psychiatric Setting. Journal of Rehabilitation of the Deaf. 10.2:15–21.

Swanson, Elinor; DeBlassie, Richard R. 1971. Interpreter Effects on the WISC Performance of First Grade Mexican-American Children. Measurement and Evaluation in Guidance. 4.3:172–175.

Teran, Miguel A.; Correa-Jones, Virginia; Benavides, Alfredo. (eds.) 1979. The Hispanics: A Missing Link in Public Policy. Des Moines, Iowa: ERIC Document #199346.

Thiery, Christopher. 1974. Can Simultaneous Interpreting Work? AIIC Bulletin. 2:3–7.

Thomson, Peggy. 1978. Good Signs from MSSD. American Education. 14.4:6–13.

Tillinghast, Grace. 1981. In-House Translators in Industry. ATA Chronicle. 10.10:28–30.

Tipton, Carol. 1974. Interpreting Ethics. Journal of Rehabilitation of the Deaf. 7.3:10–16.

Treisman, Anne M. 1965. The Effects of Redundancy and Familiarity on Translating and Repeating Back a Foreign and a Native Language. British Journal of Psychology. 56.4:369–379.

Tweney, Ryan. 1978. Sign Language and Psycholinguistic Process: Fact, Hypothesis, and Implications for Interpretation. In Gerver and Sinaiko (eds.). pp. 99–108.

Tweney, Ryan D.; Hoemann, Harry W. 1976. Translation and Sign Languages. In R. Brislin (ed.). pp. 138–161.

Varley, John. 1978. The Persistence of Vision. In The Persistence of Vision. New York: The Dial Press/James Wade. pp. 227–272. (Originally published in The Magazine of Fantasy and Science Fiction, 3/78.)

Vernon, McCay; Coley, Joan. 1978. Violation of Constitutional Rights: The Language-Impaired Person and the Miranda Warnings. Journal of Rehabilitation of the Deaf. 11:4.

Vernon, McCay; Hyatt, Carolyn. 1981. Dorsey: Symbol of Urban Deaf Condition. The Deaf American. 33.9:9–12. (Reprinted from American Rehabilitation, March/April 1981.)

Vernon, McKay; Ottinger, Paula. 1981. Psychological Evaluation of the Deaf and Hard of Hearing. In Stein, Mindel, and Jabaley (eds.). pp. 49–64.

Vernon, McCay; Prickett, Hugh. 1976. Mainstreaming: Issues and a Model Plan. Audiology and Hearing Education. 2.2:5–6,10–11.

Vetterling-Braggin, Mary; Ellison, Frederick A.; English, Jane. (eds.) 1981. Feminism and Philosophy. Totowa, NJ: Littlefield, Adams & Co.

Vidrine, Jacqueline A. 1979. Historical Study of the Neo-Professional Organization, RID, Inc. (1964–78). New Orleans, LA: Tulane University. (Unpublished doctoral dissertation.)

Walker, Lou Ann. (in press). Hidden Signs. New York: Harper and Row.

Walter, Kate. 1984. Susan Freundlich: Bringing Art and Politics to the Deaf. Whole Life Times. Jan.-Feb. pp. 33–35.

Washington Square News. 1983. What Does It Mean to be Deaf at NYU? The Washington Square News. May 4. (New York University student newspaper). p. 6. (Advertisement from D.E.A.F. and C.S.D., student organizations).

West, Lois. 1979. Breaking the Sound Barrier: Working with Hearing-Impaired Adults in an Educational Setting. Beverly, MA: Northshore Community College. ERIC Document #179261.

Wilcox, Sherman. 1981. The Myers-Briggs Type Indicator: Personality Types of Sign Language Students. RID Interpreting Journal. 1.1:39–50.

Williams, Judith S. 1976. Bilingual Experiences of a Deaf Child. Sign Language Studies. 10:37–41.

Wilss, Wolfram. 1982. The Science of Translation. Tübingen: Gunter Naar Zerlag.

Witter-Merithew, Anna. 1982. Function of Assessing as Part of the Interpreting Process. RID Interpreting Journal. 1.2:8–15.

Woll, Bernice; Kyle, James; Deuchar, Margaret. (eds.) 1981. Perspectives on British Sign Language and Deafness. London: Croom Helm.

Woodward, James. 1977. Sex is Definitely a Problem: Interpreters' Knowledge of Signs for Sexual Behavior. Sign Language Studies. 14:73–88.

Woodward James, 1979. Signs of Sexual Behavior. Silver Spring, MD: T. J. Publishers.

Woodward James, 1980. Signs of Drug Use. Silver Spring, MD: T. J. Publishers.

Wright, Jack. 1982. . . . A Part of the Deaf Community. The Deaf American. 34.8:26–30.

Yoken, Carol. (ed.) 1979. Living with Deaf-Blindness: Nine Profiles. Washington: D.C.: The National Academy, Gallaudet College.

Yoken, Carol. (ed.) 1980. Interpreter Training: The State of the Art. Washington, D.C.: The National Academy, Gallaudet College.

Young, Russell D. 1981. Sign Language Acquisition in a Deaf Adult: A Test of the Critical Period Hypothesis. Athens, GA: University of Georgia. (Unpublished doctoral dissertation.)

Youngs, Joseph, Jr. 1968. Interpreting for Deaf Clients. Journal of Rehabiliation of the Deaf. 1.1:49-55.

Yule, Meeri. 1981. Ethics Panel. ATA Chronicle. 10.10:31-32.

Bibliographic Supplement
1990 Revised Edition

Barnum, M; Siebert, B. 1984. Interpreting in Medical Settings: A Student Manual. St. Catherine's College, St. Paul, Minnesota.

Black, Henry Campbell, M.A. 1983. Black's Law Dictionary, Definition of Terms and Phrases of American Jurisprudence, Ancient and Modern. Abridged fifth edition by the publisher's editorial staff. Contributing authors: Joseph R. Nolan and M.J. Connolly. St. Paul, Minnesota: West Publishing Co.

Bowe, Frank G., et al. 1988. Toward Equality: Education of the Deaf. Washington, D.C.: U.S. Government Printing Office.

Griffin, Marie. Region II RID Representative. 1990 draft for information brochure: public education effort. Knoxville, TN.

McLachlan, Ruth. 1989. "Mini-Census" Results. Educational Interpreters and Transliterators of The Registry of Interpreters for the Deaf. (typewritten)

Quigley, Stephen; Youngs, Joseph. (eds.) 1965. Interpreting for Deaf People. Washington, D.C.: U.S. Department of Health, Education and Welfare.

Renzulli, Don. 1988. A Review of the National Evaluation System. Rockville, MD: RID informational handout.

RID National Office. 1988. Study Guide for the Written & Performance Tests. pp. 7-11 and p. 36.

Stuckless, E. Ross; Avery, Joseph C.; Hurwitz, T. Alan. (eds.) 1989. Educational Interpreting for Deaf Students. Final Report of the National Task Force on Interpreting. Rochester, N.Y.: National Technical Institute for the Deaf.

Index

About The Author

NANCY FRISHBERG was born in Minnesota and raised in California. She attended Smith College, and completed her undergraduate studies at the University of California, Berkeley, where she received the A.B. degree (with honors) in linguistics. She entered the University of California, San Diego, for graduate work to study child language acquisition. There she joined the research laboratory of Dr. Ursula Bellugi at the Salk Institute, where work had just begun on deaf children's acquisition of American Sign Language as a first language, in homes where their deaf parents signed to them. Frishberg participated in psycholinguistic studies of memory, language learning, and grammatical structure, while at the same time beginning to become fluent in American Sign Language, used by consultants to the Salk lab's research. It was during this period (1970-73) that she started to use her new language skills to interpret, with the encouragement of deaf colleagues. Frishberg received her M.A. in linguistics from UCSD, and joined the staff of the Interpreting Services at the National Technical Institute for the Deaf in Rochester, New York, as a research associate. During her two years at NTID, she participated in the instruction of student and community interpreters, educated staff and students about American Sign Language, evaluated language skills and language learning aptitudes. In 1974, she received her Expressive Interpreting Certificate, and in 1979 her Comprehensive Skills Certificate. In 1976, her Ph.D. dissertation on "Aspects of Historical Changes in Signs of American Sign Language" was accepted by UCSD.

. Since then, Dr. Frishberg has taught at Hampshire College, New York University, Fordham University, Marymount Manhattan College, LaGuardia Community College, and California State University, Northridge. She was Director of Sign Language Research at the Deafness Research and Training Center, NYU. She has done research on the sign languages of Puerto Rico, Adamorobe (Ghana), Brazil, and the Soviet Union, as well as American Sign Language. Her special research interests are in the areas of hand preference and sign language structure, language learning (by children and adults) and language evaluation and testing.

Currently President of the Sign Instructors Guidance Network (S.I.G.N.), the national professional organization of sign language instructors, Frishberg has also served on the national evaluation team for S.I.G.N., and holds the Comprehensive Teaching Certificate. She has been a member of the Registry of Interpreters for the Deaf (RID) since 1973, and has served as President and board member in her local RID chapter, New York City Metro RID. She is a founding member of the Conference of Interpreter Trainers, and has conducted interpreter instructional courses and workshops for the New York Society for the Deaf, St. Paul (MN) Technical Vocational Institute, Long Island RID, Community College of Philadelphia, Union County College (New Jersey), Gallaudet College, the Department of Social Services of Puerto Rico, Regione Lazio (Rome, Italy), and the Scottish Association of Interpreters for the Deaf, among others.

Nancy Frishberg is a consultant in sign language and interpreting and has been a practicing freelance interpreter since 1972. She is currently at IBM as a discipline specialist for the humanities.

Revised Edition Contributing Authors

MARTY BARNUM, CSC, M.A., is Program Director of the Health Care Interpreter Program at St. Mary's Campus, St. Catherine's College. Her background is in linguistics and intercultural communication.

GAIL BEDESSEM, CSC, M.A., is a teacher of the deaf at John Hersey High School in Arlington Heights, Illinois. She has been interpreting in education and other settings since 1975. She is vice-president of the Registry of Interpreters for the Deaf, Inc., for the 1989–1991 term.

GAY BELLIVEAU, CSC, Prov: SC:L, is an official court interpreter and administrative assistant for the New Jersey Administrative Office of the Courts, Court Interpreting, Legal Translating, and Bilingual Services Section. She is also a teacher of interpreting.

CHARLEEN BREWER, CSC, has been an interpreter for the Albuquerque Public Schools since 1979. She is vice chair of EDITOR (Educational Interpreters and Transliterators of RID) and a member of the working committee for the standards and certification of educational interpreters established by the National Task Force on the Education of the Deaf.

JAN KANDA, CSC, Ed.D., is an associate professor in sign language interpreter education at California State University, Northridge, and co-director of International School of Sign Language and Interpretation (ISSLI). She is the former president of the Conference of Interpreter Trainers (CIT) and is president of the Registry of Interpreters for the Deaf, Inc., for the 1989–1991 term.

KELLIE L. MILLS, CT, CSC, Prov: SC:L, is a court interpreter referral specialist/court interpreter for the Commonwealth of Massachusetts.

DONNA REITER BRANDWEIN, CSC, M.A., is a teacher of interpreting at Harper College in Palatine, Illinois. She has served as vice-president of Illinois RID, chair of the National Certification Board and is currently the region V representative to the Conference of Interpreter Trainers (CIT) national board.